I0043224

Humanity's Struggles with Inequality

More Inequality Divides
Less Inequality Unites

Carmel M. Toussaint

Copyright © 2020 Carmel M Toussaint – Phronetech Writing

This publication is in copyright. Subject to statutory exception and to the provision of relevant collective licensing agreements, no reproduction of any part may take place without the written permission of the author or his appointed representative.

Library and Archives Canada
Publisher: Phronetech Writing

The Publisher has no responsibility for the persistence or accuracy of URLs for external or third-party internet websites referred to in this publication and does not guarantee that any content on such websites is, or will remain, accurate or appropriate.

Author: Carmel M. Toussaint – More Inequality Divides - Less Inequality Unites
Book Designer: Jim Bisakowski https://bookdesign.ca
Editor: Ilex Indexing and Editing https://ilexindexingandediting.com

ISBN: 978-0-9959098-2-3

Phronetech Writing
14023 – 2408 Lakeshore Blvd West,
Etobicoke, ON M8V 1C0

In memory of my brother Ernst Toussaint who passed away during the writing of this book.

In recent years, social scientists have used new tools to analyze the motivation of human behavior. Drawing on recent findings in cognitive science, anthropology, archeology and history, their studies have revealed the source and influence of a longstanding culture of social and economic inequality spread over millennia. Throughout history, this motivation has been created by our increasing needs for power, prestige and wealth, impeding humanity's laudable goal for a better world. This book traces the evolutionary complexity of our sociopolitical system and the development of inequality in our society. In the words of the poet Robert Penn Warren, "the asking and the answering which history provides may help us to understand, even to frame the logic of experience to which we shall submit. History cannot give us a program for the future, but it can give us a fuller understanding of ourselves, and our common humanity, so that we can face the future."

CONTENTS

PART V
Evolution of Political Governance

PART VI
Economic and Political Dimensions of Inequality

PROLOGUE

The title of this book originates from an incomplete manuscript that I have abandoned titled Humankind, Past, Present and Potential Futures. My rationale for not pursuing this endeavor was the realization that it did not focus sufficiently on the main causes of the socio-economic ills affecting humanity despite the benefits of technological development. This book is about the drive of human being for self-aggrandizement that creates an unsustainable level of economic inequality by which I mean the differences among people in their command over economic resources.

History reveals that the betterment of life has been an innate objective of humanity since the first social formation. We have overcome the most challenging situations because of the uniqueness and resilience of our species. Pulitzer Prize winner Jared Diamond in the preface to his seminal book *Guns, Germs and Steel* makes the analogy that the study of world history is like peeling an onion, with the external layer being the modern world. It is indeed a logical approach to discover and explain the causes of things. The retrospective approach that I have taken provides a progressive image of the development of inequality in tandem with social and economic evolution. Both approaches underline the possibilities of our self-destruction if we ignore past lessons. Inequality remains the next frontier to cross on the road to the flourishment of humankind.

In my previous book, I discussed the evolution of humanity's well–being, the technological and politico-economic stance taken from the Renaissance to the first decade of the current century, the contribution of ancient civilizations particularly China and the economic benefits drawn by Great Britain from its colonies. I also considered the effervescent growth environment that led to the First Industrial Revolution, which in Great Britain becoming a superpower in Western Europe and later a global politico-economic leader. At its peak, the British Empire eventually controlled 25% of the world landmass and had an impact on the culture of five hundred million people. Hence, John Wilson aka Christopher North's in 1831 that the sun never sets on the British Empire.

The philosopher and social scientist Karl Marx in the preface to the *Capital: A Critique of Political Economy* commented on Great Britain's industrial development. Written while living in England, Marx foresaw Germany which at that time was mostly an agrarian society, would emulate Great Britain. This prophecy, originally doubted by the Germans, became factual not only in Germany but first in Belgium, then Italy and France - a classic case of less developed countries imitating Great Britain a country at the threshold of the technological frontier. However, by the beginning of the 20th century, the United States became the workshop of the world. Later on, as twenty nations controlled by the British Empire became independent and as a result of political events such as World War I and II, the United States supplanted the United Kingdom as the world's economic powerhouse until today.

Around the globe, the ensuing increased pressure to produce goods and services seemed to create only winners. In the context of industrial and economic development, global commercial trade benefited both producers and consumers. For the home country, the foreign market sustained capacity building in that it developed a self-propelled thrust for innovations and competition. For the receiving country, access to imported goods and services supported economic development.

If such mutual advantages were so obvious how does one can explain the persistent state of less developed countries for so many centuries? Was it by design or by accident? While the former could be considered an outcome of political ideology, the latter is more difficult to answer. Lack of governance, effects of natural disasters, geographic location and a plethora of other factors are often invoked as possible explanations. But these possible answers are all simplistic view of reality. No leader with a 20/20 vision would select a course of action leading to socio-economic stagnation. Karl Marx, among other arguments, thought that capitalism would eventually stagnate as a result of conflicts between the workers and the owners of production. Indeed, it has become more and more obvious that the financial independence of workers remains a dream as the wealth is concentrated in the "elite". Moreover, shrinking discretionary income, spiraling consumers' debt, reduction or elimination of fringe benefits and the impact of automation are all symptomatic of societal disequilibrium and increased inequality, at least in the western economy. Jared Diamond attributes the origin of the economic differences between nations to geography, cultural factors and political decisions. Hernando de Soto in *Why Capitalism Triumphs in the West and Fails Everywhere Else* attributes the economic stagnation of less developed countries, inter alias, to the lack of property rights and often the convoluted process to acquire a property. De Soto quite aptly calls property without a formal title dead capital because that property can neither be leveraged nor sold for creating or expanding a business. This, thereby increases the economic difference between the haves and the have nots.

Former US Secretary of Labor Robert Reich in the Clinton administration attributes the sources of inequality in developed countries, inter alias, not to the economic system but to the rules and regulations favoring only a segment of society and the fluidity of the property concept. One can easily see the multidimensionality of inequality and how daunting the task ahead to analyze it will be. The history of inequality will reveal its metamorphosis to over time.

We, *Homo sapiens,* communicate with each other to meet our needs, to articulate our expectations, and to express or manifest our conviviality. This unique ability of *Homo sapiens,* first manifested as oral and then written communication, differentiates us from other primates. In *Orality and Literacy,* Walter Ong states there is no adequate model in the physical universe for this operation of consciousness, which is distinctively human and which signals the capacity of a human being to form true communities.

This book reviews the emergence, development and rebalancing of economic inequality. Inequality is based on a number of related factors including technology, education, economic and social standing and luck. However, it has reached a level that compromises social cohesion. The socioeconomic impact of industrialization, the diffusion of technology in developed countries and its impact on less developed countries, globalization and its socio-political ramifications will all form part of my analysis of inequality. But first, a historical review of the chain of events leading to the current state of inequality is in order. Determining causation can be a challenge when looking at such a complex issue, hence the necessity of revisiting the past with an appropriate analytical framework.

In Part I and II, the book begins with a brief history of *Homo sapiens* and its associated cultural evolution. Historically, people have chosen various ways to secure a constant supply of the necessities of life. To protect themselves from rival bands and tribes marriage between groups or submission to a more complex polity took place.

Part III and IV review the origin of inequality in the Old and New World in six primary states. Although humans organized themselves as an egalitarian society for the greatest part of history, inequality is now the dominant feature of modern society. Around the globe, those invested with the power to protect have become richer, and capable of exchanging more goods and acquiring more land.

Part V concentrates on the origin and development of capitalism. The sheer force of competition influenced economic systems around the world. The Black Death killed almost one-third of Europe's population creating a huge labor shortage. Feudalism became no longer viable. With the rebound of population growth and commercial exchange, mercantilism became an impediment to development. Needless to say that this transformative process in most societies around the globe provoked many social upheavals in France, Russia, Great Britain. Among a few of them are the seven-year war between France and Great Britain, the birth of capitalism, the French Revolution dismantling the monarchy, the independence of the United States, the Bolshevik Revolution overthrowing the Russian monarchy with rippled effects on China, World War I and other events.

Part VI describes the economic and political dimensions of inequality and their ramification. The first quarter of the 20th century signaled a turning point in terms of the world sociopolitical profile. The establishment of two main political ideologies, capitalism and communism, each competing to maintain a prosperous socio-economic order around the world under the umbrella of social justice. The outcomes of World War II, the fall of the Berlin Wall and the collapse of the Soviet Union have proven the supremacy of capitalism. It was adopted in mitigated form in most socialist countries. A surge of democracy ensued around the globe. My focus is on the underlying forces which sustain the imbalance wherein profit is privatized and debt socialized. Consideration is also given to the maintenance of democracy or lack thereof and the rationale for the rise of populism.

For the sake of simplicity and to avoid being too technical, I opted for a narrative rather than a mathematical approach to discussing economic matters. In addition, framework of mathematical models can only be temporary given the combined effects of the current and last two decades politico-economic events. These models must be often adjusted to account for imperceptible changes yet strong enough to alter any benchmark or socioeconomic prediction. In this context, I have covered the optimal rate of inequality that is a rate where economic growth is maximized and inequality is at an optimal level.

In the current decade, inequality between democratic countries has been reduced but not within countries. The main message of this book, given that inequality is inevitable, its magnitude must be reduced from the current level currently experienced in most countries.

I dedicate this book to everyone having an interest in inequality. Gender and racial inequality are unacceptable at this stage of our civilization. It is my expectation that it will reach a wide range of readers including policymakers. In some instances, I could not avoid using technical terms or concepts. However, there are endnotes after each part and a glossary in appendix I. Conversely, sociologists and political scientists may feel unsatisfied or frustrated by the limited coverage of certain academic subjects. I hope this limitation does not affect the understanding of the topics covered.

In her book *The Wave in the Mind* Ursula K. Le Guin posits that words are events, they do things, change things. It is my hope that the message in this book will facilitate the necessary changes.

{ } Indicates that additional information is provided in the glossary note section of Appendix I.

*Indicates a note at the end of each PART

Part I
Brief History of Homo sapiens

"This is the most beautiful and satisfactory explanation of creation to which I have ever listened". (Having attended Lemaitre's seminar at Caltech on the {cosmic egg}, the mass of all the Universe at its origination - Dec 1932).

Albert Einstein

Early hominins, Language Development

Our history about the emergence of Homo sapiens can be summarized as follows:

- Big Bang occurred 13.8 billion years ago.
- Planet Earth 4.5 billion years ago.
- First bacterium 4 billion years ago.
- Emergence of life on Earth, some 2.6 billion years.
- First primates, 60 million years ago and the great apes, 15 million years ago.
- Chimpanzees, 7 million years ago (MYA)*
- *Homo habilis* 2.7 MYA preceded by Homo rudolfensis.
- *Homo Erectus* 2 MYA from Homo ergaster.
- First use of fire by Homo erectus, 600,000 years ago
- *Homo Neandertalensis* 200,000 years ago preceded by *Homo heidelbergensis.*
- *Homo sapiens* 200,000 years ago from *Homo heidelbergensis.*
- Emergence of language, 50,000 years ago.

The above chronology is based on cosmic background and fossil analysis. *Homo sapiens* evolved from the great apes, the chimpanzee being our closest relatives. Subject to more precise scientific method of fossils and artifacts analysis, the dividing line, timewise, between hominids and pongids is approximately 7 million years ago. Other factors such as geological gaps, migratory differentiation in Eurasia, interbreeding, misinterpretation of paleontological and archeological reporting have exacerbated the debates. For instance, at the time of this writing, it has been reported that *Homo sapiens* emerged 300,000 years earlier than thought.

The long evolution from the *Sahelanthropus tchadensis* and *Australopithecus bustus* to *Australopithecus afarensis* is omitted for the sake of simplicity.

Figure 1.0 and 1.1 shows the lineage of *Homo sapiens* and its expansion from East Africa. Figure 1.0 shows *Homo habilis* followed by *Homo ergaster and Homo heidelbergensis*, predecessors of *Homo erectus* and *Homo neanderthalensis* and finally *Homo sapiens*. But the history of the evolution* of *Homo sapiens* and its expansion around the globe while fascinating is also complicated. It is not within the scope of this book to provide a comprehensive review of these past events. Nevertheless, a brief explanation of the early hominins fits well in the overall framework of Part I.

Figure 1.0 The Origin and Evolution to Homo sapiens

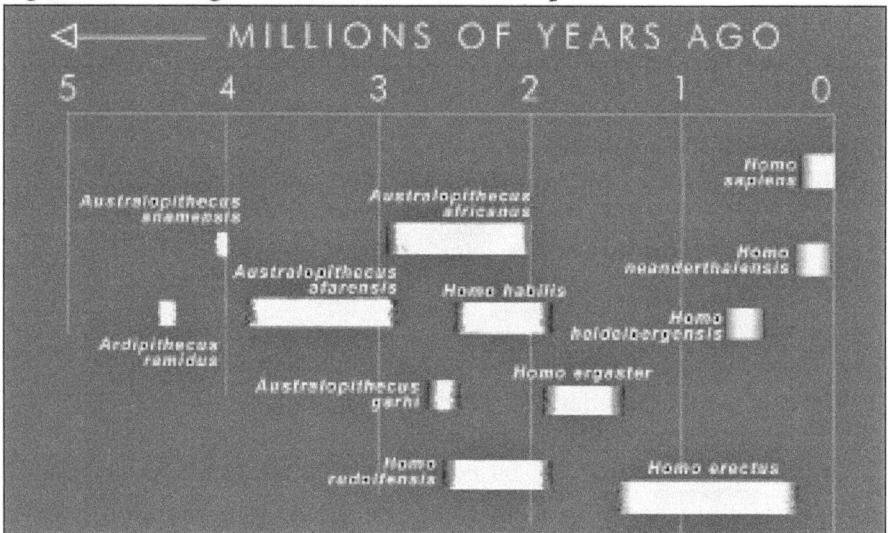

The two-part composite names in Greek and Latin for prehistoric hominins designate the origin, genus and species (See Appendix I). We owe this nomenclature to the Swedish biological scientist Carl Linnaeus. Note that Carl Linnaeus, like Aristotle, believed in the fixity of species. In his nomenclature, the first part (genus) includes groups of species that are structurally similar. The second part, species, includes groups of closely related organisms that are very similar to each other and are usually capable of interbreeding and producing fertile (capable of repro-ducing) offsprings whose own offsprings are viable (capable of living) and fertile. Conventionally, in this binomial nomenclature, the genus precedes the species. An example will make the point. Liger is a hybrid cross between a male lion (*Panthera leo*) and a tigress (*Panthera tigris*). As can be seen, the genus is the same but the species is different. When the animal's parents are from different species, their chromosomes don't align in the same order thereby making the hybrid progeny infertile.

Close to 1 MYA, *Homo habilis* (Handy Man), *Homo rudolfensis* (this species' name comes from the location where the specimen was found - East Rudolph, Kenia) and *Homo ergaster* (Working Man) were extinct. *Homo erectus* who were morphologically closer to humans emerged between 1,000,000 and 300,000 B.C. They were the first hominins to grow up to 6 feet in height and weigh more than 150 pounds making it possible for them to hunt big game such as the wooly mammoth. Archeological data shows that their brains were as heavy as the brains of modern human beings. (I. Asimov- 1920: p.5). But they also have two other particularities that differentiate them largely from all their prede-cessors. They were the first hominins to leave Africa, to tame fire and to bury their dead. As a species, *Homo erectus* survived for almost 2 million years and are considered to be the most long-lived and broadly dispersed species. By natural selection* *Homo sapiens*, meaning wise man (genus homo - species sapiens) is the only survivor of this evolutionary devel-opment until today.

Why did *Homo sapiens* migrate from Africa? The most popular theory suggests that early humans evolved in Africa and then left in successive waves. But what drove their migrations has been a matter of debate. Anthropologists believe climate change and the search for food could be the most likely reasons.

But archeological evidence of *Homo erectus* in many parts of the globe has caused much debate. Two dominant theories explain this fact: the Recent African Origin and the Multi-regional Origin of modern humans. The former is the more accepted theory on the basis of genetic analysis. The Multiregional Hypothesis holds that modern humans originated in

Africa and today share a predominant recent African origin, but have also absorbed small, geographically variable, degrees of admixture from other regional (archaic) hominin species.

In the Recent African Origin theory, the spread of the human race around the globe from Africa occurred in two migratory waves. In the first wave, *Homo erectus*, left Africa approximately 1.8 million years ago for Northern Asia followed by *Homo heidelbergensis* who settled in Europe 400,000 years later. *Homo Heidelbergensis* is deemed to be the ancestor of the Neanderthals who populated most of Europe. The time period is approximate and varies among writers.

Figure 1.1 Migration Waves out of Africa

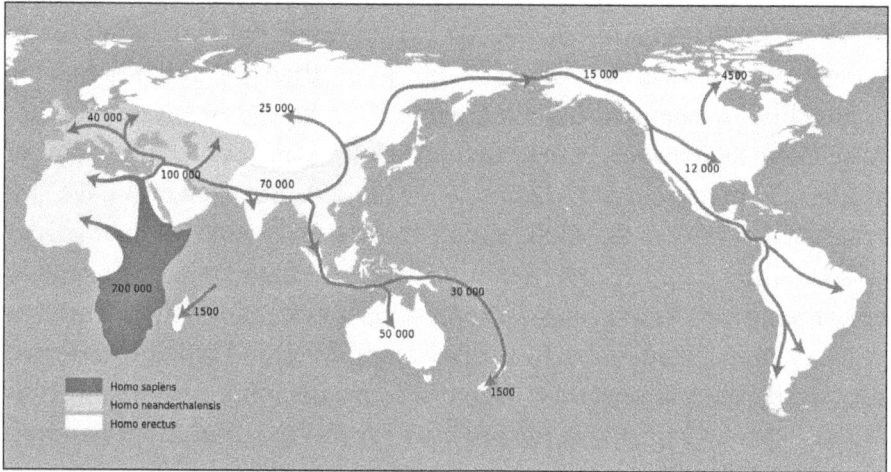

The second wave took the Southern Route which follows the southern coast of Asia and led to the lasting colonization of Eurasia and Australia around 50,000 years ago. *Homo erectus* went as far as Indonesia, sea levels have dropped as much as 300 feet making it possible to cross on foot from the Asian continent to Indonesia. For some reason, a bifurcation took place in the Arabian Peninsula. One group continued on Australia and Papua New Guinea, while another traveled northwest, crossing the Beringia land bridge around 14,500 BC to the coastal North and South America

This helps explain the Peking man discovered by the Canadian anthropologist Davidson Black. The Peking man was in fact the remains of a *Homo erectus* thereby casting serious doubt on the Out of China theory of human evolution.

Europe was populated by the Neanderthals, one of the two offshoots of *Homo heidelbergensis* who settled in the Near East and Europe and the Denisovans who appeared in part of southern China, Australia and Papua New Guinea. At that time, this area was a single continent because of the high levels of glaciation of the Paleolithic ice age. This theory also explains the presence of the Neanderthals in Europe when Homo sapiens, who continued to evolve from Homo erectus, expanded their migration to this continent. Furthermore, as can be understood from Figure 1.1, it is clear that the Denisovans were not confined solely to Siberia. The DNA analysis of remains found in Siberia can be traced to Australia and Papua New Guinea.

The opportunistic feature of evolution cannot be ignored. Evolution seldom progresses in a linear fashion. One branch may split into disparate branches, capitalizing on favorable conditions. Others may die as a result of food competition or harsh climatic conditions. Interbreeding infuses even more vigor to the debate. For example, it is now known that *Neanderthals* and *Homo sapiens* interbred. Up to 4% of the DNA of modern Europe and Middle East populations can be traced back to Neanderthals. Had they survived longer, perhaps the percentage would have been larger. Hence this quote attributed to Charles Darwin "It is not the strongest of the species that survives, nor the most intelligent that survives. It is the one that is the most adaptable to change." This is to say that while the evolutionary path to *Homo sapiens* is true, certain gaps still exist which can only be filled and explained as time goes by. As underlined by the paleoanthropologist Chris Stringer we don't know exactly when animals that can be classified as Homo sapiens first evolved from earlier types of humans. The Florisbad Skull discovered in 1932 in South Africa has been identified as belonging to an intermediate species between the *Homo heidelbergensis* and *Homo sapiens*.

The reality, out of this long transformative and expansion process, is that *Homo sapiens* remains the only survivor and in a commanding position on this planet. Evolution proceeded around the globe at different speeds subject to external pressures and competition for survival. Graph 1.1 shows the migratory path of Homo erectus, and *Homo sapiens* out of Africa. However, this theory may change as new discoveries are made and new technological methods of analysis are developed.

Language development

The fact remains that *Homo sapiens* is not only the unique surviving species of the *homo* genus but it is also believed to be the only one with the language capability which appeared between 50 to 100,000 years ago. This is not to imply that other animals do not communicate. But, in the animal kingdom, the emission of a sound by a sender suggests to an attentive receiver a representative notion perhaps alertness to danger, courting, or feeding. However, this communication does not stretch to encompass any sense of abstraction or information about past events or future volitions. By contrast, human communication is more complex, varied and includes both variety and suppleness. In my earlier book *Technology and Society – Rewards and Challenges*, I suggest that human language is an example of singularity similar to the Big Bang. Both mark a turning point causing accelerated changes. The emergence of language is referred to as a cognitive revolution. Some evolutionary anthropologists and neurologists attribute its development and perfection in *Homo sapiens*, to a genetic mutation. Needless to say, this mutation that enabled oral communication leapfrogged *Homo sapiens* to its current position of superiority. This issue deserves further consideration and additional clarification is needed about this neurological transformation including the anatomical, and psychological components. In other words, what is the interrelationship between the body and brain that could explain the emergence of language in humans? This question has long been debated at length by neurologists and psychologists.

The interrelationship of the body, mind and spirit is complex because it falls in the metaphysical realm. As such, any specific answer would be rejected by some and be offensive to others due to the absence of tangible shreds of evidence. Enormous progress has occurred in the study of the brain to scientifically explain human behavior. However, much work remains to be done to elucidate certain activities of the brain for example the formation of thoughts. In "*A Universe of Consciousness- How Matter becomes Imagination*" by Gerald Edelman and Giulio Tononi, the following quotes were extracted from the prologue of chapters 9 and 15:

"High-order consciousness (which flourishes in humans and presupposes the coexistence of primary consciousness) is accompanied by a sense of self and the ability in the waking state explicitly to construct past and future scenes. It requires, at the minimum, a semantic capability and, in its most developed form, a linguistic capability".

"...In particular, we (the authors) argue that neural changes that lead to language are behind the emergence of higher-order consciousness, and we briefly consider some aspects of the evolution of speech. Once higher-order consciousness begins to emerge, a self can be constructed from social and affective relationships...The emergence of the self leads to a refinement of phenomenological experience, tying feeling to thoughts, to culture and to beliefs..."

Philip Lieberman and Robert McCarthy in "Tracking the Evolution of Language and Speech" quoted Theodosius Dobzhansky saying "nothing in biology makes sense except in the light of evolution". Indeed, the series of morphologic changes that took place over time before the advent of oral communication is impressive. Among them are bipedalism, the straightening of the spine despite, the modification of the larynx and more importantly the appearance of the hyoid bone unique to Homo sapiens and possibly Neanderthals.

This biological development of language capability co-evolved with the development of social interaction so necessary for survival. It is my view that the development of tools and the communication of this knowledge to younger generations to survive required intense communication and cooperation as well as the ability to express a wide range of emotions from joy in success to dissatisfaction. Social interaction was a major driver of the evolution of language. From a metaphysical perspective, it is possible that the emergence of language coincides with the emergence of the soul, the latter being the expression of the mind, spirit and emotion.

The analysis of the soul correlates with an immaterial world. We remain children of Tantalus*, frustrated by the failure to grasp that which seems within reach. Depending on a person's faith the soul survives death. At the current stage of knowledge on the subject, the above statement could be seen as conjecture as opposed to theory because it cannot be scientifically proven. But, just consider this troubling question: What if *Homo sapiens* is part of a God's project in the cosmos (including Earth) with the goal of creating a similar creature to Himself for companionship? From this perspective, the emergence of the soul would coincide with the development of language* in the Neanderthals and later be perfected by *Homo sapiens*. This line of thinking is similar to the Omega Point of the Jesuit priest and scientist Pierre Teilhard de Chardin. The Omega Point is the highest level of consciousness, a spiritual belief and a scientific speculation that everything in the universe is fated to spiral towards a final point of "divine" unification.

Carvings and paintings dated from 39,000 years ago were found in a seaside cave in Gibraltar, one of the hiding places of the Neanderthals. In addition, the ritual activity evidenced by artifacts found in the burial sites of some Homo Neanderthals reflects empathy for their friends and family members and perhaps a belief in the afterlife whatever it may have meant for them. It might be worth analyzing sociability from a biological perspective. What makes human being social?

Primate brains look unusual. They are large relative to our body size. In most mammals, the neocortex occupies 30 to 40 percent of the brain volume, but in humans, the neocortex occupies 80 percent of the brain volume. In his social brain hypothesis, Dunbar calls the neo-cortex the thinking part of the brain (R. I. M. Dunbar 1996: p. 62 -71). It seems there is a quantitative relationship between brain size and the social group size. Dunbar calculated that, based on the ratio of the neocortex volume to the volume of the rest of the brain, the group size for humans should be 150.

According to Dunbar, the earliest close social formation (such as the band polity), was made up of about 35 drawn from five or six families. A mega-band might have had as many as comprehend 500 people and a tribe as many as 1500 to 2000. Based on archeological discoveries, the village size of the earliest farmers in the Near East (around 5000 BC) was 150. A similar discovery also occurred in South America. It has been suggested that managing more than 150 people requires a hierarchical structure to maintain order. A larger group of people might also have required individuals to differentiate friends from acquaintances. A friend would be someone with whom a strong connection has been established over a period of time. An acquaintance would be someone known in a particular context such as work or a ceremonial event. The key difference is the formality of the relationship in the latter compared to the former.

Returning to the discussion about migration, the typical morphology of Homo neanderthalensis appeared first in Europe about 400,000 years ago. They probably evolved from a branch of Homo erectus who left Africa heading north in that first round of migrations. The distinctive Neanderthal form continued to evolve until ~38,000 BC when the species became extinct.

Looking at the migration patterns (See Figure 1.1), *Homo sapiens* made it to Europe around 60,000 years ago where they encountered the Neanderthals who had arrived in a previous migration 300,000 years earlier. The exact cause of the extinction of the Neanderthals is unknown. Hypotheses put forward include diseases brought by Homo sapiens, scarcity of resources due to increased competition and extermination by Homo sapiens. Be that as it may, the Neanderthals existed only 28,000 years after the arrival of the *Homo sapiens.*

The hunter-gatherer lifestyle continued until 10,000 BC or earlier depending on the environmental conditions. As with every major socio-economic change in human history, this lifestyle came to an end with the most recent interglacial period. For millennia humans lived with what was naturally available i-e fishing, hunting and foraging. They consumed available resources in some cases to the point of extinction as they moved from one area to the next. With the passage of time, successive areas were depleted and the pursuit of prey required travels to more distant areas thereby complicating the hunting carrying processes. We all have heard the adage: killing the prey is the easy part, bringing it home is a totally different matter.

Historians estimate the world's hunter-gatherer population was in the range of 6-10 million by the eve of the sedentary society part of the First Agricultural Revolution in the Neolithic Period. It must be noted that the transition from hunter-gatherer to a sedentary society occurred independently in a different part of the globe at different times. Why is that? Among historians, the effect of changing climate and demographic pressure is the predominant theory.

a) Climate (in Europe, the Middle East, China, India America and Australia).

Scientists suggest that so far there have been five great ice ages, some of them lasting as long as 60 million years. The Huronian began between 2.4 to 2.1 billion years ago; the Cryogenian was between 850 to 675million years ago; the Andean-Sahara between 460 - 430 million years ago; the Karoo 360 to 260 million years ago; and the fifth one, the Quaternary extends from 2.6 million years ago to present. The most recent Great Ice Age, of which we are still a part, has much influenced the evolution and habitat of the animals known to us today. The period sometimes referred to as the Great Ice Age (about 1.7 million years ago), saw the spread of humans from Africa to the rest of the world. But the colonizing of the Americas did not take place until the most recent glacial period (about 30,000 to 10,000 years ago). The sudden and rapid development of human society began at the end of this period 10,000 years ago.

The ice ages and the concomitant climate change were less favorable for wildlife than for humans. Some animals such as the mammoths did not survive while others such as the bison moved to more temperate areas. For omnivorous, it became increasingly laborious to bring home the product of the hunt. But, climate change enhanced the growth of vegetation. In addition, better environmental conditions and the ready availability of edible plants facilitated procreation. This segued to the domestication of animals for a constant supply of meat and milk which made a sedentary lifestyle possible. Farming and pastoral activities were then born.

b) Demography

"The power of population is infinitely greater than the power of the earth to produce subsistence for man." These were the words of Thomas Robert Malthus is one of his series in the *Principle of Population* published in 1798. Since the 20th-century technology has proven this is not universally the case. Nonetheless, mass agricultural production enabled by technology should not be interpreted as a rebuke of frugality.

A population explosion occurred from the Mesolithic to the Neolithic periods but not at the same rate around the globe due to different geographical conditions. These disparities also explain the different timing of the Agricultural Revolution around the globe. A case in point is Jericho situated today in the West Bank region of the Middle East where the First Agricultural Revolution took place circa 10,000 BC but it occurred in Anatolia (present-day Turkey) and Syria circa 8,000 BC.

In *A Brief History of Humankind,* Yuval Noah Harari put forward a different theory. He calls this transformation from hunter-gatherer to farmer-pastoralist lifestyle a miscalculation by humans. The convenience of locally available food caused the population to become sedentary; in his view agriculture domesticated humans. Today we can imagine how a sedentary lifestyle required a lot of planning not only to ensure a constant supply of food but also to keep ahead of Mother Nature floods, droughts, rodents, insects. Jared Diamond posited that the agricultural revolution was one of life's unpredictable turns that set the evolution of human society in an irreversible direction. Looking through the lens of modern time, because of our resilience we have not done too badly. In my view, the advent of a sedentary lifestyle was inevitable because of demographic pressure and improved climatic conditions.

In these benign circumstances with food and land freely available, protection against threats may have not been an anticipated factor. Without strong leadership and protection, sedentary bands and tribes were vulnerable to hostile groups who took over their food reserves and resources.

Plants and Animals Domestication

Plants Domestication

While the organizational structure of the primitive societies and their way of life will be covered in PART II, I suggest another perspective of the social impact of Agriculture and the sedentary lifestyle. Based on archeological data crop domestication began at about 7,000 BC in the Near East and perhaps at the same period in China, approximately 7,200 in Mesoamerica, 6,500 in the Peruvian highlands; and 8,000 BC worldwide. This cultural convergence appearing independently in different parts of the globe must have been forced by internal factors such as population growth and culture, and external factors such as climatic conditions. The transformation from hunter-gatherer to sedentary lifestyle did not happen overnight. It took humanity 3,000 years to become fully reliant on domesticated foodstuff in the Near East which roughly represents 120 generations. The cultivation of wheat and barley in the Middle East, rice in Asia, maize and tuber in the Americas using Stone Age implements arose independently under population pressure.

Table 1.2 Plants domestication

Area	Domesticated Plants
Middle East	wheat, barley
Mesoamerica	maize, beans, squash
South America	white potatoes
North America	amaranth
China	millet, rice
Africa	sorghum

Although the domestication of plants first emerged in the Middle East, more specifically in Mesopotamia the cradle of civilization, an important fact is worth underlining. One of the most interesting parallel regions of domestication was Mesoamerica (modern Mexico and Guatemala). In contrast to the Middle East, where sedentism preceded domestication, the people of highland Mesoamerica seem to have domesticated maize (corn), beans, and squash *first* and did not become sedentary until many centuries later. Another important difference between Mesoamerica and the Middle East is the fact that the domestication process in Mesoamerica focused almost exclusively on *plants*, almost no animals were domesticated for food or secondary products. If similar types of cultural development occurred independently and at a different time they are nevertheless constrained by the environment and the specific culture of each society.

Another point worth noting is the prestige associated with hunting prowess. As I will show in PART II, in egalitarian societies a charismatic leader is respected for his hunting skill in addition to other personal virtues. The sedentary and hunting lifestyles conflicted until they aligned and resulted in a semi-sedentary lifestyle. As it often happens in history, with the disappearance of the semi-sedentary stage, the personal virtues were swallowed by the sheer urgency of daily activities.

Animal Domestication

Domestication of animals followed different trajectories in different parts of the globe. It was contingent on human culture, environment and opportunity by both parties. The following table illustrates the space and time variance of the domestication of some common animals. The length of time for the domestication process to occur suggests that the progress of domestication was slow to imperceptible.

Figure 1.3 Animal Domestication

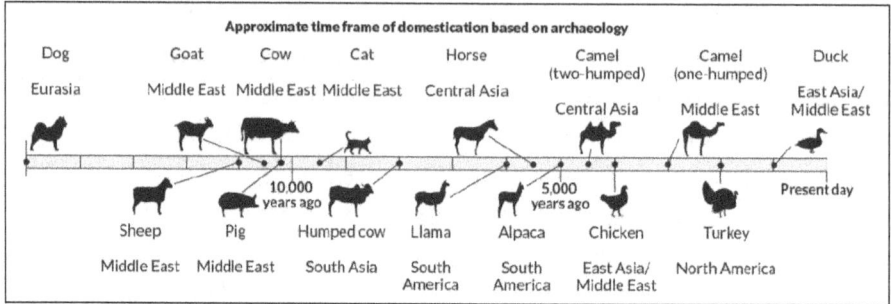

Approximate time frame of domestication based on archaeology

Dog	Goat	Cow	Cat	Horse	Camel (two-humped)	Camel (one-humped)	Duck
Eurasia	Middle East	Middle East	Middle East	Central Asia			East Asia/ Middle East
					Central Asia	Middle East	

10,000 years ago   5,000 years ago   Present day

Sheep	Pig	Humped cow	Llama	Alpaca	Chicken	Turkey
Middle East	Middle East	South Asia	South America	South America	East Asia/ Middle East	North America

Sources: D.E. MacHugh et al/Annu. Rev. Anim. Biosci. 2017; M. Germonpré et al/J. Archaeol. Sci. 2009

In a cogent paper for the Journal of Anthropology, Melinda Zeder described three different scenarios in the domestication of animals. Under the commensalism scenario, a relationship develops in which one party benefits without harming the other. The domestication of the dog is an example of such a relationship. At first, dogs were fed comestible refuse. Later, the relationship evolved into mutualistic commensalism, as dogs became a human companion.

In the prey scenario, humans fed animals which they later ate as meat. Over time, to ensure that the daily food needs were met, the domestication of animals for reproduction took place because it became wiser to select them for reproduction rather than their immediate consumption. Sheep, pigs, goats, cows fall into this category.

The third scenario of animal domestication called the directed pathway is a deliberate action to achieve certain resource-related goals to complement certain technologies. Donkeys and horses fall in this category. They have been used for hunting, transportation of heavy loads and agriculture as draft animals. As will show later, this scenario did not apply to Mesoamerica where most of the large mammals including horses and donkeys were destroyed by the migrants to the Americas.

The primary needs of the early sedentary society members were met in a rustic manner. Survival was hard work but with the development of agriculture, food became readily and reliably available. But, how these societies protected themselves and their resources from interlopers?

Was there a communal property are assigned to each group and if so by whom? What were the governing organization and the relationship between the governed and their government? PART II will answer these questions.

Endnotes

1a. Tantalus was a Greek mythological figure, most famous for his eternal punishment in Tartarus. He was made to stand in a pool of water beneath a fruit tree with low branches, with the fruit ever eluding his grasp, and the water always receding before he could take a drink.

1b. For different approaches to the development of language see Robert C. Berwick and Noam Chomsky in Why Only US – Language and Evolution. The MIT Press May 12, 2017

1c. Evolution is the process by which new species come into being.

1d. Natural selection is the mechanism by which evolution occurs: variations in the populations which spread or are eliminated based on how well they manage to survive in the environment.

1e. MYA; BC; AD. In the far distant past period, the dates are mostly approximate and are expressed in Years Ago - Millions of Years Ago (MYA).

For distant events related to the Old and New World, BC and AD are used as appropriate.

Part II
Sociocultural Evolution

No known society has ever had a completely egalitarian society.

Gerhard E. Lensky

Introduction

Most studies of sociopolitical evolution address three periods: The first is the Paleolithic period which stretched from 2.6 million to 9,600 years BC. The second is the Mesolithic period from 12,500 to 7,000 years BC. And the third is the Neolithic period, from 10,200 years to 2,700 years B.C. leading up to the First Agricultural Revolution and civilization in Mesopotamia. Another common classification of these periods is respectively Stone Age, Bronze Age and Iron Age. It is known that 99% of human history took place during the Stone Age (Upper Paleolithic period). The legacy of this period is significant in the areas of tool making, arts and social organization. There was remarkable advancement for a species that, based on the {cosmic time scale}, had recently begun to communicate orally. Tools were made and improved in the Bronze and Iron Age. Language emerged in 50,000 BC. The cuneiform script for writing was developed by the Sumerians of Mesopotamia between 3,500 and 3,000 BC; the hieroglyphic writing system was invented by the Egyptians around 3,300 BC; and the Indus script between 3,500 and 1900 B.C. Human social development was greatly shaped by these events. More will be said about the Sumerian and Egyptian civilizations from a sociopolitical perspective in PART III.

I chose 'Sociocultural Evolution' as the title of this section to reflect the change of political structure in each of the forthcoming polities being reviewed. A permanent sedentary society is recognized as the cradle of society occurring during the Neolithic period in the Fertile Crescent. As one will understand, this new way or rather inevitable way of living did not happen suddenly. A series of social transformations occurred prior to and during this societal evolution that needs to be underlined. Humans are social and competitive animals, characteristics that go back millions of years. It is customary to classify primitive societies by the way they gather food. In the beginning, social organizations consisted of separate and relatively distant units of about one thousand people with unwritten language and rudimentary technology. The groups developed a culture of customs, tradition and cooperation between members to survive. The American cultural anthropologist Elman R. Service was the first to classify primitive society into four groups according to their political organization; nomadic hunter-gatherers (bands), segmentary lineage or tribal societies, chiefdoms and early states. From this perspective, a coherent sociopolitical profile of primitive societies can be constructed. I must stress that there was not a linear continuum from band to state and some of those components continued to exist during the cultural evolution until today. The band, tribe and state polities will be analyzed in the next subsection.

Bands and Tribes

From an evolutionary perspective, one subcomponent of early society includes groups of hunter-gatherers of a few dozen dispersed over areas of about one square mile. Bands were the earliest food collectors. They were nomadic and foraged and fished to survive. Band size varied between 20 and 50 individuals, the latter being the upper limit to maintain a coherent and harmonious atmosphere in the unit. R. Dunbar's social brain hypothesis mentioned earlier supports these numbers. The small group sizes and the temporary nature of the resulted in a strong intra-bands bond. Common interests such as food requirements and survivability reinforced this bonding.

Fast forward to modern time, this hypothesis also explains the experience of an acquaintance of mine who had a network of 1000 people on social media. He thought he would become rich overnight by joining a network marketing company. For this purpose, he invited his contacts for a gathering in a hall. To his great surprise, only 10 showed up. The reality is that his relationship with his contacts was not deep enough to respond to his invitation. The digital connection seems to have replaced oral conversation. Social media gives the illusion of companionship without the demands of friendship. At the root of this profound shift in human behavior of everyone from teenagers to seniors is the insatiable appetite for immediacy and for information from or to the largest number of acquaintances deemed to be friends. However, this immediacy is overruled by the brain capacity to sustain a certain number of the relationship of a given strength at any given time. As demonstrated earlier, a close relationship cannot be maintained with more than 150 people.

Based on archeological data, bands had only rudimentary technology. They used simple tools such as wood-handled stone axes, sticks and bone hooks and fishnets to get food. They lived in a temporary encampment where they shared the product of their catches, cooked, planned and organized activities. They moved on when they had depleted their resources in an area. There was a gender division of labor. The age and gender-related roles of individuals were based on physical strength and skills. Men hunted, fished and undertook activities requiring physical strength while women gathered edible vegetation and cared for children. Leadership was charismatic. This meant band members supported a leader because of his personal character, his hunting prowess and his ability to resolve a dispute. It appears that bands generally meet once a year for the purpose of finding spouses for their younger members.

This practice known as restricted marital exchange involved two groups of hunter-gatherers exchanging young daughters and sons to create new family units. This also fosters cohesion between the two groups. But another important factor needs to be underlined. In a comparative study of 190 hunter-gatherers carried out by evolutionary biologist Minelaos Apostolou, less than 20% of men were polygamous. However, 87% of agriculturalists and pastoralists practiced polygamy. The predominance of monogamous relationships in hunter-gatherer societies reinforced stability and solidarity. In the event of a raid by a rival band, the cohesiveness of larger coalitions played an important role in the defeat of smaller coalitions. In contrast, polygamy in agricultural and pastoralist societies implies the necessity to amassing more goods, competition between members and the affirmation of the self at the expense of others as a matter of prestige, one of the bridges to inequality. From this perspective, the rise of bellicosity justified the need for a strong central authority to maintain order even in a tribe. Egalitarian does not mean pacific.

Jared Diamond reported the following response of women interviewed by an anthropologist in New Guinea: "My first husband was killed by Elopi raiders. My second husband was killed by a man who wanted me, and who become my third husband. That husband was killed by the brother of my second husband, seeking to avenge his murder" (J. Diamond 1998: p. 277)

To facilitate mobility, it appears that women breastfed their children beyond infancy to inhibit ovulation. Fewer children in the band reduced the burden of caring for additional dependent band members and reduced the pressure on limited food supplies. In the same vein, because mobility requires material possessions, no surplus resources were accumulated by any single member. The notion of surplus carries important ramifications which will be addressed later in the chiefdom polity. Overall, band members had a healthy lifestyle; they ate well and according to the anthropologist Marshall Sahlins in the "*Notes on The Original Affluent Society*", they lived well and with plenty of time for leisure. Cooperation and trust were the main characteristics of the band polity. In essence, band organization can be described as a loose society, in an egalitarian politico-economic structure.

Although common interests linked band members, disputes happened in the early communities. As in any social organization, control was necessary. Appointment of a bandleader or headman was an informal process based on the leader's social skills and other attributes benefiting the entire band.

Band societies still exist in various parts of the globe. For instance, the San or Bushmen of Southern Africa still maintain an egalitarian setting. Their roots and cultural traditions go back to 20,000 years. They are governed by consensus with no formal authority or chief, a rarity today. Leadership is recognized in those who have achieved a respectable age and moral rectitude. Hunting is teamwork and meat is distributed but not necessarily by the hunter.

Another example of an egalitarian society is the Inuit of the Arctic region of Canada. They came to North America from Asia across the Beringia land bridge when the water retreated during the glacial period. Although modern life has caught up with them in many ways, leadership remains informal and there is no absolute leader. Advice is sought from the elder in complex cases. That said, misbehavior is corrected through multiple mechanisms from ridicule to ostracism. In such a geographically remote area where constant communication is vital, isolation is very painful.

There are still a few other band societies. Some band examples are Ju/'hoansi of the Kalahari Desert in southwestern Africa, and the Mbuti Pygmies in the Ituri rainforest. These are all small multifamily bands who each live in separate territories to help them manage their resources.

Notwithstanding the foregoing, on the basis of recent joint archeological and anthropological studies, the band egalitarian concept may need to be revisited. Is it historically correct to assert that band polities were purely egalitarian? Another view has recently emerged. Given the nomadic lifestyle of hunter-gatherers, the accumulation of goods would have been an impediment to mobility. This way of living eliminated the possibility of manipulating other band members' behavior. In this way farming and animal, domestication is associated with the beginning of the emergence of surplus production and social differentiation some 10,000 years ago. But archeologists have discovered that social inequality was evident 14,500 years ago with the Natufian of the Eastern Mediterranean. They were a late culture of the Levant dating around 15,000 to 11,000 years ago. As a semi sedentary population, they may have been the earliest farmers in the world. . It was the ownership of small, resource-rich areas and the ease of bestowing them on descendants that fostered inequality. Ancient hunter-gatherers accumulated wealth and political clout by taking control of concentrated patches of wild foods (H. Pringle 2014: p.822). In other words, the wealth source was upstream instead of downstream meaning control of an area comes first in the food production process. Who has the land (or control of it) has the gold.

In 2010, archeologists T. Douglas Price of the University of Wisconsin and Ofer Bar-Yosef of Harvard University reported that ornaments, pendants, obsidians and marine shells (obviously imported from the far way) had been found in some burial sites of early Natufians. This was clear evidence of social differentiation. Those artifacts indicated the deceased had a position of power or wealth and not a common social practice. In a nutshell, inequality was evident 15,000 years ago, way before the Agricultural Revolution.

As the population grew so too did the number of bands, leading to the emergence of tribes which were larger and more complex organization. A tribe was an association of families consisting of members united by blood or marriage and their progeny, siblings, cousins, etc. Tribes had more members than bands, probably a few hundred.

Because a family tree can be quite extensive (See Figure 2.1), segmentation into smaller tribes would have occurred. Tribes like bands were the earlier producers and redistributors of food within their community. Their members were horticulturalists or pastoralists meaning a settled life with more permanent residences and structures to meet their requirements. Tribe members were farmers and migrant herders. They tended to be more technologically advanced than band members, requiring technology to cultivate food and manage domesticated animals.

The distribution of food was the responsibility of one person, known as the Big Man. This person worked as much as everyone else and got the same share as everyone else.

Tribe's technology was geared to plants cultivation for food production and the domestication of animals. The equal redistribution of food was made by a central person who came to be known as the Big Man who worked as much as everyone else and had no more than everyone else.

The Big Man had no true authority except by virtue of his ability to persuade. He would be designated the position based on his personal charisma and respect of fellow tribe members. In this egalitarian culture, the role of any big man and his members was to ensure an adequate supply of food and resources to maintain an acceptable standard of living. From this perspective, the tribal society was the first to consider hard work a matter of prestige. It should be noted that like bands there was no surplus in the tribe. Food was equally available to all. Nevertheless, keeping in mind the shortage of food in winter, some food such as dry meat, fish, staple were stored.

Figure 2.1 Tribe Lineage Descent

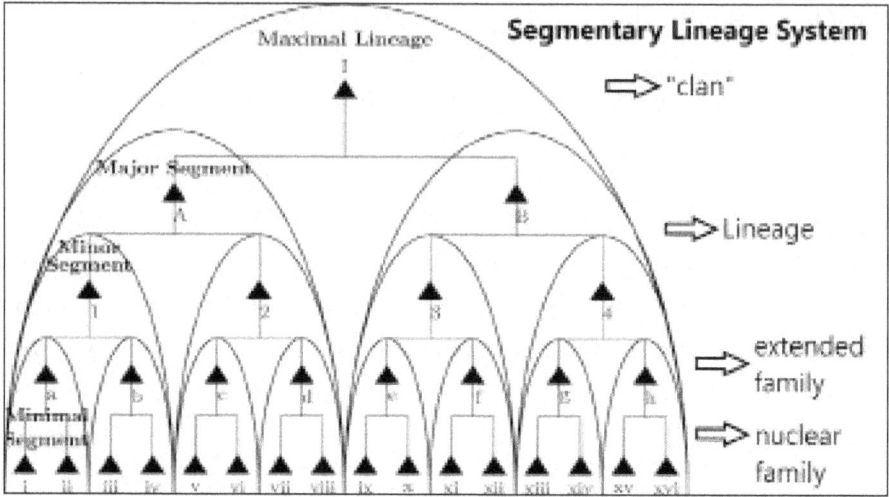

Figure 2.1 illustrates the lineage pattern of one tribal unit. The founder is at the top followed by his two offsprings. In this configuration, A and B are the primary segments with hundreds of possible descendants. This type of structure facilitates the resolution of disputes between the immediate family members and protection against outsiders. Tribal segments could rally in a united front against adversaries. The leadership of the tribe was on technical and social prowess. However, it was ephemeral and disappeared at the end of a conflict or calamity. Leadership survived as the nucleus of the primary segment.

Bands and tribes have many common features stemming from the need for conviviality and cooperation. On the trajectory of social evolution, this was more sophisticated in a tribe than a band. However, the more egalitarian nature of the band most likely contributed to the longevity of the band structure.

I could not complete this discussion about tribes without underlining an important characteristic of their members. In the words of Anglim Simon "A tribe is a society tracing its origin back to a single ancestor, who may be a real person, a mythical hero, or even a god: they usually view outsiders as dangerous and conflict against them as normal" leading to an "us" versus "them" mentality. In a nutshell, tribes provided not only a foretaste of the state but also demonstrated certain sociopolitical behaviors. Tribalism is still alive in some societies.

Men cannot abandon their religious faith without a kind of aberration of intellect and a sort of violent distortion of their true nature; they are invincibly brought back to more pious sentiments. Unbelief is an accident, and faith is the only permanent state of mankind.

Alexis de Tocqueville

Religion and Society

Before elaborating on the chiefdom polity, the next evolutionary political complexity, it is appropriate to consider religion and its influence on politics.

In a tribe, an *ancestor* could refer to a real or mythical person. This suggests a belief or relationship with a supernatural being which in turn implies a cultural behavior worth exploring. In fact, such a behavior preceded the emergence of *Homo sapiens*. It seems that religion had its origin in primitive communities 250,000 years ago. *Homo erectus* buried their dead. Archeologists have also discovered something unique in the fossilized remains of some Neanderthals. Not only did they bury their dead, in some cases plants and flowers were found with the body. Quite a sociocultural construct! The anthropologist A. B. Kehoe reports the case of a wild goat horn having been placed in the grave of a young Neanderthal child (Kehoe 1998: p 92).

Whether this attitude can be interpreted as an expression of empathy or a belief in the afterlife is unknown. However, this type of behavior is unique to human beings and has been practiced for thousands of years and preceded the establishment of modern religion as a social construct. More elaborated rituals are features of most major religions in our evolved and sophisticated society. Among the dogmas being promoted is respect, the love of others, altruism, elimination of suffering and assistance to fellow members to improve their lives on Earth with an afterlife reward within their interpretation of it.

Be that as it may, religious beliefs emerged as the exclusive impulse of humans to create a better world or the influence of a super-spiritual force to achieve this goal. There is no recorded culture in human history that has not practiced some form of religion. Each one its own god(s) and goddesses to explain the creation of the world and regulate daily life activities of proper behavior, with a peaceful afterlife as the final reward. Priest-kings were viewed either as human representatives of patron gods or elevated to the divine status of the adulation they received and the influence they had on their followers.

In the six primary states of the Old and the New World soon to be analyzed, polytheism was the norm. Religious practices dated to around 3500 BC in Sumer of Mesopotamia. Marduk was the god of Babylon. The Tower of Babel was dedicated to him. The Curse of Agade tells the story of the destruction of the city of Agade by the will of the gods due to Naram-Sin's impiety. In 3400 BC, Egyptians worshiped many deities including Horus, Isis, Osiris, Ptah and others; In the Indus Valley around 3000 BC, the Sanatan Dharma (The Eternal Order) had deities such as Brahma Vishnu and Shiva. Others emerged later between 500 BC and AD 300; In 3400 BC, Confucianism, Taoism and Buddhism emerged in China with the belief in ghost and dead ancestors (the folk religion); Prior to the Shang dynasty in 1600 BC, people worshiped many gods with one supreme god, Shangti. Head of the pantheon, Shangti was considered 'the great ancestor' who presided over victory in war, agriculture, the weather, and good government; at the beginning of the 14th century in Mexico, the Aztecs worshiped Huitzilopochtli, the god of sun as well as other minor gods and goddesses; by the beginning of the 15th century, the Incas of Peru worshiped the sun god Inti, the most important Inca's god from for whom the emperor was the living incarnation.

Although most of these ancient societies were polytheistic, each god or goddess governed a realm of human activities. Nonetheless, there was usually one who was elevated to a primary position. Religion thus became integrated with the other three cultural elements namely economics, kinship and politics, and must be considered accordingly.

With this universal albeit diverse spirituality, one wonders what religion is and where the impulse for this metaphysical concept came from. Cross-disciplinary knowledge of academics has answered this question. I must say outright, defining religion is a daunting task considering the complexity and mutability of this subject in space and time. This explains the difficulty of finding one commonly accepted definition. One definition might posit that religion is a set of rituals, rationalized by myth which mobilized supernatural powers for the purpose of achieving or preventing the transformation of the state in man and nature (A. Wallace 1966: p.107). Karl Marx referred to religion, of course, as a false consciousness intended to complete the exploitation of laborers. Sigmund Freud defined religion as a projection of unconscious processes. Each of these definitions has its own merit. In fact, they each form part of an indescribable total picture.

A simplistic and common feature of all religions and related rituals, although not universal, is the belief that human affairs are controlled by supernatural agents (s) namely gods, spirits, ancestors or other powerful invisible entities. In turn, they establish norms, values, emotion and behavior transmitted over generations like a meme. In this way, religion can be viewed as a cultural construct.

Even this premise has some weaknesses. E. B Taylor argued that narrowing the definition to mean the belief in a supreme deity or judgment after death or idolatry would exclude many people from the category of religion, and thus "has the fault of identifying religion with particular developments instead of the deeper motive which underlies them". (E. B. Tylor 1920: p. 424)

It may be more helpful to ask why people develop religious beliefs. In the last three decades, progress in cognitive science and the interdisciplinary scientific study of the mind and its processes have shed light on the enormous capacity of the human brain to acquire, generate and transmit religious thoughts and practices.

The following table was built from a summary of accounts on the origin of religion by the cognitive anthropologist and evolutionary psychologist Pascal Boyer. According to Boyer, the origin rests on four scenarios from the fact that religion provides an explanation, comfort and social order. This is facilitated by the human intellect which is illusion-prone. Under the umbrella of the actor four scenarios are represented: the mind, the emotion, the reason and the social environment.

Considering the range of scenarios laid out horizontally: explanation, comfort, order and human intellect, this table seems representative of opinion across time and space

Table 2.2 – Origin of Religion

	EXPLANATION	COMFORT	ORDER	H.INTELLECT
MIND	Natural Phenomena Experiences Origin of Things Evil and Sufferings			
EMOTION		Bearable Mortality World Comfortability		
REASON				Superstition Irrefutability Refutation
SOCIAL ENVIRONMENT.			Hold society together - Social Order Morality	

Source: Religion Explained – Reproduced with permission. (Author's modifications)

A close look at the above scenarios reveals that they are realistic in terms of describing the cause and effect of religion. Surely human beings have always sought explanations for natural phenomena and when science could not provide an irrefutable answer, our mind creates an alternate response. For example, our ancestors attributed natural calamities to the act of god or to the nefarious undertakings of bad spirits for the punishment of misbehaviors. This rationalization was a way of coping with inexplicable events. To this day, we still fear the unknown and, what we cannot understand sometimes results in self-imposed guilt. All ancient civilizations from Mesopotamia to Peru have their own explanations about the origin of things particularly the creation of the world. Through the lens of modern time, culturally they are now known as myths because nobody would today accept the creation of the universe by a sun god.

However, from a psychological perspective, religion has made the emotional response to mortality more bearable either in the sense of an afterlife continuity for the defunct depending on the religious denomination or in the elimination of suffering in some cases of terminally ill persons. Some societies attribute sickness and misfortunes to spiritual rather than natural causes. Religion lessens anxiety in that future spiritual interventions may alter the current situation in one's favor.

At the bare minimum, society as a collectivity is a sum of individuals living together in an organized way in a geographical location. It is true that religion instills a social order by having everyone adopting the same values. For instance, as will be shown later in the case of Egypt, the Maat, a system of laws of truth, balance, order, harmony, law, morality, justice, was designed and implemented to prevent chaos. In the same vein, some societies practice monogamy particularly in western civilization while others accept polygamy as a way of living based on a long-standing practice in their own culture.

Another conduit to how religion is used for maintaining the status quo of a political regime is the redistributive system of the Chiefdom polity. As will be revealed in the next Part, the whole surplus* collection in the chiefdom polity for a few at the expense of many was justified by the "spiritual" authority of the paramount chief. Hence the development of people's dependence on a central authority for a living which was the beginning of social and economic inequality.

Collective acceptance is different from individual tolerance and this latter may differ from the proponents of territorial expansion. Let's take for example a call for war which in my view was one of the conduits to how religion got intertwined with politics mostly in ancient times. While a population at large may benefit from a territorial expansion, members of the army went to war at the call of the supreme leader after consultation with the appropriate god. I doubt that this call was joyfully accepted by all soldiers particularly when death is a strong possibility or if defeated, they may be captured for human sacrifice.

It may be appropriate to shed more light on the human sacrifice also called ritualized killing that once took place in many societies around the globe (See Appendix I). As disgusting as human sacrifice looks it has been practiced by many religions but now banned. It remains that ritual is key to culture. Although no consensus exists on this term, ritual nowadays means liturgy to separate it from primitive religious practices. Ritual represents a strategic way of acting with particular social effects. It works as a mechanism that periodically converts the obligatory into desirable (V. W. Turner 1967: p.30). As noted earlier, the enormous power of the .supreme leader seen either as a representative or incarnation of a god through human sacrifice dissipates social tension, reaffirms the social status quo by his religious authority. Indeed, recent research has revealed that human sacrifice was used by the elite to maintain social stratification thereby reinforcing inequality.

The last scenario deals with the role of reason in the alleged explanation of the origin of religion which P. Boyer aptly called cognitive illusion. Most people recognize the existence of religion at least by fatalistic acquiescence. By religion, the interpretation of cause and effect is often skewed by attributing the intervention of supernatural forces to an event that could be explained by science. In essence, this attitude fits in the definition of superstitious behavior, an illusion of causality. Superstition can take place in monotheist, polytheist or syncretist adherents. This latter scenario happens quite commonly in areas where multiple religious traditions exist in proximity and function actively in the culture, or when a culture is conquered, and the conquerors bring their religious beliefs with them but do not succeed in entirely eradicating the old beliefs or, especially, practices. As a result, there are many cases of religious syncretism around the world. In China, a great part of the population follows a syncretic religion. Out of all Chinese believers, approximately 85.7% adhere to Chinese traditional religion with either Mahayana Buddhist or Taoist at the same time. In Haiti, Catholicism and Protestantism adherents represent respectively 57% and 30% of the population. However, Haitians believe in Vodou's existence. This is not to say that they get involved in the vodouistic rituals. One might accept the existence but not get involved in the ritual activities. Overall in 2015, Christians represented almost 33% of the world population, followed by Muslims at approximately 24%. Only 16% of people worldwide are not affiliated with any particular religion. Perhaps increased social interaction has caused this shift.

Irrefutability remains the hallmark of some of the religious claims. While everybody would agree they are preposterous, people continue to believe in them because evidence to the contrary is not palpable. The cause of these claims is attributed to supernatural forces whose existential evidence cannot be proven. So understandably, in a cultural setting, it is easier to believe in those claims than to refute them.

I believe in the separation of things. Let's look at the role of reason and the cultural effect of social interaction on religion. As mentioned earlier, cognitive science has made enormous progress at explaining the functioning of the mind particularly in the formation of thought, intuition, feeling, choice and myriad behavioral activities. Why do we fear walking alone particularly at night in the forest? Why any strange sound or total silence suggests sometimes an imminent threat? The experimental psychologist Justin L. Barrett posits that the human brain is equipped with what he called Hyperactive Agency Device Detection (HADD) as part of human nature skepticism. It is a filtering mechanism of HADD to eliminate biases and flaws of realities. In fact, methodological doubt precedes rationalization. HADD reflects an expansion of thinking capacity. It is triggered when confronted with an ambiguous situation such as a strange movement, pattern or object particularly if this latter moves by its own volition as perceived by our visual system. Our brain attributes liveliness to that object not necessarily from a biological but from a psychological viewpoint that is a thing that produces a specified effect without track. This thing qualifies as an agent.

As part of the HADD process, the incumbent reacts instantaneously. We imagine what this agent can do. It is better to act on the side of safety or survival than negligence. J. L. Barrett and other scholars have speculated that HADD plays an important role in the development of religion and superstition recognizing that further research is required to support their position with more robust evidence. Indeed, this theory can be modified or expanded by the further discovery in neuroscience, hopefully without an effect in the opposite direction.

As noted, religion has been explained as a natural phenomenon. Moreover, the anthropologist Robert N. McCauley in his book *"Why Religion is Natural, Science is Not"* posits that there is far more risk for humanity at pursuing scientific creations than clarifying the origin of religion. However, in this whole debate, more importantly, the philosophical dimension needs to be underlined.

It is relatively easy to explain the origin of some of the phenomena that we can hear and/or see. For instance, thunder caused by lightning is essentially a stream of electrons flowing between or within clouds, or between a cloud and the ground but not by Govannon, a Welsh god of blacksmiths in Celtic mythology. What about what we can't see? Scientific development has enabled the understanding of gravity which is the force by which a planet or other body draws objects towards its center. The force of gravity keeps all of the planets in orbit around the sun. Electricity is a form of energy resulting from the existence of charged particles either statically as an accumulation of charge or dynamically as a current. The list can go on and on in the physiological and biological fields. These are clear explanations of phenomena in the natural realm.

This debate becomes more complex if I move to the supernatural realm. For instance, what is a soul? The Oxford and Cambridge dictionaries have come to basically the same definition respectively the spiritual or immaterial part of a human being or animal, regarded as immortal; the spiritual part of a person that some people believe continues to exist in some form after their body has died. Both seem to imply the survival of the soul after the physical death of the body. "A soul-centered theory is a view that meaning in life comes from relating in a certain way to an immortal, spiritual substance that supervenes on one's body when it is alive and that will forever outlive its death"(Thaddeus Metz 2013: 2.2). In philosophical parlance, religion, inter alias, gives meaning to life by practicing the virtues and values accepted in a society to access a peaceful afterlife. Conceivably, this may explain the variety of religious faith in different civilizations around the globe on what the adherents believe is the truth. But what is truth? From the Greek philosopher Aristotle (384-322BC) to Pontius Pilate the Roman prefect of Judea tenure (AD 26-36) or even in today's justice system, this question has been of utmost importance to humanity for millennia. Aristotle simply defined it as "to say of what is that it is".

We believe in what we can see and in what we can't see as well with our naked eyes including extra sensorial perception. As mentioned earlier, chemistry and physics respectively give evidence of the building block of matter and electricity. In the metaphysical realm, the presence or absence of religious faith separates believers from non-believers. Indeed, some religions had existed for millennia, others came and fell out of "style". Let's now consider two of the most important religions. In the less distant past in 4 B.C. or perhaps earlier, at Bethlehem, in the suburb of Jerusalem, Jesus was born. In AD 29, He was crucified. This is a fact. In Arabia, a young man named Muhammad (570-622) began preaching a new religion called Islam. On September 20, 622 he was forced to flee his home city of Mecca for Medina. This was the hegira (from an Arabic word for "flight"), and from that day, his followers, the Muslims, count their years (I. Asimov 1989: pp. 61 & 68). This also is a fact. I am not certain when the theology proper doctrine (God's revelation of Himself to human) was introduced probably in the 3rd century but in reality, it boils down to what people choose to believe. It is my hope that this short section will help people from following or not a religion as passive automata. Dogmatic practices without foundational truth become a system of religion without power.

Chiefdoms

As I have pointed out, for the greater part of our history, we lived in an egalitarian society. The advent of the chiefdom form of social organization was a major shift with significant long term consequences. I cannot overemphasize this statement. With the advent of the chiefdom polity, people had to live with different tribes, different customs and comply with a non-charismatic leader. Moreover, people had to accept being treated differently. In other words, from this point onwards the product of the work of many was taken by a few for their own benefit. This was the official birth of inequality and its related institutions. As I will show, inequality can be economic, social or political. Economic inequality refers to people's different positions within the distribution of income, pay or wealth in the economy. Social inequality covers the relational processes in society that have the effect of limiting or harming the social status of a group, class or circle of people. Political inequality refers to structured differences in the distribution and acquisition of political resources. The most common approach is to understand political inequality as differences in political voice and participation. (L. Bartels – J. K. Dubrow).

Over time, as part of the demographic forces, many tribes particularly those of a few thousand members population consolidated in chiefdoms, a more complex form of social organization. However, this transformation should not be seen as a general trend or unilineal continuum in that some tribes and even bands continued to exist independently. Moreover, some tribes in the chiefdom because dissatisfied and reverted to their prior social organization.

The most succinct definition of a chiefdom in anthropology is by Robert L. Carneiro: "An autonomous political unit comprising a number of villages or communities under the permanent control of a paramount chief" (Carneiro 1981: 45). I will come back to the paramount chief in a moment. A chiefdom was characterized by a central authority that was responsible for the redistribution of food. In return, the central authority headed by a paramount Chief provided protection and social order. Chieftainship was based on kinship. The position was inherited and rarely bestowed based on prowess or special abilities. However, the ability to maintain and secure a chieftainship position was required. As a representative of a god, he must display the ability to pass on success in agricultural production, arts music and all his undertakings. Conversely, a bad harvest could have been detrimental to a chief.

Chiefdom was a ranked society. People are locked in specific rank at birth based on their lineage. The paramount chief occupied the highest level and received better goods and resources. This social ranking was reinforced by occupational category wherein certain high functions could be performed by the closest descendants of the chief. These permanent positions were the beginning of endogamous nobility still visible in some countries today. Chieftainship could also be obtained by marriage.

Around the world, this model of central authority was supported by a new factor of social integration: religion. The population size of a chiefdom could reach several thousand although smaller chiefdom polities existed, however less productive than the larger ones. As a result of a demographic explosion more tools were developed to enhance agriculture, irrigation, crafts, arts and music for the upper class. Disputes between parties, common because of the population size, were settled by the supreme chief.

Returning to the role of religion in this new organizational structure, many rituals including sacrifices were performed by the paramount chief who was ascribed with supernatural powers, the spoke-person of the gods. Ceremonies and rituals had been carried out in-band and tribe egalitarian societies for many purposes such as finding a partner, worshipping an ancestor and gods. However, ceremonial events became more frequent and elaborated in chiefdom as the paramount chief playing the role of a priest. As mentioned, humanity's search for spiritual connection and fulfillment goes back to millennia. Animism, totemism and other social constructs remain part of many cultures today.

In chiefdom societies, a political organization could be simple or complex depending on the size of its population and structure. A simple chiefdom would be made up of a few villages (clans). The supreme chief would be aided by a chief assisted by three or more representatives. These chiefs would be responsible for the collection of the surplus production which would be remitted to the chief. Those lesser ranking representatives got their power and privileges from the intermediate chiefs who like the supreme was divorced from food production. A complex chiefdom would consist of a group of simple chiefdoms and be ruled by a paramount chief. The central authority resided with a paramount chief. The collection and retribution of food and resource were carried out by minor chiefs who were responsible for the villages in their vicinity. More importantly, these little chiefs ensured the continuity of the flow of goods to their superior chief who passes them on to the supreme chief. Both the lesser and intermediate chiefs enjoyed a privileged position commensurate with their role. Such an economic system required a lot of resources to support the lavish lifestyle of the paramount chief and his "acolytes". This quickly became a source of internal dissension and competition between rival chiefdoms. Such stresses build until they overwhelmed the decision-making apparatus at which point the system collapsed or developed a new decision-making apparatus. This suggests a punctuated rather than a gradualist conception of cultural evolution (T. K. Earle 1987).

As a result, chiefdom's politico-economic organizational structure was inherently unstable. Chiefdoms were often conquered and absorbed by more powerful chiefdoms. And, internal dissensions would compromise its stability when things like a bad harvest or an epidemic disease undermined the authority of the paramount chief. This demonstrates the importance of two factors: the rivalry between chiefdoms in the race to maintain or extend their territories, and the fundamental role played by religion in the veneration of the paramount chief. Without these factors, it would indeed be difficult to understand the veneration of the paramount chief to a point that the commoners accept the global transfer of the fruits of their hard work to a minority. Chiefdom marked the beginning of systemic inequality which is the institutionalization of a system that syphons goods from the masses, namely the commoners, to an assertive elite whose wants to exceed their needs. Let's analyze this situation. This is a " "storable-stealable surplus" (E. L. Mendonsa 2016: p.323).

In a complex chiefdom, the position of the paramount chief (and the associated wealth) was transferable to one of his children. However, the work resource remained limited and access to prestigious goods was at the whim of the paramount chief. In such a social organization the workers' position is fixed. It is a situation where one group is systematically assigned an unequal status in relation to other groups. This relationship is perpetuated and reinforced by a confluence of unequal relations in roles, functions, decisions, rights and opportunities. This begs the question of what was this surplus product and who were the stealers?

Based on archeological excavations and in concert with anthropologists, it was determined that acephalous society of the Paleolithic period did not carry any surplus. Hunting products were shared by the hunter(s) and consumed by the members. In this communal system, each member depended on the whole social organization. In addition, it was unwise to store food because such a practice would negatively affect mobility and was unnecessary because of the abundance of Mother Nature. This frugality did not extend to seasonal fruits, nuts and meat drying which could hardly be called surplus within the meaning of a stored food system. What then is this resource surplus in the chiefdom polity?

The notion of surplus occurred during the Neolithic period starting in the chiefdom polity but with a different connotation. The surplus in question was derived from the commoners, be they agriculturalists, pastoralists, craftsmen or anyone else working for producing extra goods collected by the minor chiefs for the paramount chief. Those extra (aka surplus) goods collected were seen as a tribute to the chief by the workers for the use of the land occupied by the commoners. The mass thus became dependent on the higher authority for survival in contrast to those in the communal system of bands and tribes.

The accumulation of resources gave the paramount chiefs enormous wealth and bargaining power for acquiring prestigious goods from external traders. Although coveted by all, these goods were given to selected ranking officials to consolidate their loyalty to the political system. Craftsmen and artists work exclusively for the paramount chief creating luxury items such as ceramic, pottery, leather goods, baskets, cookware and jewelry. The items could also be used for exchange in commercial transactions. Commodities exchanges were distinct from gift exchange. This latter "places the recipient under an obligation to the donor, who, for the time being, has a measure of advantage over the other person" (Service 1975: p.73). Commodities in the chiefdom polity "are exchanged strictly in relation to other commodities without any implied residual obligation or relationships between the people involved" (D. Bell 1991:156). Those prestigious goods acquired by commodity exchange were symbols of the power of the paramount chief affirming the legitimacy of rule over the people in the chiefdom.

Another important feature of commodity exchanges is the tacit strategy of maintaining peace. Both parties involved in the exchange process develop a friendship. This phenomenon can be seen as the precursor of the "doux commerce" (lit. gentle commerce or soft commerce). It is a concept that originated from the Age of Reason in the 18th century stating that commerce tends to civilize people, making them less likely to resort to violent or irrational behaviors. This theory is also called commercial republicanism meaning trading between two free and equal commercial partners.

With regards to the stealers, this refers to the conflicts and raids of sedentary farmers and nomad pastoralists in the early period of settlement necessitating some form of protection a quasi-unanimous shield against this plague. Raiders have quickly realized that land productivity is proportional to the number of people working on it. Laborers captured during those raids were a bonus that could be used as a sacrifice to the victor's gods. Over time, this consensual arrangement for protection between the commoners and the paramount chief became coercive and exploitive as we will see in the next sociopolitical organizations: the state

I could not avoid making an analogy between symbiosis in the biological field and inequality in this early sociopolitical arrangement. The most popular definition of symbiosis is an interaction or relationship between two different species sometimes beneficial or detrimental. In the case of endo-symbiosis, the species live inside the other such as protozoan living inside termites and help to digest wood. In the case of ecto-symbiosis, the species live on the surface of the other such as lice that live on the skin and blood of the host. Symbiosis has three components; Mutualism: a symbiosis in which both organisms benefit. For example, in the distant past wolves, evolutionary the dogs' ancestors, assisted humans in hunting and in return humans fed them. Commensalism: a symbiosis in which one organism benefits without helping or harming the other. A case in point a spider web on a tree does not affect either organism; Parasitism: a symbiosis in which one organism benefits at the expense of the other. Ecto-symbiosis and parasitism are both harmful. In my view these types of symbiosis perfectly describe inequality. More importantly, despite the complexity and "perfection" of inequality in various forms in modern times, it (inequality) is destroying society. To paraphrase the biologist Louis Pasteur, the role of the infinitely small is infinitely big.

It has been argued that workers in a redistribution system received items that they could not otherwise obtain in exchange for their labor. This is because the paramount chief had more contacts and purchasing power. The reality was that access to those prestigious products was very limited. Basically, the commoners' surplus was "siphoned off" to sustain the lavish lifestyle of the paramount chief and his acolytes and to maintain the loyalty of those lesser authorities who also do not work. Surplus occurred in the Neolithic Agricultural Revolution and granted demographic forces, a socio-political transformation had taken place. Disputes could no longer be settled by the Big Man because of the size and dispersion of the population. This evolution, among other factors, has led to a stratified society with centralized authority as the surplus products of many were allocated to the few

Societies at different evolutionary stages confront different challenges and possess different properties and dynamics. Chiefdoms could be found around the world in Hawaii, Africa, the Southeastern United States of America, the six chiefdoms of Hispaniola in the Caribbean and South America. Some of these ancient civilizations were destroyed during the colonial period. However, surviving chiefdoms do not necessarily evolve into a state. For example, the tribes of Papua and New Guinea were consolidated after World War II and became independent from Australia in 1975.

State Formation

Earlier, I have mentioned the term storable-stealable-surplus, coined by E. L. Mendonsa, was one of the key features of the chiefdom polity. I also raised the notion of the consent followed by the coercion of the commoners giving their hard-earned farming and herding products to the few called the elite, in return for protection and security. In addition, the paramount chief, sometimes assuming the role of the high priest, was accepted by the commoners, and through many well thought manipulations including human sacrifices, as descended from the gods. This was a powerful strategy because psychologically it was difficult to dislike or distrust the gods regardless of the commoner feeling about the paramount chief. In the state polity, autocracy and theocracy were both institutionalized not only to maintain social order but also for the purposes of aggrandizement and expansion.

Before going into the intricacies of state as a politico-social organization, I would like to provide a brief perspective of the demography of society at the dawn of the Neolithic period. As can be seen in Table 2.2 the global population rose from a few thousand in the Lower Paleolithic period to 5.3 million in the Mesolithic period. Moreover, the human population increased more than twofold during the Neolithic period, reaching 12 Million. Several methods have been used to estimate the prehistoric population. One approach is to study episodes of settlement aggregation, migration and dispersal. Another is to attribute to a given area the population density recorded in a recent period among other people of similar culture living in a similar environment and culture. According to Professor Jean-Noel Biraben de l'Institut national d'études démographiques de Paris, population distribution in the prehistoric era was much closely linked to the size of the territory populated, the climatic variations than the limited technology. I support this concept. The expansion effect of Homo sapiens into new territories in the Middle Paleolithic period and the accelerated population growth thereafter were largely due to better stone tools.

Table 2.2 - Estimated Pre-historic World Population

CULTURAL STAGE	ESTIMATED POPULATION
Lower Paleolithic	125,000
Middle Paleolithic	1 million
Upper Paleolithic	3.3 million
Mesolithic	5.3 million
Neolithic	12 million
First Millennium A.D.	300 million

Source: Jean Noel Biraben: Population and Society No 394 – Oct 2003 & Massimo Livi-Bacci: World Population

The population growth evidenced in the above table parallels the cultural and economic evolution of the society. The political evolution from chiefdoms to state was a substantial change. It brought with it the growth and refinement of inequality, stratification and the institutionalization of the separation of the ruler from the ruled. How can this political transformation, which emerged independently in different geographical locations, be substantiated? What are the drivers of this political metamorphosis? Archeologists, anthropologists and sociologists have shed light on this matter. In the words of the politician and historian Niccolò Machiavelli: "Everyone who wants to know what will happen ought to examine what has happened: everything in this world in any epoch has their replicas in antiquity". Even the Bible obliquely mentions the formation of a state. Put in another way, the historical process is a manifestation of evolutionary complexity. David J. Snowden and Mary E. Boon, in an article published in Harvard Business Review (Nov 2007) identified the following aspect of complexity:

1. A complex system involves large numbers of interacting elements.

2. The interactions are nonlinear, and minor changes can produce disproportionately major consequences.

3. The system is dynamic, the whole is greater than the sum of its parts, and solutions can't be imposed; Instead, they arise from the circumstances. This is frequently referred to as emergence.

4. The system has a history, and the past is integrated with the present; the elements evolve with one another and with the environment; and evolution is irreversible.

5. Though a complex system may, in retrospect, appear to be ordered and predictable, hindsight does not lead to foresight because the external conditions and systems constantly change.

We have a past, a history. We live our lives not just "be in the moment". This uniqueness of human mental capacity for creativity explains our survivability and eventually, our expansion beyond the confines of our planet. For better or worst we are shaped by the institutions and values inherited from our past. History is not a meaningless tale. It needs to be told and retold. Understanding the historical evolution of our sociopolitical system will allow us to better understand ourselves and to cope with current challenges. This echoes a quote from the poet and American activist of the preceding century Penn Robert Warren "History cannot give us a program for the future but it can give us a fuller understanding of ourselves, and our humanity, so that we can better face the future".

In the myriad definitions of state, it is indeed difficult to come up with one definition that would satisfy all the arguments about this form of polity around the world. As a result, there is no academic consensus on the most appropriate definition of the term because each definition sustains different political strategies. Cultural anthropologists Henry J. M. Claessen defines a state as a centralized socio-political organization for the regulation of social relations in a complex, stratified society divided into at least two basic strata, or emergent social classes - viz. the rulers and the ruled – whose relations are characterized by political dominance of the former and tributary relations of the latter. This configuration is legitimized by a common ideology of which reciprocity is the basic principle. I have retained J. C. Classen's definition because it is far more detailed and comprehensive. Although the terms state and government are used interchangeably in the public discourse there is a great difference between both. The former is a non-physical entity, the institutionalization of leadership. The latter is a bureaucracy instituted to rule by right of authority and is the agency of the former (E. Service 1975 pp. 71-102)

As a non-physical entity, a state is characterized by four attributes: (1) a non-homogenous, permanent with no minimum population, culturally and ethnical speaking (2) a defined territory with no minimum size (3) a government with a power limited by its constitution (4) sovereignty within the territorial limits of the state. For modern states, I must add population surveillance and monitoring as other attributes. The first two criteria constitute the physical basis of a state and the last two its political basis.

State polity, like the Neolithic agricultural revolution phenomenon, emerged independently at different geographic locations around the world. Several theories have been advanced in the last few decades about the origin of this new polity. One fact is certain, the emergence of the state polity reflects a cultural evolution and a new level of complexity of information processing and decision making, in line with the (complexity's) characteristics mentioned above. Max Weber defined a state as a compulsory political organization with a centralized government that maintains a monopoly of the legitimate use of force within a certain territory. But this definition of state among many is not about its origin. Because of the importance of the state polity until today around the world, I thought it appropriate to briefly address its origin.

The multitude of publications on this matter from Plato to Francis Fukuyama and others underscore its importance. Most scholars dealing with this issue have adopted a multi-causal approach with many different factors having an impact on this political evolution. Among them are justice, production, population pressure, geography, and coercive forces, which have been raised to explain this political evolution. Although none of these factors taken individually explains the origin of state around the globe, a brief review of some of them seems necessary.

Food production is often mentioned as one of the main factors causing the evolution of a complex society. Archeologist and philologist Gordon Childe posits that the development of food production led to fundamental social transformations which created other levels of complexity resulting in the development of the earliest cities and states. In other words, agricultural production can be viewed as the root cause of both urbanization and social complexity.

More sophisticated food production drives and then sustains a larger population. The development of subsistence based on plant and animal domestication was as dramatic as any of the big cultural transformation of the more distant past. Indeed, some hunter-gatherer societies had population densities from 0.1 to 1 person per square kilometer. Agriculture permitted the density to rise between 40 and 60 fold in major European countries in the mid18th century. As a result, social interactions became more complex changing the social organizational profile of society.

The effect of food production, social interaction complexity and population increase has been the subject of much debate. But which came first? Did food production drive population growth causing organizational change or did an increase in the population and social complexity drive food production?

An increase in population density and social interaction complexity cross-pollinate in successive loops and feed each other. Population growth enhances social complexity (different politico-social organization) which requires more food production looping back to population growth as seen in Mesopotamia and China. The chiefdom polities of Mesopotamia and China were able to undertake infrastructural works such as large irrigation projects, trade networks and technological development to enhancing food production which in turn accelerated population growth.

Socioeconomic and political reality are intertwined which becomes more evident with the evolution of political entities. The preceding pages underlined the emergence and development of inequality between the commoners and the paramount chief and the elite in the chiefdom polity. Now I will address the causality of the emergence of the state, the most popular political entity until modern times and how it functions. My goal is to identify the underlying social challenges in the primary states. The state polities, like the ones listed in table 2.3, were formed without the influence of neighboring countries. These state's societies developed in regions where no states existed before. The internal process of this emergence and relation with only non-state have been the subject of much debates among anthropologists. In addition, the spontaneous emergence and sparse dispersion of states in time and space, as you can see in the following table and map, add more energy to the debates

Table 2.3 Table of Primary States with Region and Approximate Time of Formation

STATE	ARCHEOLOGICAL SITE	DATE
Mesoamerica		
Oaxaca Valley-Mexico	Monte Albán	ca 300 BC- AD 100
Peru		
Virú Gallinazo-	Virú Valley-Coastal Northern Peru	ca 200 BC-AD 200
Egypt		
Hierakonpolis-Egypt	Upper and Lower Egypt	ca 3500 - 3100 BC
Mesopotamia		
Uruk	Susiana – Susa	ca 4000 - 3300 BC
Indus Valley		
Harrapa	Eastern Pakistan	ca 2600 - 2000 BC
China		
Erlitou	Central China (Shanxi & Henan)	ca 1900- 1500 BC

From an anthropological perspective, I will consider the most important theories and hypotheses of state formation. Human society has come a long way since the first social formation in the band polity.

Gary Ferraro and Susan Andreatta provide a detailed description of Gordon Childe's voluntaristic theory One of the most detailed descriptions of the archeologists Gordon Childe voluntaristic theory. This theory of state formation posits that "the introduction and development of intensive agriculture (stimulated by the introduction of the plow, irrigation, metallurgy during the Neolithic period created food surplus. These food surpluses, in turn, freed up a certain segment of the population from the tasks associated with food production, allowing them to engage in a wide variety of new occupational roles such as wavers, traders, potters, and metal workers. This dramatic increase in occupational specialization necessitated a wider form of political integration to mediate between and protect the varied special interest groups and to provide the economic superstructure to enable them to work in an efficient and complementary fashion". Implicit in this definition is the idea that people rationally and spontaneously gave up their individual freedom to a political entity for the common good with the expectation that the benefits of doing so would be greater than the cost. This is consistent with the spirit of Rousseau's Social Contract which I will cover later.

The difficulty with this theory lays in the concept of surplus. This is an elusive term which requires clarification. I suggest that surplus is associated with forced labor for over-production, the precursor of a land tax. Archeologist Vincas P. Steponaitis has proposed a model for extrapolating the amount of surplus (in effect a tribute) mobilized to support the political establishment in a centralized society the number of levels in a regional hierarchy – the degree of political centralization. Hence "power" means control over resources. He posited that "it is reasonable to expect that in general the degree of political power will be closely related to the amount of tribute that can be extracted, for these two variables are intrinsically interdependent. One of his findings was that the degree of centralization at the apex of a three-level hierarchy that emerged during the Late Formative times was pronounced: one regional center appears to have controlled roughly three times more tribute in food than the average local center. Additionally, the evidence suggests that approximately 16% of the total population in the study area consisted of non-producers supported by the tribute.

In the context of an egalitarian society, neither bands nor tribes had surplus production. It was unthinkable that a surplus production would occur in a band because the products gathered were shared and consumed when collected remembering the tribe's small size. Nature was to a certain extent the warehouse notwithstanding very few items to counteract environmental limitations. Excess production in food or commodity in the tribe polity occur by consent for specific purposes such as gift exchanges and was limited to the same value to avoid embarrassing the receiver. In addition, food production was hard labor considering the rudimentary agricultural implements of the time. If a surplus was produced to feed the European settlers during the Age of Discovery, it was more likely done by coercion. G. D. Jones and Robert R. Kautz argue that the potential to produce a food surplus is inherent in any agricultural system, its actualization however depends on economic incentives or political coercion.

A case in point is the Cubeo Indians of the Northwest corner of the Amazon Basin. They cultivated manioc to meet their own needs. They were capable of producing more but in keeping with their lifestyle, it was unnecessary (I. Goldman 1979: p. 3-5). In the case of manioc, subsistence can be measured by the amount converted directly to manioc cake and tapioca porridge. Farinha, a byproduct of manioc was mainly used for trade. No surplus existed. The development of agriculture does not automatically create a food surplus. There was no social stimulus to do so (Carneiro 1970: pp.733-736). States are created or expanded by military force as weaker polities are subdued to satisfy the need of the victor, which in the case of the Cubeo Indians, was the Spaniards.

Before turning to J. J. Rousseau, let's consider the position of Aristotle on the origin of the state. He believed that it naturally evolves from the city-state as a political unit. First, there is the pairing of individuals for reproduction and self-preservation followed by the formation of households which consolidate into villages. Self-sufficiency is achieved for the sake of a secure life. This continuum is imposed by nature. Humans, being a social animal gifted with language, have the natural impulse to live in this setting and the great political benefactor is the lawgiver of the city-state. This political framework lifts human beings from savagery. From this perspective, Aristotle sounds like a harbinger of Thomas Hobbes who stated that life outside society without law and order would be solitary, poor, brutish, nasty and short.

Aristotle's concept is difficult to understand. If the process leading to the state is a natural process the means do not justify the end because the benefactor overtly sanctions gender and class inequality for the sake of living a good life. The surrendering of women to men and slaves to their masters are questionable concepts at best. Only adult citizen males could participate in the political process. There is nothing natural about this! It is just a conveniently built social construct supporting gender imbalance and class discrimination.

This lack of clarity about "natural" leaves a challenge for scholars of its possible meanings. In Political Naturalism, the political scientist Ernest Barker suggests that Aristotle meant "natural" in the extended sense that it arises from humankind's natural inclinations to live in communities. However, the communities remain unfinished until a lawgiver provides it with a constitution. It is my view that if Aristotle's theory were implemented at its face value, this approach would have led to totalitarianism.

Another way to view Aristotle's theory of state is from a political complexity evolutionary perspective. By the 4th century BC, most countries in the ancient world had evolved into state political organizations. However, earlier forms of societal organization including bands, tribes and chiefdoms had not entirely disappeared from Europe, Central Pacific or Australia They were still in existence during Aristotle's lifetime. The simplest explanation seems to be that, geographically, Athens was already surrounded by state polities. The intermediate chiefdom polity involving autonomous villages and states had disappeared by his time. Conceivably, Aristotle wanted to describe the components and the modus vivendi in a state as a natural institution in which humans would flourish.

Another proponent of the state arising from nature instead of being the outcome of the evolution of cultural institutions is Jean Jacques Rousseau. In the *Social Contract,* he posits that people surrender their rights and freedom to a central body i.e the government for a higher purpose namely the common good in the absence of which the aggressive pursuit of self-interest would infringe on the rights of others. The Social Contract can be seen as an instrument to eliminate the problems created by society. However, history has not revealed any state formed on that basis. Nonetheless, the social contract may have inspired the founding fathers of the US Constitution by ensuring the sovereignty of people in the free choice of their government.

Rousseau and Locke diverge on the issue of private property. Rousseau did not find anything natural about property unless preceded by a social contract with the state. Otherwise, society incurs the risk of corruption and envy because of its insatiable appetite for profit. Locke extends ownership of one's physical body to property. No collective agreement is needed to certify a property right. In summary, Rousseau's position supports equality while Locke's enhances inequality.

Another form of voluntary consent is hydraulic theory. According to the hydraulic theory of Wittfogel and Stewart "large scale irrigation requires centralized coordination and direction of effort, which, in turn, leads to greater political integration...Irrigation is a major cause of the emergence of centralized political authority and supra political organizations and, as such *a* major cause of the development of early states and civilizations".

The implicit assumption therein is that farmers from many villages cooperated to create large scale irrigation projects instead of their ineffective individual projects. The administrative and bureaucratic levels required to manage these projects became the foundation of the state polity. However, archeological and historical data has revealed that primary states in Mesopotamia, North China and Mexico emerged long before the development of large scale irrigation projects.

But, cause and effect can often be confused particularly if the subject at stake and the chronology of events are not deeply analyzed. Small-scale irrigation existed in many parts of the world before the rise of states (J. Diamond 1997: pp. 283-284). Construction of large scale irrigation systems did not accompany the emergence of the state polity but came significantly later in the above-mentioned areas and Madagascar. In most of the states formed in the Maya area of Mesoamerica* and the Andes, irrigation systems always remained small-scale ones that local communities could build and maintain themselves. Thus, even in those areas where complex systems of hydraulic management did emerge, these projects were the consequence not the cause of state polities. While the effects of irrigation cannot be minimized such as the required human resource and budget management, the hydraulic hypothesis cannot be viewed as the cause of a state polity.

If population size is of paramount importance in the formation of states, other factors such as warfare need to be underlined in the causality of state formation. In a paper "The Circumscription Theory", R. Carneiro wrote that "when the population is growing in a region tightly hemmed in by physical barriers such as mountains, deserts and oceans, the pressure exerted by this growing population is prevented from dissipating by escaping into new surrounding regions. The initial effect of this heightened pressure was to increase the frequency and intensity of warfare as villages competed for scarcer and scarcer land". The ultimate effect of this warfare was to bring about a categorical change in the political structure of the enclosed population". This explains in certain cases the evolution of chiefdom to a state polity.

In the paper mentioned above, Carneiro noted that not all circumscribed areas became a state. The prime mover for the emergence of the state was the coercive force. Circumscription must be understood as a mechanism or an enhancing condition to the emergence of a state. Social circumscription entails an increased population density caused by the combined effect of resource concentration and environmental circumscription. This pressure caused villages to impinge on each other resulting in warfare which resulted in a change of the political landscape from tribes to chiefdoms and ultimately to state.

Circumscription can be caused by environmental, resource or social conditions. The core characteristic of environmental circumscription is embedded in the brief description of the theory described above. Basically, it occurred in some areas because of the ecological setting.

Indigenous areas such as the Nile, Tigris-Euphrates and Indus Valleys in the Old World, and the valleys of Mexico, the mountain and coastal valleys of Peru in the New World have one common feature: they were all areas of circumscribed land. It was also where the first primary states emerged.

Let's look at the Amazon basin and the coastal valleys of Peru through the lenses of the circumscription theory. When inter-tribal warfare occurred in the Amazon Basin, the defeated tribes could easily retreat and settle in unoccupied land for rebuilding a community. This type of warfare is known as "fight and flight" in which the defeated are not subjugated by the victor. The multiplication of this type of outcome explains the spread of horticulturalists in the entire Amazon basin. However, the situation was different in the Peruvian coast area. Based on archeological evidence, we know that villages were confined to 78 narrow valleys backed by mountains, fronted by ocean and flanked on either side by desert, a classic definition of circumscribed area. By demographic pressure, more villages were developed as long as land was available until all usable land was occupied. As methods to increase land yields such as tiling and irrigation became less effective, land expansion by the conquest of another tribe became inevitable. However, in the Peruvian Coastal area fight and flight was no longer a possible alternative to the defeated tribes. They became subordinated to the victor and, if not exterminated, forced to pay a tax in kind by producing more food than before.

As this kind of subordination increased over time so did the political integration. Tribes evolved to chiefdoms, the most powerful chiefdom became a state and the most powerful states became an empire. Nonetheless, this continuum should not be taken as a general unilineal political evolution. I do not see territorial expansion as a cause of state formation but a consequence of it. Nonetheless, the six primary states of Spencer is used as a reference point in this study of inequality.

Obviously, not all areas of the world were or are circumscribed. However, warfare is a trademark of human society and it has led inevitably to more complex political integration. Did the taking of land begin before population pressure became a factor? The endowment is one of the answers. Societies well-endowed with arable land and resources still compete over more of the same. The fight over várzea* is an example that can corroborate this statement. Archeologists have also noted inter-village competition among the Olmec of Mexico over deposits of obsidian and jade or some other high valued commodities to obtain them. This latter example shows that resource concentration is not limited to fertile soil.

Resource concentration and environmental circumscription are concomitant issues. It has been observed that resource concentration often accelerates the political evolution process. In the Olmec area of southern Mexico, chiefdoms and even states arose before they did further west in the Oaxaca Valley. The concentration of wild food resources enjoyed by the Olmec seems to have led to an early buildup of the population followed by competition over its choicest parts. As a result conquest war led to a more complex political organization.

In this context, there is clearly a symbiotic relationship between resource concentration and environmental circumscription. However, it has been observed that resource concentration alone while enabling large and complex societies to arise does so slowly. The crowding together of villages as they grow in size and proliferate in number in an unbounded area produces a similar effect as crowding in an area of environmental circumscription. Without a physically circumscribed perimeter to constrict the population, it simply takes longer for the population to fill the whole area. Social circumscription occurs when the population reaches this point.

In summary, the voluntaristic* theory under which the hydraulic and automatic* hypothesis can be grouped was found inappropriate as a causative factor of state formation. Only coercive force with the precondition of warfare, the prime mechanism and the circumscription setting, the proper conditions provide a robust explanation of the origin of state. That said, generalizations are often dangerous. For instance Papua, New Guinea, despite population increased and warfare in a circumscribed area became a sovereign independent state in 1975 only when Australia relinquished its territorial administration. There are other circumscribed areas such as Chibok in Northeastern Nigeria which evolved to statehood without warfare (R. Cohen 1984: p. 336). Then there are the populous and circumscribed environments of the high island of Polynesia where state did not emerge (D. Webster 1975: p.465). But these examples do not reduce the important role of coercive force in the formation of the state as many countries around the world have gained their sovereignty but through war.

Consideration of coercive force as a common instrument for the origin of state permits to recognize the contribution of evolutionary biology to the understanding of the emergence of state. In 1972, the paleontologist and evolutionary biologists Stephen J. Gould and Nile Eldredge proposed the Punctuated Equilibria theory. They suggested that significant and rapid shifts leading to radical change were the result of accumulated tensions followed long periods of relative stability. Hence the name punctuated equilibrium. Gould and Eldredge challenged Charles Darwin's theory of evolution. They suggest that the phyletic gradualism of Darwin's evolutionism theory is not evident in fossil records and that most species will exhibit little evolutionary change for most of their geological history.

Social scientists usually adhere to one or the other of the above theories. On the one hand, those supporting Darwin's gradualism are found among the conflict theorists led by sociologists Lesly Ward, Albion Small and Frank Oppenheimer. They were strongly influenced by Darwin's conflict and survival theory which they combined with an emphasis on the permanent subjugation of losers by winners – that is the state is a product of conquest as well as conflict-inspired selection-and-survival (E. Service 1975: p.41). On the other hand, sociocultural evolution never proceeds in a linear fashion; other scholars have concluded that in an organizational system stresses such as population growth, food production and maintenance of power cause difficult choices and can result in a total system collapsed. A radically new organizational system then re-emerges with a totally different structure. This basically reflects the concept of punctuated equilibrium.

I will illustrate the forgoing with the following situation. Earlier, I have mentioned that the chiefdom was an unstable political form of organization because the central authority or parts thereof could not be delegated without risking insubordination and insurrection. The paramount chief only option to maintaining his dominance was to rule his entire organization from the center. Charles Spencer estimated the effective and sustainable limit of a chiefdom's territory had a 25-30 km by foot from the center of command to go back and forth. In addition, this restriction adversely affects the decision-making process. This eventually led to a problem of population density, limited territorial growth and resource scarcity. "The compounded effect of these factors over time drove the chiefdom organization to a threshold that made it predisposed for a radical change". Accumulated internal conflicts raise the chiefdom stress level to the highest provoking aggression and attack on other chiefdoms in the vicinity. As mentioned earlier, the repeated success of the victor led to the emergence of a super chiefdom having all the political and bureaucratic characteristics of a state.

Natufian civilization is a good example. Between 9000 and 7000 BC better weather conditions facilitated cultivation in the Levant. This resulted in an agricultural surplus, the precondition for an elite detached from the food production process and the necessity for a strong control agency.

There were large villages with an estimated population of 300 to 500. Stability for groups of this size required adherence to occupational, recreational and religious in order to maintain a unified society and they did. Whether the Natufian chiefdom evolved to state is currently a subject of much debate. According to archeologist J. E. Arnold* social complexity is "the specific control of labor by non-related individuals, the institutionalization and legitimation of social hierarchy, the stability of a hereditary and centralized power". Using this definition the Natufian culture did not qualify because the archeological record, markers of a complex organization such as stable authorities, hereditary hierarchy, specific labor control, were not evident. Nevertheless, the Natufian civilization displayed some features including sedentary semi-sedentary a simple form of social hierarchy and division of labor according to perform activities that made it an intermediate stage of a complex political organization. Since the notion of surplus production is socio-politically associated with the chiefdom polity, it can be assumed that the Natufian next stage would have been the state.

{Radiocarbon} dating revealed that the appearance of the Natufians coincided with the beginning of a warm period which started 14,500 years ago. This period facilitated the growth of pistachio, and other nuts, olives, emmer wheat, barley all of which could be easily stored. Sophisticated stones and wood houses were built with storage bins for this purpose. As such, storage, as a way of life became a stimulus for change (E. L. Mendonsa 2016: pp.28-29).

The Natufian transformation embodies the spirit of the punctuated equilibrium theory. Being on a threshold of change, the demographic and ecologic pressure provoked a sudden radical change not totally identifiable at first glance. Nevertheless, the Natufians have transformed polity as shown by their proprietorship, settlement, infrastructural work and institutional mechanisms to maintain internal peace and order in the population. The success of the Natufian society led to its demise. The short duration of the Natufian phenomenon and its replacement by the Neolithic cultures suggest that the unique characteristics of the Natufian created an uncontrolled momentum. The Natufian population not only did not starve, they flourished and kept growing. The population growth presumably led (at least in the Mediterranean zone) to a growing sense of proprietorship of land, especially with their growing dependence on agriculture. Sedentism brought about many changes in settlement patterns, including greater investment of energy resources in habitation structures and storage facilities. Under such conditions of population growth, when each group defends its territory and strives to differentiate itself from its neighbors, the need for group identity increases and encourages the appearance of unique characteristics in each social group. As more and more people were forced to live in close proximity to one another, the establishment of strong institutional mechanisms became inevitable to prevent anarchy and control emotional behavior and information exchange within the group. The strengthening of all these trends cumulated in the appearance of a new cultural entity – the Neolithic Complex.

Endnotes

2a. The surplus produced in some late Paleolithic societies and more commonly after the domestication of plants and animals (the Agricultural Revolution) was comprised of food that could be stored and was subject to theft. Hence, E. L. Mendonsa calls it a storable-stealable-surplus. It was a major stimulus to the development of a political organization, first in corporate kin groups and subsequently in Chiefdoms.

2b. It may be useful to expand on gift exchange in view of its intended consequence. Gift exchange creates a permanent social obligation between the parties involved in the process. Duran Bell mentioned the case of a daughter given in marriage. A solid bonding is created in that the family link with the daughter is not broken in addition to the organic link with the new family. Commodity simply reflects the skillfulness of the trade or wealth in the exchange process in relation to other commodities – no string attached.

2c. Várzea is the rich alluvial soil found along the banks of the Amazon River.

2d. Voluntaristic Theory: At some point in their history, certain people spontaneously, rationally and voluntarily gave up their individual sovereignties and united with other communities to form a larger political unit deserving to be called a state. This is the automatic theory supported by Gordon Childe. But the development of agriculture easily produces conditions necessary for the development of a state. However, the development of agriculture does not automatically create a food surplus. (R. L. Carneiro. A Theory of the Origin of the State).

PART III
Inequality in the Old World

Introduction

The Book of Genesis (10: 6-12), New King James Version has reported the exploits of a mighty hunter called Nimrod son of Cush, great-grandson of Noah and King in the land of Shinar. He organized the first secular government in the city of Babel (10:10-12) and expanded it to Assyria, Nineveh and other cities. He instituted a system whereby one or a few at the top profit from the labor of the majority under them. Soon there were many cities, each ruled by a self-willed king. Not content with one city, ambitious rulers, seeking greater wealth and power, armed a portion of their manpower and by aggression subjugated adjoining cities. Thus nations were born followed by empires.

There are still some debates about when the Book of Genesis, part of the Pentateuch, was written. According to modern scholars, it was probably produced in the 6th and 5th centuries B.C. In it, one can trace the political developments of that millennium. In the context of sociopolitical history, this section will emphasize the impact of the development of social stratification in the primary states. Again, by definition, these states were created without contact with other state societies to act as a model or stimulus.

For the sake of simplification, an empire is a centralized, socially stratified government in which a monarch controls a number of states and territories of a diverse population in contiguous and or remote locations. Like the origin of the state polity, not a single factor can sufficiently explain the emergence of the empire. Instead, it is a combination of many inter-related factors yet applied differently according to the context. Human behavior being is shaped by society and vice versa, therefore, it should not be surprising that coercive force was a key driver in the emergence of empires.

In the course of history, empire as a polity has existed for millennia. An empire is "a particular form of domination or control between two units set apart in a hierarchical, inequitable relationship, more precisely a composite state in which a metropole or core state dominates a periphery to the disadvantage of the periphery" (G. Steinmetz 2017 p.1). It seems that achieving large polities was the unlimited force of evolutionary political complexity In the governing of peripheral spaces and populations, the peripheries were typically subjected to different legal and administrative practices than the core. Scholars agree that military, economic and cultural means or any combination were the reasons for the emergence of empires, the administrative structure of the metropole and the culture that legitimized sovereignty over the vanquished. The generation of wealth was crucial to supporting the empire's political structure. The economy of early empires were mostly agrarian and the trade of grains, artisanal products and metal provided additional resources needed for the entire kingdom.

In PART II, I have exposed the sociocultural evolution of egalitarian societies (band and tribe), ranked societies and the chiefdom (hierarchical dominance of a leadership structural elite) to state and then empires consisting of a group of states under a supreme authority. Demographic and environmental pressures, aggrandizement and warfare were identified as causal factors of this sociopolitical evolution. Tracing the emergence and development of inequality in state and empire until modern times could be a daunting task. For this reason, I had to be selective in what I examine considering the number of existing empires at that time and the theme of this book. For this reason, the following criteria were used for selecting the appropriate ruler in Mesopotamia, India and China, three of the six primary states: duration of the empire or dynasty, stability of the political culture in subsequent governments, territorial expansion and unification of the empire. I suggest that territorial expansion and a long mandate relate to strong leadership and acceptance of the ruler's vision for the country. This vision adopted by subsequent rulers magnified the political culture then facilitated the identification of socioeconomic ills including inequality.

Correlation is not always easy to establish in social science when many events affect the development of a sociopolitical process. Keeping this in mind, the review of the primary states in Mesopotamia, Egypt, Indus Valleys, China in the Old World - Mexico and Peru in the New World (Fried M. H. 1967: p. 231) will be preceded by a look at earlier events to assess possible cause and effect relationships.

I keep repeating that these early states were created without any contact with each other or acted as a model or stimulus in the creation of other states, but there are some troubling facts. For example, although some scholars would argue that the earliest civilizations in the Andes (Peru, Bolivia) and Mesoamerica (Mexico. Guatemala) may have some contact with each other, overwhelming evidence suggests they arose as states independently of early civilizations in the Near East (K. V. Flannery 1972: pp 399-426). In addition, it is unproven, that Mesopotamian urbanization exerted an influence on the urbanization of the Indus Valley which may have had an influence on the urbanization of China. It remains a strange coincidence that the city of Harrapan's design and orientation is similar to that of China (T. l. Norman 2009: p 96). A common conjecture is that the three may have had some contact through the trade routes. Nonetheless, coercive forces under certain geographic and ecologic constraints (R. Carneiro 2012: pp.10-27) seem to be the predominant theory. My examination of the review of the evolution of inequality will shed light on the ramifications of historical events and the institutions created.

The fall of Constantinople in May 1453 signaled the end of the Eastern Roman Empire and the consolidation of the Ottoman Turkish Empire. This was a vast territory that spanned southeastern Europe, Asia Minor, the Middle East, and North Africa paralyzing land and maritime transportation. Considering the quantity and variety of goods traded, the European market was, economically speaking, severely affected. I will expand on this point at the beginning of the next chapter. Being accustomed to luxury items, exotic fruits, spices, and other raw materials created a dependence on them; just think today of the world's reliance on coffee, tea and other imported items that are taken for granted. The

East-West trade of that time could be considered a forerunner of today's global trade.

I will now consider the four primary states in the Old World namely Mesopotamia, Egypt, Indus Valley and China.

Mesopotamia

Mesopotamia, known as the cradle of civilization, seems appropriate for an examination of the roots of inequality. Mesopotamia occupied the land between the Tigris and the Euphrates Rivers and is actually the name of an area rather than a country. Map 3.0 shows its location in Western Asia surrounded by the Mediterranean Sea, the Zagros Mountains and the Arabian Plateau. Map 3.1 more specifically locates Mesopotamia between the Tigris and Euphrates Rivers currently part of Iraq, Kuwait and infringing on Saudi Arabia, Syria and Turkey. The most important city-states in Mesopotamia were: Kish, Babylon, Uruk and Ur. It might be useful to remember that a city-state was a self-governing political entity that may include smaller areas falling under its jurisdiction. The importance of a city-state can be understood by the size of its economy, its buildings and the influence of the spiritual being(s) on people's activities. These four city-states were prominent features of Mesopotamia and left behind a significant cultural legacy.

In the areas adjacent to the rivers, the soil was very fertile. The combination of the rich mud carried by the rivers down from the mountains and the silt deposited over a wide area during the spring floods justified this area's name of Fertile Crescent. Drainage and irrigation systems further enhanced farming making it extremely productive. This in turn, since 5,000 BC, drew settlements of people and an over-capacity of food production. This surplus production in turn facilitated the emergence of other occupations such as craftsmanship, scribes, priesthood. Overtime, cities emerged with populations ranging from a few to one hundred thousand. As always happens in society, this population growth contributed to more complexity in the government political organization to maintain a stable society. As a result, cities evolved to city-states, territorial states and then empires. But I must emphasize that demography and agricultural surplus were only secondary contributors to these political evolutions. The period 2900 to 2350 B.C. in Mesopotamia is known as the early dynastic period. During this time, Sumer was divided politically between competing city-states, each controlled by a dynasty of rulers. City-states warred between each other to gain access to water, agricultural resources, timber and metals. It followed that weaker cities were absorbed by more powerful ones leading to the formation of more complex polities.

Map 3.2 also shows the major oldest cities, city-states and territorial states in Mesopotamia in 2500 BC. Eridu, Ur, Uruk and Larsa were actually within sight of each other, competing for resources and dominance with about a dozen other city-states, such as Lagash, Umma, Kish, Adab and Shurrupak.

Map 3.0 Mesopotamia

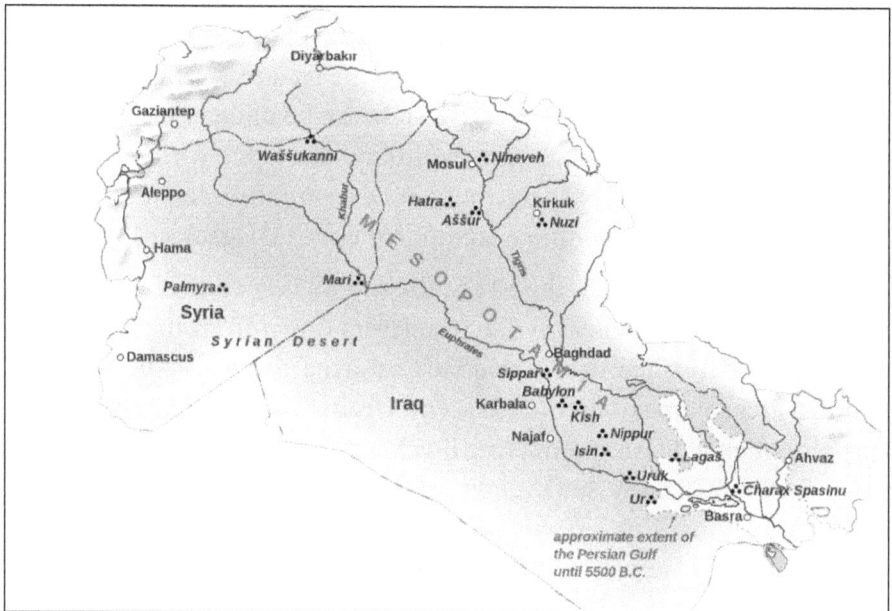

Map 3.1 **Sumer**   Source: John D. Croft.

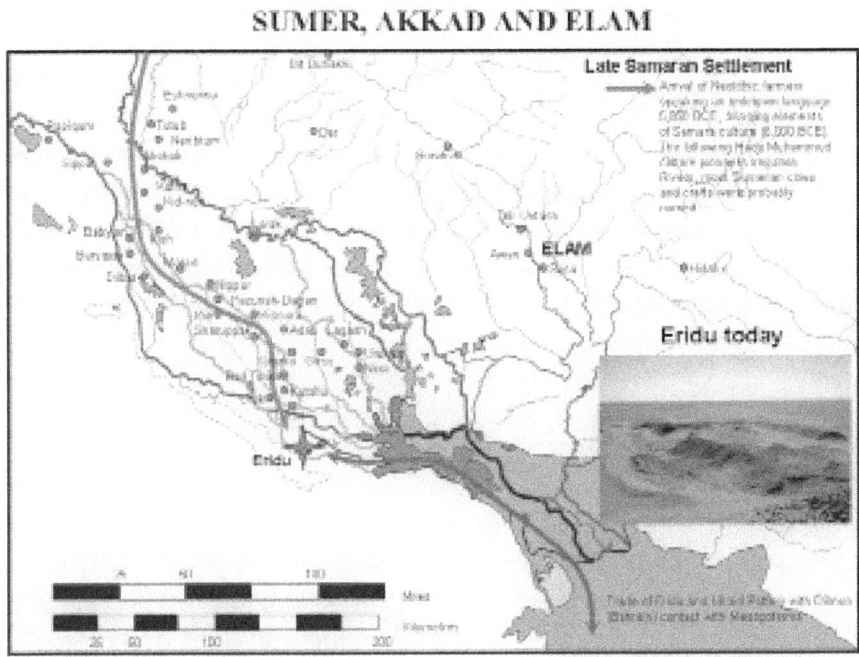

In Southern Mesopotamia, Sumer is known as the cradle of civilization. An unknown author describes the Sumerians as a mysterious group of people, speaking a language unrelated to any other known human language, using written communication and living in cities whose names such as Ur, Lagash, Eridu speak from a distant and foggy past. The origin of the Sumerian is still a mystery. Some believe that they came from Anatolia*. Others suggest they came from India and were Caucasian in origin or perhaps came from Dilmun the Island of Bahrain in the Persian Gulf.

By 4000 BC the Sumerian civilization had an advanced system of writing, spectacular arts and architecture and had developed skills in astronomy and mathematics. The structural complexity and grandeur of the three-story mud-brick ziggurats of Ur are fascinating. How could science and technology use to design and construct these buildings be so advanced? I strive to separate historical facts from myths and propaganda. No one could answer this question.

The most powerful cities and city-states included Eridu, Kish, Uruk, and Ur and Nippur. It is believed that Eridu was one of the oldest cities in the world and the first city in Mesopotamia. At its height, it was also one of the most important cities for trade and religion. Kish, not as old, was also strategically important. The king of Kish was considered pre-eminent in Sumer because of the city's position at the juncture of the two rivers. Whoever controlled Kish ultimately controlled the irrigation systems of the cities downstream. Uruk was the seat of Mesopotamia's creative arts and the capital of Sumer ruled by king Gilgamesh*. Nippur was not the capital of any city-state but played an important political role because no royal rule over Mesopotamia could be considered legitimate without recognition in its temples. Ur was home to many great artisans whose artifacts still survived. It is also the birthplace of Abraham according to the Holy Scripture.

Northern Mesopotamia was made up of hills and plains. The land was fertile due to seasonal rains, and the rivers and streams flowing from the mountains. Early settlers farmed the land and used timber, metals and stone from the mountains nearby.

The purpose of providing the preceding background is twofold. First, it gives a perspective of the social complexity of Mesopotamia and ecological advantages. Second, it facilitates an understanding of the challenge of governing this land or any part of it until today. I will focus more on the Akkadian empire and its social structure and implications than the entire dynasty.

Over the course of three millennia, Mesopotamia experienced many different forms of government. Around 2300 BC Sargon the Great rose to power and established the city of Akkad. When the powerful Sumerian city of Uruk attacked Akkad, they fought back and eventually conquered Uruk. Sargon then went on to conquer all of the Sumerian city-states and united northern and southern Mesopotamia into a single country under a single centralized government. The rationale for this political strategy has been debated by many scholars. Some suggest that Sargon was more preoccupied with the military expansion of his empire than with conquered city-states in one single state. Be that as it may, Sargon created the first and largest empire by conquering what he called the "Four Corners of the Universe". After the displacement Ur-Zababa for an unknown reason, Sargon was crowned king, and he embarked on a career of foreign conquest. He carried his conquest north of Assyria subjugating the cities up to the mountains east of Elam west of Mari and south of Sumer to the Persian Gulf. By unifying Northern and Southern Mesopotamia in a single entity, Sargon formed his empire and named Akkad the capital and ruled Mesopotamia for approximately fifty years with a dynasty spanning over a century:

Sargon	2334 -2279 BC
Rimush	2278 -2270 BC *Dates are approximate.*
Manistushu	2269 -2255 BC
Naram-Sin	2254 -2218 BC
Shar-Kali-Shari	2217-2193 BC

Social Structure

Figure 3.2 Social Structure of the Akkadian Dynasty

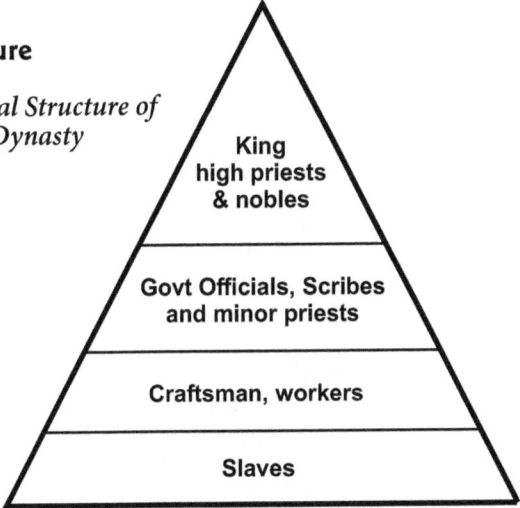

King
high priests
& nobles

Govt Officials, Scribes
and minor priests

Craftsman, workers

Slaves

The first ancient Semitic speaking empire introduced a four-layer centralized form of government to keep control of its vast territory. At the top of the pyramid figured the king with a semi-divine status, absolute authority and his family. The second layer consisted of the priests and priestesses (communicators with the gods) nobles, top officials of the army and scribes - the upper class. The third layer, encompassed farmers, craftsmen and merchants - the middle class. The slaves made up the fourth class.

King Sargon consolidated his dominion over the conquered city-states by replacing the opposing rulers with noble citizens of Akkad, his native city to ensure loyalty. Furthermore, in a brilliant political strategy, he appointed his daughter Enheduanna as the high priestess of the goddess in the important Sumerian city of Ur to improve the political climate between the north and the south. The presence of a strong military force in the Sargon Empire ensured a period of stability which permitted the construction of roads to improve trade and improvement to irrigation to increase agricultural production. Trade and agriculture were two important sources of revenue for the empire and led to a variety of new work opportunities. But were these opportunities available to all? In other words, what were the barrier(s) to upward mobility?

Before answering these questions one must remember that during the Sargon dynasty the Akkadian language of the north and Sumerian languages of the south co-existed. Without entering into the controversy about the origin of these languages it is fair to say that in the third and early second millennia BC, southern Mesopotamia Sumerian and a number of Semitic dialects in northern Mesopotamia, there was a continuum of Semitic languages and dialects spoken. That said, the Akkadian dynasty used the language of Akkad as a written language, adapting Sumerian cuneiform orthography for this purpose in a complementary manner. Hence the introduction of complex tablets that only educated people could decipher. But education came at a cost that only the upper class, sons of the nobility, government officials, priests and rich merchants could afford. And it took twelve years to learn the cuneiform language!

As mentioned earlier, Sargon and his successors replaced the local elites with their own people in the upper class. In the words of anthropologist Piotr Michalowski in the Life and Death of the Sumerian Language in Comparative Perspective, centralized schooling at the capital undoubtedly created a situation in which access to bureaucratic careers involved Akkadophones or bilinguals. As a result, this barrier prevented the less fortunate male from accessing bureaucratic careers. The language of the conqueror became also a matter of prestige associated with high social class, formal education, and ceremonial occasions.

Gender differential treatment was also deeply rooted in Akkadian society. Boys were taught reading and writing, math and history as well as geography, zoology, botany, astronomy, engineering, medicine and architecture depending on their future employment. Girls were not taught to read and write unless they were princesses or training to be priestesses.

These cases of language barrier and gender differential treatment fit in the definition of systemic discrimination starting in the ancient world. In summary, the freedom and status of women were limited particularly if they or their parents are poor. Daughters of rich families could be involved in business and have responsible duties subject, of course, to the will of their husbands. (Marten Stol 1995: p.140). At the bottom of the pyramid were the slaves. Slavery was part of the social fabric since the inception of agrarian Uruk as shown in the Warka Vase described by the historian and archeologist Senta German (See note in appendix I). Slaves were captives of war, law offenders, debt defaulters, and deportees whose skills could be used in public work projects. It is noteworthy that slaves could purchase their freedom, eventually own property and take part in business. However, I did not find any evidence of their access to the upper class.

Sargon died circa 2279 BC perhaps of old age or battle wounds. The circumstances of his death are as foggy as his early childhood. He was succeeded by his son, grandson and great-grandson who all fought to maintain the legacy of Sargon. However, several rebellions coupled with a severe drought referred to as the Curse of Agade* lasting for almost 300 years, put an end to the dynasty.

Fast forward to Cyrus the Great (550-530 BC), the Persian leader conquered Medes and united the Iranian people under one ruler for the first time. Cyrus became the first king of the Persian Empire and went on to establish one of the largest empires in the world thereby meeting the selection criteria for identifying the roots of inequality. His reign witnessed the first serious contacts between the Persians and Greeks and the permanent loss of political power by the peoples of the old centers of power in Mesopotamia.

I have introduced the Persian Empire as part of the Mesopotamia review because geographically it included what is now known as Israel, Jordan, Iran and Iraq. The social structure established by Cyrus and subsequent rulers had its origin in Brahma, the Hindu god of creation. It was believed that people were born into the specific social class of their occupation which is fixed for that person's life until he/she is reborn. Classes (also known as castes) were Brahmins, Kshatriyas, Vaishyas and the Shudras respectively the priests, the ruler administrators and warriors, artisans and merchants, tradesmen and farmers, and the general labor class. This structure is silent about the slaves which might have been war prisoners.

However, it appears they were not subject to hard labor or used as a human sacrifice. Needless to say, that upward mobility was almost impossible. This type of social structure will become clearer in the review of Indus Valley

This system borrowed from India and introduced by the Indo-Arians was used to maintain power through a regimented structure solidified in religious belief. Nevertheless, the ruler of the Persian Empire practiced a policy of tolerance towards the people of the conquered countries. He did not execute them but scattered them throughout the kingdom to prevent rebellion. Cyrus even allowed the Jews who had been relocated by the Babylonians, to return to Israel.

I have to wonder whether inequality in the modern countries that were part of ancient Mesopotamia is related to its past? This is a challenging question considering the many historical events and the resulting path that the current sovereign countries formerly part of Mesopotamia have taken. A comprehensive delimitation encompasses mostly Iraq, Kuwait, the eastern part of Syria, Southeastern Turkey and regions along the Turkish-Syrian and Iran-Iraq borders. So many sovereign states! The region contains too many states to permit conventional country-by-country treatment (R. Owen 2004: xii).

One of the ways to solve this is to reconsider the core definition of the land "between rivers" (Meso Potamia). In the words of archeologist Dominique Collon former curator of the British Museum, Mesopotamia was the name of an area rather than of a country corresponding to mostly modern Iraq. It was also part of modern Iran, Syria and Turkey and in the recent past the State of Israel. Expressed differently Mesopotamia was the motherland of the many cultures that flourished in ancient Iraq including the Sumerian, Akkadian, Babylonian and others whose influence spread to neighboring countries from 5,000 B.C. Biologically, using a motherland metaphor, some commonalities and behavior are expected to be passed on to those cultures. So the task at hand is to identify whether they are common to Iraq, Iran, Syria and Turkey e.g. religion, race and landscape or specific to any of those particular countries. The comment of the late social scientist D. D Kosambi shed light on this complex situation when he said in another context "ancient empires incorporated contiguous territories which allowed some broad-based similarities that crossed their frontier. Nevertheless, disparities persisted". It is safe to say that religion, language, bellicosity, land and more importantly social stratification and inequality remain those commonalities with the ancient world.

As is often the case for countries in the Middle East, historical events and the resulting social impact leading to their creation are numerous and complicated. Lately, too many players including international powers have added extra layers of complication.

In a nutshell, the Assyrian dominance in Mesopotamia ended with the Battle of Nineveh in 612 BC. The concerted forces of Medes and Babylonia led an attack against the Assyrian capital of Nineveh and as a result, this major city was sacked after a three-month siege. After the fall of the Assyrian Empire, Mesopotamia was ruled by a succession of foreign dynasties from the Macedonian to the Roman Empire. Monolithic Assyria was finally dissolved when it was conquered by the Arab Islamics in the mid-7th century starting with the capture of Mecca and Medina in AD 630 by the Prophet Muhammad. One of Muhammad's successors, Osman is credited as the founder of the Ottoman Empire.

When the Ottoman Empire was defeated, the Sykes-Picot Agreement of May 1916 with the assent of Imperial Russia, allowed the glorious European victors to partition the defeated territory in order to protect their interests and to assist the various Middle East occupants within their self-determination process. Lebanon, most of Syria and control of Morocco, Algeria and Tunisia went to France. Great Britain was allotted the rest of Syria, the mandate for Palestine and control of Iraq, Iran, Egypt, Jordan and the south of Yemen. The control of Iraq lasted twelve years (1920-1932). The Armenian provinces of Erzurum, Trebizond, Van, and Bitlis, with some Kurdish territory to the southeast went to Russia. The geographic borders between these countries became official when they became independent states. Notably, no international power took responsibility for the millions of Kurds * in Iraq, Iran, Syria, Turkey and elsewhere in the Middle East, as part of this land partitioning exercise.

World War I led to the formation of independent countries in the Middle East. World War II had almost the same effects. Turkey became independent in 1923, followed by Syria and Lebanon became in 1943. In February 1947 Great Britain gave United Nations responsibility for Palestine. On May 14, 1948, Israel became an independent state. The atrocities committed on the Jews in the concentration camps increased the momentum for an independent state. Iran became an independent state in 1979.

In Iraq, a Hashemite* constitutional monarchy was organized under British protection in 1921 and three Hashemites ascended the throne: Faisal I (1921-1933), Ghazy I (1933-1939) and Faisal II (1939-1958). On October 3, 1932, Iraq was granted independence. After a period of relative calm, the monarchy was overthrown by a coup in 1958 and replaced with a republic. The next decade witnessed a series of short-lived governments until the Ba'ath Party came to power in 1968 under the leadership of Ahmad Hassan al-Bakr and Saddam Hussein who became President in 1979. Iraq's abundant oil revenues greatly facilitated the country's economic development. New schools, hospitals were built and housing facilities were modernized.

Iraq's aggressive foreign policies and repressive civil liberties affected its relationship with the neighboring countries particularly Iran and Kuwait. In 1980, Iraq embarked on a costly eight-year war with Iran. A US-led military coalition liberated the latter from Iraq in 1991. Kurdish rebellion in the north and Shi'ite Muslims (See Endnote about Shiite and Sunni) uprising in the south of Iraq raised some concerns in the international community because of Iraq's heavy-handed military response. In 2003 another US-led coalition invaded Iraq on the account of their alleged possession of a weapon of mass destruction and their ties with terrorism – democracy needed to be protected. The coalition forces quickly controlled Iraq's major cities and captured Saddam Hussein, On November 5/ 2006, Saddam Hussein was sentenced to death by the Iraqi High Tribunal for killing 148 Shiites from Dujail. No weapons of mass destruction were found.

On May 12/2018 elections were held in Iraq. Populist Shi'ite cleric Muqtada al-Sadr was elected and he chose the Shi'ite veteran Adil Abdul-Mahdi as Prime Minister.

The following observations can be made if Iraq, Iran, Syria, Turkey and Israel are taken as a proxy for Mesopotamia. Religion continues to play an important role in this part of the world. Before the Arab Islamic conquest in the mid-7th century, Iraq like the rest of Mesopotamia was polytheistic, worshipping a variety of gods and goddesses at local shrines and temples. With the passage of time under the Abbasid rulers (750-1258), religion continued to be a dominating force in Iraq. Iran is generally recognized as the birthplace of Zoroastrianism which has both monotheistic and dualistic features. The Assyrians worshipped one main god Assur and many secondary deities such as Ishtar and Adramelech. Nonetheless, the Assyrians were among the first to convert to Christianity and to spread Eastern Christianity to the Far East. However, they became a minority religion in their homeland following the Muslim conquest of Persia in the 8th century.

The Kurds, one of the indigenous peoples of the Mesopotamian plains and the highlands, live in what is now south-eastern Turkey, north-eastern Syria, northern Iraq, north-western Iran and south-western Armenia. This explains the intra and interstate frictions on the major issues concerning the Kurds in these countries and the role of the Western powers in the process. During the Kurdish Civil War (1994-1997) factions from Iran and Turkey, and Iranian, Iraqi and Turkish forces were drawn into the fighting, with additional involvement from American forces.

I briefly mentioned religious profile as the first commonality between the selected modern countries representing Mesopotamia not from an ethical perspective but because, as it will become clear later, as a practical instrument for the justification of passion. As a case in point, it was esti-mated that about 275,000 Assyro-Chaldeans* in Syria, Northern Iraq, Iran and Turkey were killed by Ottoman troops between 1914 and 1918. The combined population of the Assyrians of the Ottoman Empire and Persia before the genocide was about 600,000. It was reduced to 325,000, with very few survivors in Turkey or Iran by 1930.

The second commonality between the proxy countries and Mesopotamia seems to be war. As I mentioned earlier, states have competed with each other since their inception. The first recorded war in history was between Sumer and Elam in Mesopotamia in 2700 BC and later between Assyria in the north and Babylonia in the south until they were unified under Sargon of Akkad (2334-2279 BC). Historically, countries went to war to acquire natural resources to maintain the well-being of their inhabitants, to protect or expand their territory, to consolidate and secure their (geographic) position or simply for cultural hegemony in a particular area. The Middle East is not an exception. This part of the world has been the seat of ongoing tension and bellicosity for millennia. Before addressing the main reason for this continuing tension I would like to illustrate the impact of these socio-political confronta-tions with the following facts.

1. For eight years (1980-1988) Iraq and Iran warred over the control of the Shatt al-Arab, the waterway that forms the boundary between the two countries weakening thereby the economy of both countries.

2. The relationship between Iraq and Syria is at most lukewarm since Bashar al-Assad became president of Syria in 2000. The point of contention was the participation of Syria in the coalition that forced Iraq out of Kuwait in 1990.

3. In Turkey the ongoing sectarian armed conflict with the Kurds since 1980 remains unresolved. I should mention that Iran and Iraq have also fought Kurdish separatism Representing 18% of Turkey's population and 98% of Sunni* Muslim, the Kurds through the Kurdish Workers' Party* aims to separate from Turkey or to have greater political rights inside the republic. The number of casualties in this conflict for both sides was significant and it had a huge negative impact on Turkey's economy in the range of $300-400 billion.

4. Finally but not least, there is the war against the State of Israel since its creation on May 14/1948. The next day following its declaration of independence Israel was attacked by Egypt, Transjordan, Syria, Lebanon, and Iraq all of whom were unwilling to accept the existence of this country. In the last six decades, Israel has been forced to protect itself 14 times to maintain the integrity of its territory.

In short, Iran, Iraq, Turkey Syria and Israel have a long history of conflicts which has an impact on their social structure and economic performance. According to the Economic Research of the Federal Reserve Bank of St Louis, the Gini coefficient for Iran, Turkey, Israel, for 2016 were 40.0, 41.9 and 38.9 respectively. However, as pointed out by F. Alvaredo et al, the Middle East* inequality can no longer be considered higher when based on surveys rated on historical or international standards; Based on their robust study, the Middle East seems to stand as the most unequal region in the world. The authors of this study have acknowledged the limitation of their study because of the quality of the data available. It is important to clarify the difference in inequality both within countries and between countries. The former concerns the repartition between the different social classes within a country's society. In this context, inter-country inequality is the comparison between the Middle East* and other countries. Another clarification worth mentioning is that the Alvaredo et al study covers income inequality but not wealth inequality. This latter is more difficult to undertake because of privacy laws.

Most similar studies concern income inequality and not wealth inequality although social inequality derives from both. Laws protecting personal information limit access to the necessary data for the calculation of wealth inequality. Social inequality refers to the distribution impact of wealth and income as well as the overall meaning of luxury of each person's existence within a society. Lack of wealth in certain areas prohibits these people from obtaining the same education, housing and health care as the wealthy in societies where access to these goods and services depends on wealth. In this sense, social inequality means any impediments or processes in society that limit or harm a group's social status, social class and social circle.

Chart 3.3 Top 1% income share: Middle East compared with other countries

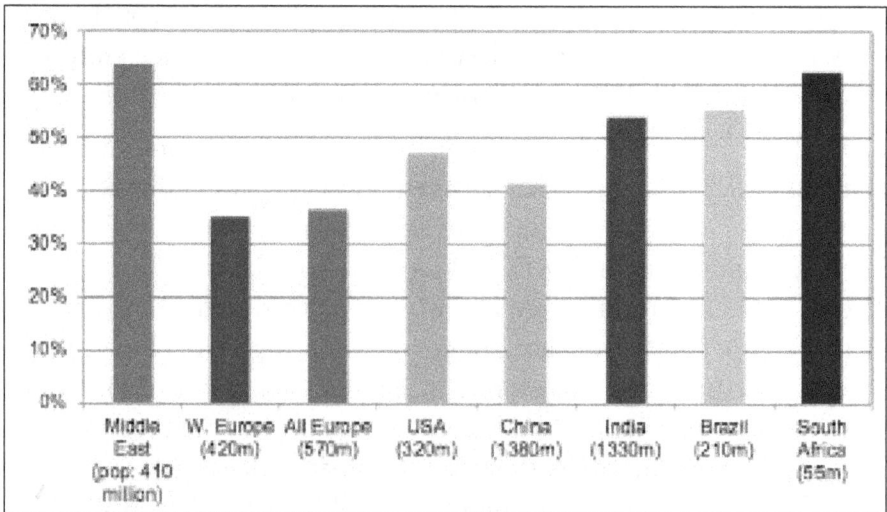

Source: Measuring Inequality in the Middle East 1990-2016: The World's Most Unequal Region? Facundo Alvaredo Lydia Assouad Thomas Piketty. April 2018.

As can be seen in the above bar chart, income inequality in the Middle East* is obvious when it is compared with Europe, the United States, China, India, and Brazil. The share of income flowing to the top 10% (the elite) is approximately 63% in the Middle East, 35% in Western

Europe and 47% in the United States. The difference is not significant when all Europe is factored in the comparison. It should be noted that the large lower class has very little income to live on, only 9%. The situation of the middle class, a hot topic in political discourse particularly during an election period, is better off in Europe than in America.

Considering the enormous socioeconomic ramification of oil, it would be of interest to consider how this resource leads to inequality particularly in developing countries where it is the primary export commodity and source of revenue. For developed and developing countries, many roads may lead to inequality depending on the political structure of the country and the distribution level of the workforce in the primary, secondary and tertiary sectors.

The production and commercialization of oil reserves are known to require large capital investments involving the state and international private and public investors. Oil has always been in great demand requiring cadres of skilled workers on demand. It is not difficult to see the active role of politicians, private sector lobbyists, and environmental activists in issues such as import and export permits, corporate tax advantages, use of temporary foreign workers and so on. Hence the source of money benefiting a few known as rentiers, including politicians who use their position for personal gains.

The international sale of oil generates large revenues and raises also the exchange rate of the exporting country that has more exports than imports. However, as a result, prices of locally manufactured goods become less competitive in international markets and eventually lead to a decline in manufacturing. Known as the Dutch disease, this economic consequence reinforces the country's dependence on oil. It also creates an unemployable labor force, unless retrained to meet the skill requirements of the oil industry.

When the economy of a country largely depends on oil, its commercialization may have adverse socioeconomic consequences particularly in the absence of a diversified manufacturing base. This explains the position of some authors positing that an oil-dependent country may experience moderate growth and reduced inequality during the boom period. Generally, countries with natural resources as the main export commodity have low economic growth. Following the boom period, increased inequality may emerge particularly if the price of oil falls. A robust and dynamic macroeconomic policy framework balancing and unifying the components of the country's economy are needed to prevent an economic collapse.

Given the serious consequences of reliance on oil as a main traded commodity, I have provided in the Notes of Appendix I the case of Venezuela in South America. In fact, with some variances, it has also happened in Europe and many countries in Africa.

But why so many conflicts in the Middle East? This is a question which has preoccupied most political analysts.

Whether or not the Middle East is prone to war is not the objective of this book. However, in the context of analyzing the causes and effects of inequality, it is something that must be considered. Indeed, wars carry the potential to change political regimes, social structures, population composition and social dislocations leading to economic and social inequality. The Middle East has been in a persistent state of conflict for millennia.

So, is the Middle East prone to war?

In their large sample of countries representing the MENA*, Sørli et al found that MENA surpassed Europe, Africa, America, Asia and Oceania in a number of conflicts in more than half of the study period (1960-2012). Sadly, Africa and Asia have won the honor of the top position in the subsequent decades. According to Sørli et al the incidence of conflict in the Middle East has declined since the end of the 1980s, as is the case for other regions reviewed.

I also wanted to find out whether the Middle East is prone to war within the confine of the five countries cited earlier. From a cause and effect relationship, it is my view that war causes inequality and vice versa. The most likely causes of social unrest, rebellions and grievances are the accumulation of injustices, repression and suffering. Indeed the number of conflicts and wars in the Middle East decreased in the last two decades of the 20th century. However, a sharp increase emerged in the 2002-2012 period. The turbulence started with the US-led coalition forces invading Iraq in 1990: the 1995-1997 Kurdish Civil War in Iraq and Turkey; the 2011- present Syrian civil war and the ongoing Israeli-Hezbollah conflict. The first decades of the new millennium were a bloody period, particularly for Iraq, Turkey, Israel and Syria.

In the Middle East, 321 wars took place resulting in 1.5 million casualties* during the six decades between 1947 and 2012. M. G. Marshall cautions that the casualty numbers are simply estimates spread over sixty years. But these are not small numbers since the number of casualties represent 2.7% of the selected five countries population in 2012. This percentage is slightly less than World War II's casualties of 3% of the world population in 1940 which was 2.3 billion. The Middle East's 1.5 million casualties include a few large numbers such as

- Kurds ethnic war in Iraq (ended in 1993) - 150,000
- Kurds ethnic war in Turkey (ended in 1994) – 40,000
- Eight-year war between Iraq and Iran (ended in 1988) – 50,000
- Iraq/Kuwait war (1990) – 100,000
- Iraq continuation of the Sunni/Shia sectarian conflict (2011) – 65,000
- The confrontation between the ethnic-Sunni militants and Islamist Extremist against Assad's ethnic Alawite regime (2011) -275,000.

The causes of most interstate conflicts are often known, particularly those that are internationalized. But the real causes of intrastate conflicts resulting in civil wars can be less evident because of propaganda or distorted for the sake of political correctness. The literature on the subject suggests that the ramifications of certain endogenous factors such as internal politics, religion, ethnic fractionalization, the country's economic resources or any combination thereof may be the cause. Nonetheless, one of the leading experts on this matter suggests that "the true cause of much civil war is not the loud discourse of grievance, but the silent force of greed" (Collier 2004).

The continuum power – prestige – status is the classic conduit to inequality. Collier's theory is of great importance to the analysis of inequality. In a nutshell, he posits that the risk of conflicts is higher in countries relying mostly on exported commodities with a sizable proportion of low educated young men between the ages of 15-24 and experiencing an economic decline (Sørli et al). The propensity for rebellion is also more associated with an authoritarian political regime than otherwise. These factors were confirmed by a robust statistical analysis followed by policy recommendations to counterbalance the effects of greed motivated rebellion.

Let's look at greed motivated rebellions in the many civil wars in these selected countries through the lens of Collier's theory.

In the Sørli et al (2005: p.146) study, of the 19 states selected to represent the Middle East only Israel qualified as flawed democracy on the Democracy Index*. For the purpose of the discussion, I have retained Iraq, Iran, Syria, Turkey and Israel as a proxy for the Middle East. Political scientist Samuel Huntington stated that the Middle East region remains the world's authoritarian stronghold and has yet to experience a wave of democratization (S. Huntington 1991). I will come back on this point in a moment but for the time being what has caused this system of government? Could historical continuities be invoked? As enunciated earlier, most rulers and their governments in ancient Mesopotamia were authoritarian rulings over a segregated social structure. But since then, political and religious developments such as the emergence of the Ottoman Empire, the spread and penetration of Islam have changed the course of history. In the modern Middle East, there have been some improvements in the status of women. Recall that in Mesopotamia, women did not have equal access to many areas of life (M. Stol. pp.123-144). And in the Quran Islam men and women as moral equals in the sight of God.

The cultural evolution including the proliferation of higher education has continued to improve the social status of women. But I believe that more must be done in the Middle East and certain other countries. Nonetheless, many studies have proven that authoritarianism and Muslimism are linked: ... "the evidence shows that Muslim countries are markedly more authoritarian than non-Muslim societies, even when one controls for other potentially influential factors; and the station of women, more than other factors that predominate in Western thinking about religious systems and politics, links Islam and the democratic deficit" (M. S. Fish 2002: p. 37).

Can democracy be achieved in Muslim countries? I believe in the separation of facts. Few Muslim countries are democratic. For example, Indonesia a Muslim majority country has adopted a democratic regime. The Republic of Senegal with approximately 92% of its population being Muslim, is another example.

Samuel Huntington stated that Muslim countries are especially prone to violence. Since violence has proven to be a hindrance to the achievement of democracy, it would be useful to review Huntington's statement empirical analysis carried out on this matter. M. S. Fish (2002: pp. 18-20) conducted a comparative analysis of the mean scores on the stability and lack of violence index between Catholic and Muslim countries. The results have shown that violence is not significantly lower or higher in Catholic countries than in Muslim countries. They are no more prone to war than other regions around the globe. This result begs the question of why most Muslim countries in the wide definition of the Middle East as well in my restricted version respectively 19 out 21 and 4 out of 5 maintain an authoritarian system of government. According to the Democracy Index 2019 study, Israel (#28 worldwide) was the only democracy in the Middle East. Perhaps economic performance supports this democratic achievement. Indeed, the durability of Israel's economic performance had shown a consistent growth from 2010 to 2017.

Scholars argue that authoritarianism can explain the democratic deficit in the Middle East. Political analysis suggests that the confluence of two factors, one rooted in ancient socio-economic institutions and one ironically in the abundance of natural resources explains the prevalence of this system of government.

In politics, past practices tend to subtly become part of subsequent political cultures and then find their way in some institutions. Many political scientists have emphasized the effect of past institutions on current societies: (Acemoglu & Robinson 2012: pp.298-301), (M. J. Sørli et al 2005: pp. 146-7), (T. Kuran 2011: p. 6). The latter has defined the institution as "a means of socially produced regularities that shape and are in turn shaped by individual behaviors".

A case in point is "waqf" also known as hubous, an alienable financial endowment under Islamic law for a specific purpose determined by its founders or donors, with no intention of reclaiming the assets. Any fixed assets e-g land buildings could be part of such an endowment. Generally, endowments are managed to keep the principal intact while a small part of the investment income is available to use each year. T. Kuran identified three categories of waqf of increasing importance and complexity: a family, a charitable and an imperial waqf. The beneficiaries are usually associated with or related to the family of the waqf's founder such as a poor neighborhood or a larger constituency base.

In spite of its dedication for good cause e-g mosques, housing, schooling, hospitals and so on, waqfs are not tax-exempt*. Waqf are intended to last forever unless there is an expiry date set in the charter or is nullified by a religious judge because of illegal activities against Islam or the properties are damaged and cannot be used as intended by the waqf's founder. The sacredness of waqf's assets, contrary to private properties, prevent them from being confiscated. It is important to underline a few points in the rules set by the founders to govern the wafq. The selection of corporate officers is beyond the power of the beneficiaries. Even the court can be powerless in a litigation case between the corporation and the beneficiaries be they tenants, universities, hospitals or the like because often little is known about the rules set by the founders. The beneficiaries also have difficulty forming political associations such as tenants association to promote and lobby for common interests. The effect is a textbook definition of repression despite the pious objectives of the charity corporation.

An important reason for the waqf's longevity is their financial capacity. The waqf Islamic law goes back to medieval times, also known as the Islamic Golden Age during the 8th to the 14th century. Financial information about waqfs in each Muslim country of the Middle East has proven to be hard to get. However, it appears that the asset value of waqfs in Turkey was estimated at 52.4 billion in 2017.

Table 3.4 Waqf Properties in Turkey

Type	Number of Properties
Mosques	4,400
Dormitories	500
Business centers	453
Hotels/caravansaries	150
Shops	5,348
Apartments	2,254
Other properties	24,809
Total	37,917

Source: Islamic Research Institute/Islamic Development Bank (IRTI/IDB)

The Finance Ministry rarely grants tax-exempt status. Out of more than 4,000 new waqfs established during the republican era that is the first quarter of the 20th century, a mere 195 were granted tax-exempt status.

Waqfs have hindered democracy by eliminating the emergence of socioeconomic change initiatives in the community and by installing a culture of powerlessness. One of the pillars of democracy is the right to choose and the people must have a say in important factors affecting their lives through the electoral process. Political economist Joseph Schumpeter has defined the democratic method is that institutional arrangement for arriving at (political) decisions in which individuals acquire the power to decide by means of a competitive struggle for the people to vote. The waqf's structure and the rules' secrecy nullify this power.

Over time waqfs have become less common in the modern Middle East and have also been subject to many changes. Governments came to the realization that Waqf's objectives can be met by a public entity. In Egypt and Turkey, the powerful control position of the caretaker has been diluted by the installation of caretaker boards. Furthermore, the sacrosanct protection of waqfs from nationalization can be removed on the basis of non-adherence to its mandate or corruption. Nonetheless, the social damages of the waqf system still persist. In Iran, Iraq and Syria and other Middle East authoritarian countries, the system has infused a lack of trust in the political system and an absence of opponent groups to counterbalance authoritarianist regimes.

The second factor is oil, the main source of revenue for the majority of Middle East countries. This natural resource is owned and commercialized by authoritarian regimes. If oil and fire must be kept isolated, oil, wealth and democracy do not always entertain each other companionship. A combination of factors can make oil to be labeled a curse. One may tend to think that an abundant and well- needed natural resource should facilitate democracy, economic development thereby reduce inequality. However, this is not always the case. M. Ross lists that three factors explain the link between oil and authoritarianism: a rentier effect, a repression effect and a modernization effect. Let's briefly look at each of them.

The rentier effect is associated with the large cash flow generated by the export. It provides Middle East governments with the flexibility to indirectly win the consent and support of their citizens through tax reduction. I must add that not all Middle East countries are major rentier recipients. Saudi Arabia annually earns at least $30 billion in oil revenue; more than enough money to appease the population or at least to give a sense of wellness. However, this inducement is also a reinforcement of the political status quo. It weakens the formation or emergence of political opponents, an important dimension of a vibrant democracy

Oil revenue also gives Middle East countries the means to build a large military capacity perhaps for protection from external adversaries and for intimidation of potential discontents. Military expenditures of the Middle East countries are among the highest in the world. Appendix I has a table of military expenditures of the Middle East countries from 2008 to 2018 as a percentage of their Gross Domestic Product (GDP). They are the highest in the world. Oman, Saudi Arabia, Israel and Jordan occupy are the largest spenders on military arms and equipment well above 5% of their GDP. For comparison purposes, the military expenditure of NATO countries as a percentage of their GDP is approximately 2.2% of their GDP except for the United States at 3.4% in 2018.

Finally, the modernization effect refers to the socio-cultural behavior in the context of economic development. Quite rightly, M. L Ross has emphasized the rentier, repression and modernization effects and their combined impact of demobilizing the population. Sociocultural opportunities are lost in authoritarian regimes particularly in education. This in turn negatively affects social interactions and participation in a modern economic structure. It is known that as the economy develops old structures are shattered and people become available for new patterns of socialization and economic aspirations. (K. W. Deutsch 1961: p. 494). Lack of education is an impediment to cultural development and work opportunities.

Conceivably, education like most human activity in authoritarian regimes is controlled. The religious education system uses texts provided by the state and must be adhered to. Informal education and access to technology are facilitated by social media, the Internet and on-line universities. Authoritarian systems enhance economic inequality by the unequal access to knowledge and training required for gainful employment.

In summary, the Middle East, as found in the study of F. Alvaredo et al, remains the most unequal region in the world. The combination of historical events, political culture, natural resource management and the related institutions can partly explain this situation. Another factor that must also be acknowledged is the involvement of international powers in this geographic area. This was vividly evident in the role of Russia, France, and Great Britain in the partitioning of the Ottoman Empire territory in the Sykes-Picot Agreement. Britain's presence in the Middle East was motivated by three reasons; the first was the desire to protect access to India, which meant controlling the Suez Canal and the Persian Gulf; the second was to protect their mandate in Palestine, where they had pledged to establish a Jewish homeland. This of course necessitated further clarification by Sir Winston Churchill in a White Paper*; the third reason was to protect their access to oil in Iran and Iraq (Robertson 2015: pp. 270-271). More recently, the interference of international powers in the Middle East was seen in the warfare activities in Israel, Iraq and Syria.

From a socioeconomic perspective, in 2016 most of the five countries selected as a proxy for the Middle East displayed a relatively high level of income inequality as measured by the Gini index: Iran 40.0, Turkey 41.9, and Israel 38.9. No information was available from the World Bank for Syria and Iraq. The long-term socioeconomic imbalance for these countries remains foggy due to the combination of many factors including religious sectarianism, oil revenues and the type of political regime. Somehow these factors seem to support each other in the maintenance of income inequality. It is not by accident that only Israel is listed as a flawed democracy in the Middle East. Of the oil-exporting countries, 60% are authoritarians.

Egypt

The next primary state in which the emergence and evolution of in-equality are reviewed is Egypt, another old civilization in the North East corner of Africa close to the Mediterranean Sea. Based on the discovery of Aterian tool-making, human settlement in Egypt dates back to at least 40,000 BC. Egypt has a long, rich and vibrant culture spanning over three millennia or even earlier if the Badarian*(I. Shaw 2000: pp.39-43) culture, an Egyptian Pre-dynastic Neolithic culture dated about 4400-4000 BC in Upper Egypt, is considered. Archeological evidence has revealed early agricultural practice in this area more specifically in the region of Badari, hence the name's origin. In the same vein, I must also mention the Naqada culture, an archaeological culture of Chalco-lithic Predynastic Egypt (ca. 4400–3000 BC), named for the town of Naqada. Moreover, possibly an earlier civilization preceded the Badar-ian culture but, chronologically speaking, there is no consensus among scholars on this issue. The Tasian culture is possibly the oldest-known Predynastic culture in Upper Egypt, which evolved around 4500 BC. The Tasian name came from the burials found at Deir Tasa, a site on the east bank of the Nile.

As you will discover in the following pages, it was necessary to review the works of archeologists and anthropologists on the remains of these civilizations to understand the origin of inequality in ancient Egypt. This was a challenging task considering that writing came along almost 3300 years later. The archeologist Gil Stein in the prologue of the book *Before the Pyramids – The origins of Egyptian Civilization* underlined that archeological evidence had to be supplemented with the "interpre-tation of the relatively small number of artistic depiction of key events and processes."

You will recall in PART II my explanation, based on archeological evidence, that hunter-gatherers did not live in an egalitarian society contrary to the popular belief. It would be of interest to identify in which period social differentiation occurred in Egyptian earliest sociaties and the related archeological evidence. Granted that demographic forces are insufficient for a society to become non-egalitarian perhaps ranking may occur to ensure a certain social order. In fact, the opposite is supported by most anthropologists. Social organization precedes population growth.

*Graph 3.5 Map of Lower and Upper Egypt**

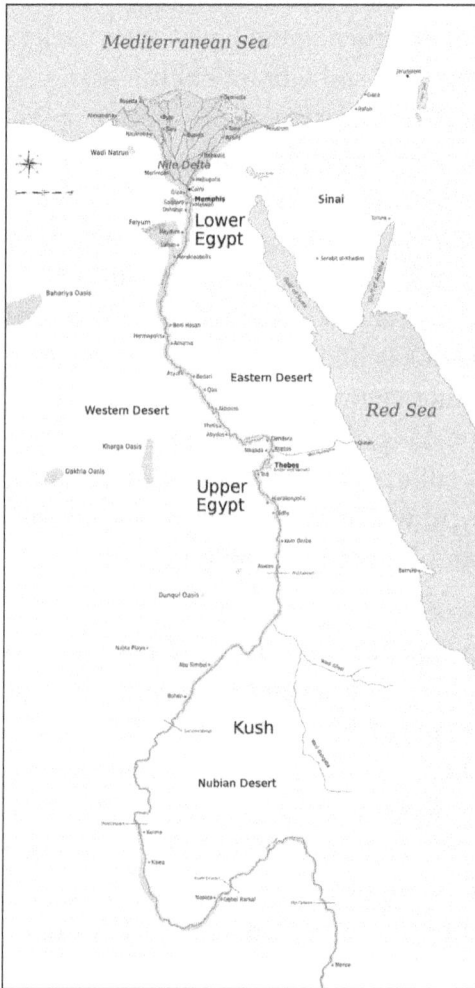

With respect to the Badarian culture (4400-3800 BC) little can be said about their population size and dwellings. However, based on data gathered from the analysis of the bodies at hundreds of burial sites in Upper Egypt it seems that a difference does exist between the setting and artifacts at these locations. More specifically, the tombs linked to the Badarian culture in Upper Egypt before the unification, that is the early Pre-dynastic period, consist of two groups; one more populated with very few goods, the other far less populated but quite noticeable in terms of size, grouping, decorations and offerings to the deceased. It can be argued that this arrangement reflects the grouping of elite members compared to the ordinary preceding group members. It is then possible to assume the beginning of social inequality in Upper Egypt at that time.

Concerning Lower Egypt, the ruling must be more nuanced. There is no conclusive evidence in the oldest cemeteries of the sedentary communities in this region that could indicate the existence of social inequality

An important issue needs to be raised. There are many types of inequality e-g economic, ethnic and social. What kind of inequality existed in the Pre-dynastic period? The limited information on the Badarian culture does not permit a detailed analysis of the social differentiation shown in the mortuary data in Upper Egypt. Nonetheless, many scholars have ruled out the existence of a formal authority based on a chain of command which is one of the characteristics of a state polity. There was a certain degree of social inequality in the Badarian, but going no further than rank based on prestige in communities not yet very attached to the land. Very little evidence was found of craft specialization or social stratification and of an object that could be interpreted as an expression of authority instead of merely prestige (J. J. Castillos 2010. However, in Naqada I period(4000-3500 BC) and subsequently the archeological data has revealed the presence of formal authority as witnessed by the presence of the first type of mace head, gold and stone vase unlikely to be found in an ordinary tomb but the elite. In the interpretation process, due consideration was given to separate social practice from social differentiation .

Why then social stratification occurred in Upper Egypt? For the sake of avoiding repetition, I will not elaborate in great detail on part of the state formation process; the accumulation of goods coincides with the presence of aggrandizers using their wealth to purchase in the first stage the submission of others and later coercive force to conquer neighboring countries for resources until the victor reaches a unique state polity in the pertinent geographical area. However, recent archeological findings have revealed a different scenario in the case of Egypt since some of the key events preceded the invention of writing circa 3,300 BC.

How did the Egyptian state emerge? A new school of thought has assessed the ramifications of a horde of existing events such as craft specialization, long-distance trade, political economy, urbanism, social complexity, bureaucracy and centralization which imminently lead to state formation. These events occurred in autonomous regions of Egypt and served as a catalyst to less developed regions to a point where many proto-states were developed. The "Two Lands" concept may be more an idea than a reality. The development of long-distance trade, urbanism and conceivably the active "lobbying" of Hierakonpolis, Naqada and Abydos elites led to centralization favoring the emergence of statehood. This does not rule out inter-regional conflicts but they did not play a substantial role in Egypt's state emergence. Narmer, the first king of Egypt, is historically known for unifying lower and upper Egypt, two regions as shown in the above map*. It is more a consolidation of many proto-states.

Predominantly native Egyptian rules lasted until the conquest by the Achaemenid Empire in the sixth century BC. Narmer Empire met the preset selection criteria as a primary state for studying the development of inequality. It might be helpful to remember that these criteria include territorial unification, duration of the empire or dynasty, the persistence of political culture in subsequent governments

The name of the king's first dynasty of ancient Egypt still remains unclear. Archeological evidence seems to support Narmer as the first king while Mene's name is also referred to in archeological records. Nonetheless, based on recent archeological evidence undoubtedly was a factual king of ancient Egypt. Perhaps Menes was only an honorific name as it continued to be mentioned later during Hor-Aha's reign (3020-2975 BC) Narmer's son. The First Dynasty (3150 to 2613 BC) started with Narmer who is also known as the last king of the pre-dynastic period and unifier of the Two Lands: the North, the Lower Egypt more rural with rich agricultural fields with Memphis as the capital of Egypt and the South, Upper Egypt more urbanized with Thebes which later became the capital under the reign of King Akhenaten (1353-1336 BC). Both regions developed simultaneously. However, agricultural development, population growth and trade allowed the North to absorb the South for its needs.

Egyptian mythology inspired or influenced many religious rituals and provided the ideological basis for kingship. As most Egyptians were illiterate they may therefore have had an elaborate oral tradition that transmitted myths through spoken storytelling. As the myth goes, the pharaoh as Horus in life became the pharaoh as Osiris in death, where he was united with the other gods. New incarnations of Horus succeeded the deceased pharaoh on earth in the form of new pharaohs. The lineage of Horus, the eventual product of unions between the children of Atum (Ra) an important deity in Egyptian mythology, may have been a means to explain and justify pharaonic power. The gods produced by Atum were all representative of cosmic and terrestrial forces in Egyptian life. By identifying Horus as the offspring of these forces, then identifying him with Atum himself, and finally identifying the Pharaoh with Horus, the Pharaoh theologically had dominion over all the world. The notion of Horus as the pharaoh seems to have been superseded by the concept of the pharaoh as the son of Ra, the deity of the noon sun during the Fifth Dynasty.

My purpose in going into so much detail was to facilitate the understanding of the King's authority over his people. He was seen not as a representative of god but as a god himself.

The genealogy of Narmer, like other kings of the Pre-dynastic Period (6000-3100 BC) is unclear the same as his military performance. It is reported the god-king had a son, Hor-Aha who succeeded him, from his wife Neithotep a princess of northern Egypt. With respect to his conquest, some authors contend that the unification was gradual over a one-hundred year period while others posited that it occurred by force. According to the war theory as the origin of state formation, I believe that the latter is more plausible in that weaker city-states were conquered by stronger ones as was the case in many states of the Middle East prior to evolving to an empire. Indeed, archeological evidence supports that Upper Egypt was reduced to three major states Thinis, Naqada and Nekhen, the Egyptian name of Hierakonpolis. As the inter-city state war continued, Naqada of Upper Egypt was absorbed leaving Thinis and Nekhen the final competitors for supremacy. Regardless of who the other monarch was, Narmer wan the final battle. In fact, monuments belonging to the king Narmer have been excavated at Abydos, a royal cemetery in the Thinite nome now the famous Umm el- Qaʾab cemetery near the ancient city of Abydos.

As both god and human, Narmer had absolute authority on Upper and Lower Egypt. He owned all of the lands, made laws, collected taxes, and protected Egypt against foreigners. As 'High Priest of Every Temple', the King represented the gods on Earth. He performed rituals and built temples to honor the gods.

An era of prosperity developed during King Narmer's reign. Like most ancient societies Egypt's economy was agrarian. The Nile was the lifeline of the inhabitants for water supply, fishes, waterfowls and the black silt deposit left each year on the river banks after the flood which makes agriculture possible. By carrying out sacred rituals and ceremonies, the king assured order, protection of the people, and the seasonal Nile flood. When trouble occurred, such as a low flood or plague, Egyptians believed the king had failed to perform his duties adequately.

King Narmer instituted a centralized form of government to control the land. He organized the territory in divisions called districts or nomes, 22 in Upper Egypt and 20 in Lower Egypt. Each nome was ruled by a governor (nomarch) accountable to the royal highest representative which is the vizier. The governor owed his post and loyalty to the king. Since no monetary system existed yet in Egypt, the king paid his most important government officials by granting them estates. This innovative administrative structure lasted for thousands of years after Narmer's dynasty. More importantly, the vizier must ensure that the laws were implemented to the letter. This priority can also be seen in the reign of Hor-Aha the son and successor of Narmer to the throne. Hor-Aha instituted at least annual visit to each nome with his vizier not only to verify adherence to the law but also to magnify his power and visibility to his subjects

This interaction of the center with the regional polities coupled with trade development created a stimulus to the development of the formal hieroglyph writing later on. It is reasonable to say that limited cuneiform writing existed to account for grain production collected in the form of tax by the government for redistribution and for bartering.

King Narmer (3150-3100 BC) ruled over Egypt as a theocratic government. Conceivably, he did not create this political structure since religion was inexorably interwoven with kingship in ancient Egypt. In the ancient empires reviewed thus far, the ruler was either secular or a spiritual leader representative of the gods. In this section on Egypt in which the ruler is seen as divine, god's incarnation I will review the social and political implications and their repercussions with the passage of time.

For the Egyptians Narmer was the incarnation of the god Horus, one of the two deities (Horus* the Elder and Horus the Younger). He was assisted by a vizier who is responsible for supervising the implementation of the law, managing the central bureaucracy, the different monarch members and major building projects. The other layers of the pyramid consist of what is known today as the middle class from the merchants to the commoners followed by the slaves at the bottom of the pyramid.

Myth and religion are often associated. At the beginning of the section on Egypt, I have deliberately expanded on mythology because of its ramifications on the social structure and governance of that country in ancient times. As I have said earlier, king Narmer personified the god Horus on Earth and was also seen that way. His main role was to pursue and create an ideal kingdom in Egypt and he chose Maat to achieve this purpose. Maat refers to the ancient Egyptian laws of truth, balance, order, harmony, law, morality, and justice from the goddess Maat of ancient African indigenous inhabitants of Egypt in the Pre-dynastic Period (5500-3100 BC). Egypt's name was Kemet at that time. Archaeological evidence in coffin texts during the reign of Narmer has proven the administration of the forty-two Laws of Maat dating from this period (see Appendix I). I have found this instrument of moral ideal for personal behavior relevant even today particularly laws 8, 29, 31, 35, 36, and 37 although the values embedded therein are thousands of years old.

As shown in Figure 3.6 Egypt, as most ancient countries reviewed thus far was a stratified society in which the king/gods, the vizier, the nobles the priests, the scribes and were part of the highest layers followed by the traders, the skilled workers and the artisans. Narmer did not need to maintain a standing army. Favored by its geographical position between the Sinai desert and Mesopotamia, isolated by the great desert of Africa, Egypt enjoyed a peaceful period until almost the end of the Old Kingdom c. 2200 BC. Armed forces, if needed, could be formed from farmers, and commoners at the call of the king. Conceivably, a coherent action against an enemy could not be taken without a high unit of command, which in this case went to a general. The commoners, encompassing the brick makers, pyramid builders and farmers, figured at the bottom of the pyramid followed by the slaves' layer.

As stratification often varies in scope and degree in different countries, it is pertinent to assess the impact of the hierarchy on ancient Egyptian society.

Figure 3.6 Social Structure

*During the Early dynastic period Egypt's rulers were knowns as "Kings". The title "Pharoah started only in the new kingdom (~1570-1069 BC)

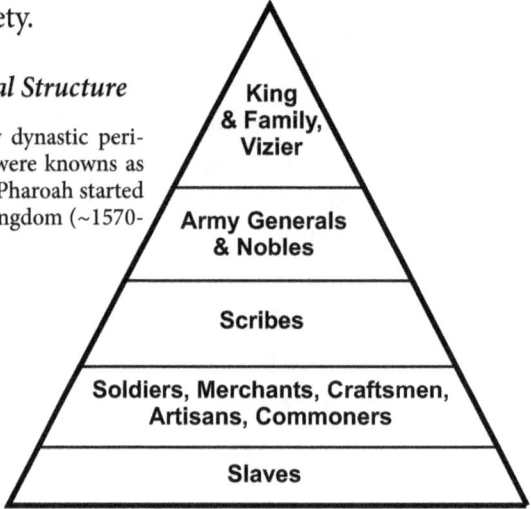

King & Family, Vizier

Army Generals & Nobles

Scribes

Soldiers, Merchants, Craftsmen, Artisans, Commoners

Slaves

Most studies of the ancient Egyptian society during the Narmer reign display several hierarchy levels. At first glance, those settings may suggest a very rigid social structure. The reality was quite different. Ancient Egypt reflected a relatively progressive society. This should not be surprising since according to Kemet cosmology Maat was designed to avert "Isfet" meaning injustice, chaos and violence and to maintain truth. Although occupational categories were well defined and people tended to remain in the profession of their parents it appears that upward social mobility was possible from the lowest level upward if the education criteria for the position sought were met. I must underline that the position of scribe required a high level of education on history, law, science and the fact that hieroglyphics encompasses more than seven hundred symbols to represent orality. It could be rare but not impossible for a lower-level person to achieve the position of scribe excluding other positions in the bureaucracy.

Narmer dynasty is remembered in history for not practicing gender inequality. The prominence and influence of women in Ancient Egypt are well known. For instance, Narmer being from Lower Egypt, the presence of Neithhotep the first Queen of Egypt from Upper Egypt played a clever strategy by Narmer but also an important role for Neithhotep in maintaining a balance between Upper and Lower Egypt. Women in the middle and upper layers worked as doctors, government officials, or priestesses. Even after the reign of Hor-Aha women occupied high positions in the Old Kingdom. History tells us of some famous Egyptian woman names such as Pharoah Hatshepsut (1473-1458 BC), the mono-theist Queen Fertiti (1370-1330 BC) and Pharoah Cleopatra (51-30 BC).

Women enjoyed a better quality of life the higher they were on the social pyramid. On the one hand, this translated into social dignity because of the high social status. Within the family concept, a spouse is a beloved partner, the relations with whom are to be mutually balanced and aimed at providing for psychological harmony between husband and wife as two autonomous friendly persons. Several papyri indicated the capacity of Ancient Egyptian women to gain wealth independently from their husbands. A husband could lawfully treat his wife as his legal "child," if he did not want to give any of his riches to his relatives. This way, the wife could acquire the greater part of his riches if they had no children together, or 66% if they had children. The Ancient Egyptian culture believed that a content and delighted home life ought to be the standard. They believed that it could be only accomplished by a husband and his wife, indulgent and administering to one another according to the guideline of Maat.

Women could obtain a marriage contract, divorce agreement particularly if she had accumulated assets on their own before marriage. No ancient civilization has reached such a level of wisdom in equal rights between genders as witnessed by the Greek historian Herodotus. It is most unfortunate that the social position of women deteriorated from 664 BC until today in some countries. The disintegration of the political and socio-economic situation of Egypt led to gradual deterioration and disintegration of the family relations.

As can be seen in Figure 3.6 slaves represented the lowest social layer in Ancient Egypt and mostly throughout the ancient world. Historically, slavery had carried the connotation of forced labor or the most humiliating and repetitive work as a war prisoner. It has been seen in all the empires reviewed so far surpassed only by the ancient Indus Valley civilization with the "untouchables" to be analyzed later. In some of those so-called closed societies, an individual is barred from any possibility of moving up in the stratification ladder because of the social status of his parents.

Delineating slavery in Narmer's Dynasty and Pharaonic Egypt is complicated because of the different classes of servitude over the course of dynastic history. One could become a slave in a number of ways granted being captured in war, other causes of falling into slavery include selling oneself to pay off a debt, being sold as punishment for a crime, being kidnapped and sold into slavery in another ".region, or being sold by a family member to relieve a debt. Slaves had no single ethnicity nor were they solely employed for manual labor. Slaves kept house and depending on their skills managed large estates, tutored young children, tended horses, served as accountants and skilled jewelry makers, and could be employed in whatever capacity their master saw they had a talent in. The salient factor in ancient Egyptian slavery is that a slave who worked diligently for his or her master could eventually buy their freedom.

Although women's social discrimination did not appear to take place in the Narmer dynasty, economic inequality between members of the lower class is evident. Even that far back the elite members had found a way to use the empire institutions to enrich themselves as will be seen in the causes of the collapse of Narmer's empire.

Despite King Narmer's diligence to avert ifset and his many accomplishments his dynasty collapsed in 2613 BC. Most historians attribute the collapse of this empire to environmental factors and the climatic disintegration of the central authority.

In a comprehensive paper on the first factor, the impact of the sediment reduction, perhaps imperceptible at the beginning of the first dynasty but accelerating by the end of the Old Kingdom adversely impacted agricultural production (Ralph O. Allen et al 1993). The authors posited that at "about 4,500 BP (*2550 BC*) well after the unification of the Two Lands (Upper and Lower Egypt), the Nile sediments were again deposited in the area far beyond its banks, but the total amount of sediment was far less. We have observed that there was a difference in the trace element ratios between the pre-5200 BP (*3250 BC*) Nile sediments and those deposited after 4500 BP (2550 BC). The observation made at Nekhen (also called Hierokonpolis) is important for understanding the pre-dynastic period and could be explained by a model involving major changes in the climate of Central and East Africa and reflecting the local conditions in Southern Egypt. Major climatic changes disrupted this society. It is my view that the reduction in agricultural production led to famine and social unrest contributing to the fall of Narmer's Empire.

The second other important factor is what I would call the impact of the trilogy of power, prestige and wealth; more on this phenomenon in the rest of the book. These three elements, sometimes at the source of greed, overlap each other so complexly that it becomes difficult to recognize their individual effect. As I have mentioned in the preceding pages, unless exempted by the king, estate owners paid taxes in the form of grain, cattle, or other agricultural products. The king's treasury consisted of storehouses for these products to be used in the form of government workers artisans and others, donations to temples, and trade goods in foreign commerce. Egypt had no forests, so it imported timber from Syria and Lebanon and traded with Nubia, a land extending from southern Egypt far into the African interior, for luxury items like ivory, incense, spices, gold, and animal skins. But as said the English historian and politician Lord Acton "Power tends to corrupt. Absolute power corrupts absolutely". This aphorism explains the behavior of some of the elite component by the end of the Old Kingdom (2686-2181 BC). The provincial viziers became less vigilant as their position became more comfortable. The enormous wealth of the government was spent on these massive building projects and the priests, as well as the monarchs and provincial governors, were becoming wealthier. As their wealth grew, so did their power, and as their power grew, they were less and less inclined to care very much what the king thought or what his vizier may or may not have requested of them. The rise in power of the priests and monarch members meant a decline in that of the central government which, combined with other factors, brought about the collapse of the Old Kingdom. While social inequality may have been prevented by the Maat system it was ultimately powerless to repress the elite's greed.

Both the Old and Middle Kingdom maintained a strong central government. Conceivably, because it cannot be proven, this political culture was inherited from the former to the latter. While the Pyramid of Menkaure, the Pyramid of Khafre and the Great Pyramid of Khufu are, inter alias, the legacy of the Old Kingdom, the Middle Kingdom (2055-1650 BC) is quite rightly called the Golden Age due to the long period of economic, social and political stability by a strong central government. Indeed, trading, arts and literature flourished in the Middle Kingdom starting in Mentuhotep II's reign. He is known as the first pharaoh of the Middle Kingdom and the unifier of Lower and Upper Egypt by making them administratively more visible in creating agencies for both parts of Egypt.

As is in the Old Kingdom, the economic success of this period raised the greed of the elite. Regional governors, priests and other high bureaucrats grabbed more power, debilitated the public funds thereby making the central government weaker. In addition, the expansion and control of the Semitic people in the far north of Egypt substantially reduced the capacity of the King to govern. The Middle Kingdom ended with the defeat of the Semitic people in 1552 BC signaling the beginning of the New Kingdom.

There is no consensus on the precise period of ancient Egypt's New Kingdom. Although {radiocarbon dating} provides a range estimate for the beginning date between 1570 BC and 1544, many scholars seem to limit the New Kingdom in the 1570-1069 BC period. It was Egypt's most prosperous time and the apogee of its power, the period that the King's title was changed to Pharaoh. Among the most known pharaohs of the 18th Dynasty figure Hatshepsut, Thutmose III and Amenhotep III. Although women had a relatively high status in ancient Egypt a woman becoming pharaoh was rare. As a regent for Thutmose III, Hatshepsut was the second woman pharaoh preceded by Sobekneferu who reigned as the pharaoh of Egypt after the death of her brother. Hatshepsut is credited for her major contribution to Egypt's prosperity and the longest-reigning woman pharaoh (1479 to 1458 BC). Amenhotep III ruled Egypt from June 1386 to 1349 BC and is remembered for the stability and prosperity of Egypt during his reign. As an astute diplomat, he used his wealth to manipulate the rulers of other countries to get what he wanted. He maintained the honor of Egyptian women in refusing requests to send them as wives to a foreign ruler. Many impressive Egyptian monuments were built during his reign.

The political structure in the New Kingdom period remained relatively identical to the preceding period in that highest officials were often members of the same families, whose members held important positions at court and across the country; the vizier, the scribe, the professionals, the generals, and the priests constituted the elite under the pharaoh; the middle class encompassed the artisans, the builders, the soldiers. At the lowest level were the slaves, the servants and the farmers working on the properties of the elite. In the preceding period, people tend to continue the profession of their father. However, the prosperity in the New Kingdom period created more work in so many areas that upward mobility was possible. Nonetheless, the pharaoh and the elite were the prime beneficiaries of this era of prosperity.

Rameses III who had reigned from 1186 to 1155 BC was the last strong pharaoh of the New Kingdom. From Rameses IV to XI, the political situation deteriorated due to the increased religious and financial power of the priests of Amun. In fact, they fulfill the role of intermediary with the gods diminishing thereby the role of the pharaoh. Moreover, the High priests held more land than the pharaoh and had a strong grip on the provinces.

The decision of Rameses II to move the capital from Thebes to Tanis in the northeastern region of the Nile Delta accelerated the decadence process by giving free hand to the High Priest of Amun wealth increased in tandem with popularity. This situation was a reminiscence of the decadence of Narmer in the Pre-dynastic period. Greed, the combined effect of power, prestige and wealth from the rulers of the provinces brought an end to Narmer's dynasty, so did the Amun priests to the Rameses dynasty.

Predominantly native Egyptian rule ended in the Third Intermediate Period (1069-664 BC) with the advent of the Achaemenid Empire (550-330BC). It became the first world power by conquering and uniting Mesopotamia, Egypt and Indus Valley. The Achaemenid Empire was succeeded by the Macedonian ruler Alexander the Great and Egypt became one of the provinces of Rome at the death of Cleopatra, the seventh pharaoh of Egypt. It remained under Roman rule until AD 641 except for the short 10 years (AD 619-629) control period by the Sasanian Empire the last kingdom of the Persian Empire before the rise of Islam.

Medieval Egypt 639 to early 1500

In medieval Egypt, the twenty- year period reign of the Rashidun refers to the first four caliphs following the death of the Islamic prophet Muhammad (Abu Bakr, Umar, Uthman ibn Affan, and Ali). The Rashidun was replaced by the Umayyad following the first Muslim Civil War. The Umayyads ruled the Islamic Empire for almost 90 years. The Abbasids, the third caliph reigned for nearly 200 years. They came to power at a time in which science and culture flourished under the reign of the caliphate. In religion, belonging to Sunni Islam is a major difference from the previous dynasties and there lies the attitude towards Muslims and non-Muslims who resented religious discrimination.

Support for the Abbasid Revolution came from people of diverse backgrounds, with almost all levels of society supporting armed opposition to Umayyads rule. Both Sunnis and Shias supported efforts to overthrow the Umayyads, as did non-Muslim subjects.

Thereafter, a series of dynasties from the Tulumid (868-905) to the Mamluk (1210-1517) ruled Egypt until the Ottoman sultan Selim I conquered Cairo in 1517 absorbing Egypt in the Ottoman Empire.

Pre-Modern Egypt

The Muslim conquest of Egypt lasted until 1867 except during the short period of French occupation (1798-1801). Muhammad Ali, a junior commander of the Albanian contingent of Ottoman forces inflicted major damages to the French army. From a practical perspective, Egypt fell under the control of the United Kingdom until the end of World War I (1914-1918) followed by a period of occupation that lasted until 1954. However, in 1922 Egypt was declared independent by the United Kingdom. Although the Medieval and Pre-Modern Egypt narrative present a brief summary of the key chronological event, for the sake of clarity and completeness the meaning of the independence granted to Egypt in 1922 needs to be explained. It is not sufficient to describe the societal change, the underlying forces shaping this change process must also be described

The Ottoman's implication in World War I started in 1914 by their attack of the Russian Fleet in the Black Sea and the Russia-controlled port city of Odessa thereby siding with the Central Powers (Germany and Austria-Hungary). The opposing consisted of the Allies that is France, Great Britain, Russia, Italy, and Japan and from 1917 USA. The Central Powers lost. In addition, the Ottomans lost the Gallipoli peninsula after the successive attacks by the allied in 1916 and the Russian forces. These attacks severely weakened the Ottoman economy and devastated its land, leaving some six million people dead. By 1916 even before the end of World War I, it seems that the fate of the Ottoman Empire was already sealed when France, the United Kingdom with the assent of Russia drafted the partitioning of the vanquished territory in the Sykes-Picot Agreement. As per this treaty, the United Kingdom got, inter alia, control of Egypt. Further involvement later of the United Kingdom in Egypt's political affairs will be more understood.

Two political parties emerged by 1907 that increasingly became vehicles for Egyptian nationalism: The People's Party (Al Hizb al-Umma) and the National Party (Wantani Party). In 1919 the exile of Saad Zaghlul, leader of the Wafd Party, another secular nationalist political party caused a countrywide revolution extending even to Sudan, a country bordering Egypt to the North, against the British occupation of Egypt. A series of strikes organized by the leaders of the political parties, well described by S. Dunes and J. Laird, paralyzed the functioning of the government. The United Kingdom was forced to declare limited independence to Egypt in 1922. Although, as a result, a constitutional monarchy was established, the United Kingdom kept control of certain key areas such as Foreign Affairs and National Defense until 1954. Egypt became a modern nation in 1953. Equally important, however, is the socio-economic development of the preceding 150 years.

When Muhammad Ali became Egypt Viceroy in 1805 he initiated a series of changes and initiatives which subsequently led people to name him the Father of Modern Egypt because of the substantial changes or better, a rupture from the traditional past. He developed agriculture by nationalizing the land, initiating large irrigation and crop diversification projects, rationalizing marketing and workforce for this purpose. He also nationalized all industries from textile to military weapons to reduce Egypt's dependence on imports. As a result, Egypt later became a major producer of cotton* in quantity and quality supplying almost 30% of UK needs.

This industrialization was halted by the imposition of free trade on Egypt based on the Anglo-Ottoman Agreement. This agreement allowed cheap British exports to enter the Egyptian market while the foreign exporters closed their market to imports. From 1836 to 1916 Egypt continued to invest in agricultural crops, irrigation, ports and commercial navy projects funded by the large increased price of cotton due to the demand caused by the American Civil War (1861-1783). Nonetheless, when the demand fell after the war, Egypt had to raise taxes in addition to heavy borrowing to finance these projects. Viceroy Isma'il Pasha (1863-1879) resorted to taking foreign loans and repaying them with shares of the Suez Canal. Domestically Isma'il also got financing by selling land to rich Egyptians. This was de facto the creation of an elite class which, as history has shown, usually supports the highest political power.

Modern Egypt 1953 to present

More important, however, are the institutions created after the 1919 Egypt Revolution. To be more precise the seeds of these institutions germinated even before the revolution resulting from various incidents including the Dinshaway* incident but the nationalism eruption manifested since 1920. Within two years from the revolution, three major initiatives can be seen as the forerunner of the nationalist policy of the second President of Egypt Gamal Abdel Nasser in 1954. First, the creation of a national bank in 1920 namely Bank Misr. The core idea behind this creation of this entity which emerged during the Revolution was to have more control over the economy, Second, the creation of The Egyptian General Agricultural Syndicate in 1922 to have more leverage over the foreign merchants export of cotton crop and to increase its resilience of the economy to external shock by more diversification. Third, the creation of the Egyptian Federation of Industries for the industrial development of Egypt. It was felt that through this syndicate the cultivators would have a voice on the financing of cotton production.

However, the creation of these institutions revealed another social perspective that is the invigoration of the middle-class political expression. Although at first glance these institutions particularly the Bank Misr and the Egyptian General Agricultural Syndicate may appear to be the creation of the elite but the reality was quite different. The confusion might have come from the profile of the middle class in the first two decades of the 20th century. It was composed of disparate groups with internal cohesion but no intragroup commonality. They encompassed merchants, artisans, civil servants and members of liberal professions and urban petit bourgeois on their way to attain the status of a distinct social class. Israel Gershoni in his contribution to Asian and African Studies used "effendiyya" to identify the agglomeration of these groups to identify the urban middle class. In his words, the term *effendiyya faithfully reflects and expresses their self-perception as a single social body. Hence within this term, we may include the variety of social actors and elements which comprised the urban middle class....It renders it a real social entity different and distinct in several principal aspects from both the Egyptian upper class and lower class* (G.R. Warburg and G. G. Gilbar 1983: pp.228-230).

In Egypt and the Fertile Crescent the effendiyya social force encompasses the western dressed and educated people at primary, secondary and tertiary levels.

Figure 3.7 provides a brief description of the Upper, Middle and Lower social class and their complex interaction during the 20th century in Egypt. I usually present a nation's social structure in a pyramid but in the case at stake, the variety of inter and intra relationships between the different classes prevents me from doing so. A descriptive narrative will precede visual representation. It will become clear that the notion of class encompasses a mass of individuals related by the type of work and possessing similar power to affect this mass. The driving force of this power transcends the conventional stratification lines and wealth. Power can then be viewed in terms of the relationships that classes have with each other or in terms of social structure.

The ruling class included the ruler, the ruling families, the tribal nobility such as the Abaza family*, the native landlords, the high clerics (religious and educational support system) and the military elite. As part of the upper class, there was also an economic elite comprising an indigenous aristocracy and a landless rentier elite, a group of foreign industrialists and businessmen which by reciprocal beneficial relation with the upper-class groups supported the indigenous class.

The middle class referred to as "effendiyya" earlier encompassed the bureaucratic, bourgeois and cleric classes. The bourgeois middle class was composed of merchants, traders and businessmen focused on their activities in the bazaar. In terms of identifying the interplay of attractive forces, the wide occupational composition of the Egypt middle class deserves further consideration: the bureaucratic component tended to be associated more with the ruling class perhaps for practical reasons such as decision implementation or tenure security - the bourgeois and cleric middle class could exercise enormous influence on the mass.

Finally, the lower class the most populous in that society comprehended mostly the peasants, the nomads and the workers, industrial workers later on. Compared to the other components of the lower class, historical events negatively affected the socio-economic condition of the peasants in the 19th century, a turning point in the socio-economic and political foundation of modern Egypt. As part of the transformation to increase export of cotton Peasants were dispossessed of their land and distributed to the ruling elite of large and medium-size landowners.

Generally, a product or service is the sum of disparate sets of voluntary work but sometimes it may also represent a sum of exploitation. For instance, corvée labor in irrigation projects (J. Tucker 1979: pp.251-2) took another toll on the time needed by the peasants to make their land economically productive. This displacement caused them to abandon their primary occupation for governmental projects. This absence caused them to become landless and were forced to move to the urban area, joining thereby the group of poor and unemployed people. Those peasants* who survived this ordeal and capable to keep their property were unable to pay the land tax due to the fall of cotton price after the American civil war. The combined effects of these policies benefited a few at the expense of many. Indeed, by 1906 40% of privately owned land was owned by 1% of the population

Some explanations are required in order to clarify the meaning of these centripetal and centrifugal arrows which, by the way, are a simplified representation of power between the different social entities shown on this graph. What is important to remember is that the limitative authority between each entity is seldom fixed. Therefore the concept of class will pivot more around interaction and relationships than sharp lines of differentiation and demarcation. This creates a permeability between the class lines to the point that an individual, such as a non-bourgeois middle class, may represent more than one class. This enhances class mobility in that a successful dual-class representative could have a snowball effect on members of a lower class. In the words of J. A. Bill, this culture allowed slaves and soldiers to become sultans and shahs.

This social practice prevailed up the revolution of 1952. On 23 July 1952, a military coup led by Mohammed Naguib Gamal Abdel Nasser terminated the constitutional monarchy of Egypt and Sudan of King Farouk and established a republic form of government. Sudan became an independent nation. The modern Republic of Egypt was founded in 1953. The British occupation ended with the complete withdrawal of British forces from the Suez Canal in 1956. The revolutionary government adopted a nationalist, anti-imperialist agenda, which came to be expressed chiefly through Arab nationalism, and international non-alignment. For six decades Egypt will be ruled autocratically by three presidents: G. A. Nasser (1954-1970), Anwar Sadat (1971-1981), Hosni Mubarak (1981-2011). In 2012 Mohamed Morsi became the first democratically elected president of Egypt beginning a new era for democracy.

Figure 3.7 Analytic view of the Islamic Middle Eastern class Structure

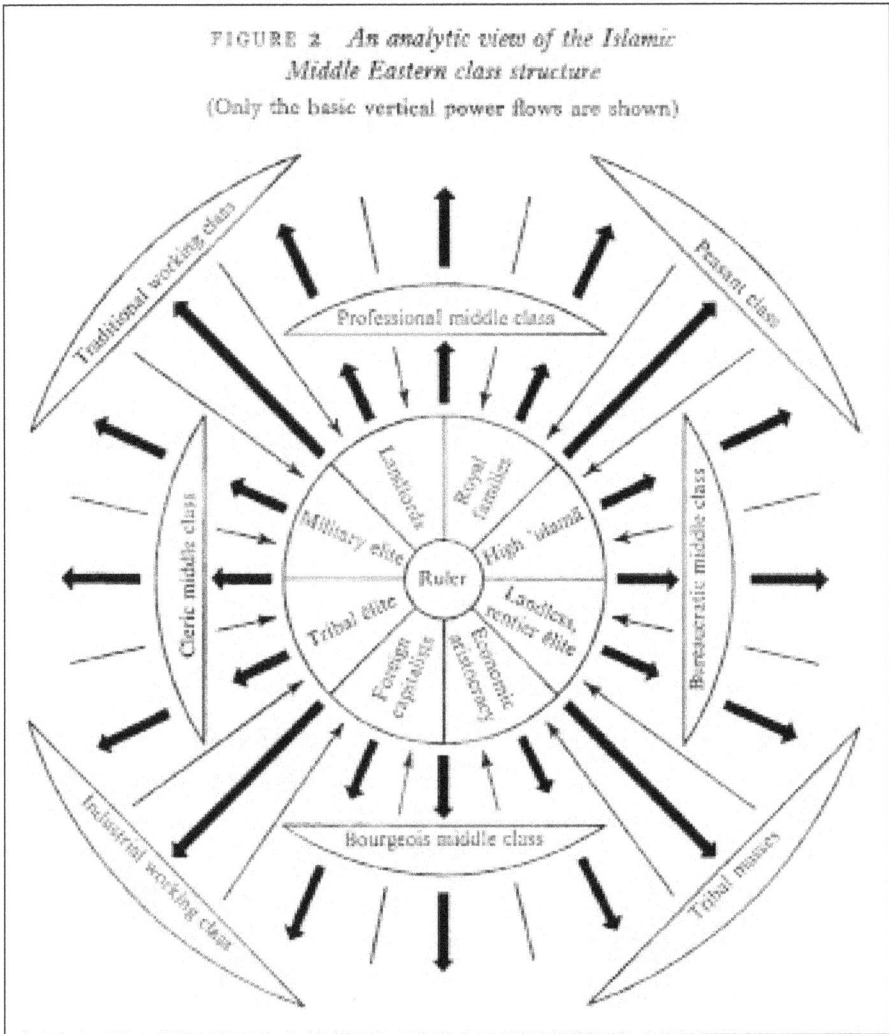

FIGURE 2 *An analytic view of the Islamic Middle Eastern class structure*

(Only the basic vertical power flows are shown)

Traditional working class · Peasant class · Professional middle class · Cleric middle class · Bureaucratic middle class · Landlords · Royal families · Military elite · High 'ulama · Ruler · Tribal elite · Landless, rentier élite · Foreign capitalists · Economic aristocracy · Industrial working class · Bourgeois middle class · Tribal masses

Source: International Journal of Middle East Studies

Nationalist political initiatives in line with Nasser's ideology, what really has been achieved in terms of reversing social inequality particularly given his socialist economic approach to govern?

It is difficult to answer this question without sounding either a partisan or opponent because of the many changes undertaken. With the passage of time, the sheer urgency of historical events has a knack to fade away. As a socialist, or rather a populist to use a renewed attribute, Nasser quickly undertook myriad activities to improve the living conditions of the middle class and the poor including the construction of schools and health care facilities. He also launched a land reform to redress the inequality of the peasants and small landowners. By the time Nasser became president less than six percent of Egypt's population owned more than 65% of the land in the country, and less than 0.5% of Egyptians owned more than one-third of all fertile land. The implementation of these policies necessitates a new brand of public servants and technocrats thereby enlarging the middle class.

There is a large body of literature on Nasser's land reform. It is mostly known as a failure because his policy has not reversed the concentration of land issue to the advantage of the "privileged" class. There is more inequality in landholdings in contemporary Egypt than there was at the time of Nasser's revolution (R. Bush 2007: p.15). Indeed, Nasser's successors also failed which resulted in land ownership was more obvious in rural than in urban areas. Nevertheless, the living conditions in the periphery has improved.

Agriculture accounts for approximately 36% of overall employment in Egypt and 22% of commodity exports. Additional indirect revenues from the Suez Canal resulting from the oil price increase in the 1980s positively affected the economy but as it often happens, increased importations made locally produced goods less competitive affecting farmers and industrial workers.

On the women's civic rights issue, women were given the right to vote in 1956 by Nasser. The economic rights of women were met by Nasser's successor almost a decade later. Nonetheless, the patriarchal family system remained immutable. "Women's organizations became associated with the authoritarian state structure ensuring that women's rights were part of a larger state-led developmental strategy, all restricted by state authoritarianism" (Sika, N. and Khodary, Y., 2012: pp. 91-100)

I thought appropriate and timely to underline the Egyptian women's role in the political arena. In the aftermath of the 1919 Egyptian Revolution, as part of a strategy to continue the occupation of Egypt and control the population, British officials painted peasants, students and women as terrorists. Each of them had supported the Revolution in their own way. Jane Linhares has thoroughly described the British strategy in the international community in this respect.

Women's feminism and nationalism had existed at the turn of the 19th or even earlier. Contrary to to the description of the British officials women were not illiterate and unintelligent as evidenced by the Society of Women Progress and the many articles they published. In the words of Beth Baron:" For the first time in Egyptian history, according to many accounts, women were thrust from the private realm onto the public stage. The revolution is thus often taken as the first expression of nationalist sentiment on the part of women, as well as the crucible of the women's movement. Yet women's participation in the events of 1919 was a continuation and extension of the activities of the previous decades."

Overall, the above sequence of events is linked with the authoritarianist type of regime prevailing in the Middle East and North Africa. The 2015 Human Development Report of the United Nations Development Programme provides a definition that seems to encapsulate this situation: "Development is about enlarging people's choices – focusing broadly on the richness of human lives rather than narrowly on the richness of economies.." Perhaps the turn of events would have been different if a cooperative approach was adopted to bringing the small landowners closer to the government as a counterbalancing force to the privileged class. A mutually beneficial position to both parties could have been reached thereby avoiding turning full circle.

By 1961 there was even more land concentration than in 1952. The land reform of subsequent Egyptian governments has not been successful either.

Table 3.8 Egypt Gini Index

	1990	1995	1999	2004	2008	2010	2012	2015
Gini Index	32.0	30.1	32.8	31.8	31.1	31.5	29.8	31.8

Source: worldbank.org

From an overall socioeconomic perspective, there is little difference between the 1990 and the 2015 most recent Gini Index. The lowest index conceivably coincides with the Arab Spring, the most recent democratic wave and its ramifications in the Middle East and North Africa. Hosni Mubarak had to resign and a year later Abdel Fattah el-Sisi was elected president in May 2014 and reelected in March 2018. Expansion of the Suez Canal was one of his main projects to enhance economic recovery. The new canal was opened in 2015 in a ceremony attended by several international dignitaries. Revenues from the suez Canal are expected to jump from 5 billion dollars to 12.5 billion dollars annually. Egypt's revenue from the Suez Canal for the 2017-2018 financial year was $5.585 billion.

The future of Egypt resides in its leader's ability to maintaining social peace and improving the Egyptian living conditions by restructuring the economy for a more balance wealth redistribution.

Indus Valley

A As one of the oldest and richest civilizations the Indus Valley Civilization (IVC), also called Dravidian civilization, has its roots in the Harappan civilization which occurred at around 6000 BC. The Dravidians were the largest population component of the entire Indus Valley particularly in the central and northern parts of the country. The IVC was roughly contemporary with the other riverine civilisations of the ancient world: Egypt along the Nile, Mesopotamia in the lands watered by the Euphrates and Tigris and China in the drainage basin of the Yellow River and the Yangtze. The following chart illustrates the timeline of the Pre-Indus Valley civilization, the third primary state considered as part of the review of humanity's struggles with inequality.

Figure 3.9 Timeline of Pre-Indus Valley Civilization

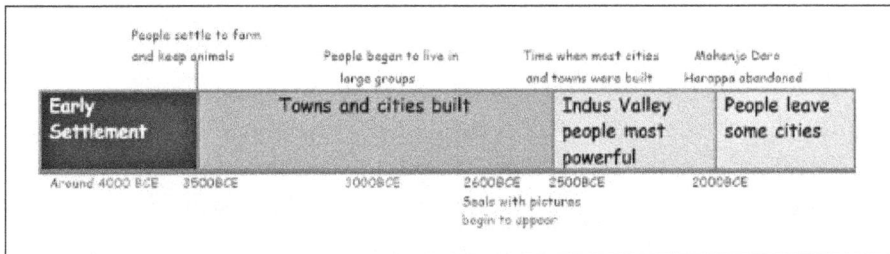

Indus Valley Civilization in the Mature Harappan Phase 2600-1900 BC had an estimated population of approximately 5 million inhabitants. The coordinated work of archeologists and social anthropologists in their analysis of the Indus Valleys' archeological sites have provided detailed information about Indian society in terms of behavior and social evolution. Still, very little is known about the first inhabitants of IVC. Genetic data suggest that they migrated from Africa and settled in

Southern India 50,000 years ago. They had a very complex culture and worshipped all forms of life. In addition, the Dravidians displayed no trait of bellicosity and were skilled farmers.

Based on archeological studies, many important discoveries were made at Harappa and Mohenjo-Daro. Further analysis has raised some crucial issues which cannot be clarified until today. Most of the pertinent information found in carved stamp seals and pottery cannot be deciphered. The Indus script is not comparable to any other known language. However, it is known that this civilization was located in the northwestern regions of South Asia extending from Afghanistan to Pakistan and Northwest India.

The IVC was as developed as ancient Egypt and Mesopotamia civilizations. Migration is even conjectured from many countries of the Middle East. As mentioned earlier, it is possible, yet unproven, that Mesopotamian urbanization exerted an influence on the rise of civilization in the Indus Valley and that later on may have exerted an influence on the beginning of urbanization in China

At around 1500 BC Indo-Aryans migrated to the Indus Valley from the North in such a large number that the term invasion is instead used by some authors although no trace of war was ever found. Preceding the Indo-Aryans* were the Hittites and possibly other groups from the Middle East.

Like Egypt, the geographical position of the Indus Valley facilitated the development of agriculture. The land flourished along with the system of monsoon-fed perennial rivers in the basins of the Ghaggar-Hakra River in northwest India, and the Indus River flowing through the length of Pakistan. In addition, it is known that by 2600 BC dozens of well-planned towns and cities with water and sewer systems were established; Harappa and Mohenjo Daro being the major ones. Between 2500 and 2000 BC the IVC was at its peak. Evidence of commercial transactions was found with the Near East as recorded in Sumerian documents dated 2000 BC. Craft and Agriculture, craft, and trade were the ICV's main sources of revenues. John Haywood wrote in the *Chronicles of the Ancient World* "The Meluhhaites (Indus Valley people), the men of the black land, bring to Naram-Sin of Agade all king of exotic wares".

It seems that there was a real cultural continuity between the late Indus Valley phase and the Copper Age cultures that characterized central and western India between 1700 and the 1st millennium BC. Those cultures form a material bridge between the end of the Indus civilization proper and the developed Iron Age Civilization that arose in India about 1000 BC. The Indus Valley culture belongs to the Bronze Age (3000 BC – 500 AD).

Sociopolitical Structure

As part of the administrative structure, it appears that Harrapa and Mohenjo-Daro were each ruled by a "governor". However, no information is available about the nature of the relationships between them. How then the Harrapans were "governed"? Put in another way, did the Harappan lived in an egalitarian political system? Although it may appear to be so, at least up to the migration or invasion of the Indo-Aryans* by 1500 BC, some contradicting facts make it difficult to provide a definitive answer to this question.

House size, which is one of the approaches used in social statistics in absence of better information for identifying socio-political class differential in ancient societies, tends to favor the egalitarian hypothesis. Indeed, the similar size of baked bricks residences based on archeological excavations in Harappa and Mohenjo-Daro sites confirm it. Furthermore, archeological excavations in Harappa and Mohenjo-Daro sites did not reveal artifact of any value with the dead which suggests the absence of class stratification. In addition, in most ancient civilizations army generals were always part of an elite. No evidence of weapons and soldiers and no sign of violence was found in the remains in both sites.

Another finding requires explanation. Archeological excavations undertaken in 1964 displayed forty-four skeletons scattered all over the city many of them in a body positioning suggesting a massacre by the Indo-Aryans invaders. This alleged massacre at Mohenjo-Daro is highly questionable. Based on information recently available, water contamination by insufficient maintenance of the sewage system resulting in cholera and malaria appears the appropriate explanation. The archeologist Jane McIntosh (McIntosh 2007: pp. 396-398) made a comprehensive analysis of the collapse of the Harrapan civilization. She posited that seepage of wastewater from the drains, among other things, may have contaminated drinking water in the numerous wells, and a few cases could have escalated rapidly into a major epidemic of malaria and cholera. As a result of this calamity, the inhabitants could not keep up with the number of dead. Residences and streets became the burials for these abandoned corpses.

However, a few practices and facts appear to shift the balance towards a stratified society. One of the main emphasis of Indus cities was on hygiene. About one in three private dwellings had access to an individual water well. Conceivably, only the fortunate of powerful ones could afford such a luxury.

Wastewater was disposed of through underground canals to a large reservoir with a settlement system to prevent clogging. The construction of such an infrastructure and its maintenance suggest at least an administrative structure with a chain of command and a reporting system. In addition, most cities were protected by thick walls surrounding a citadel. Granted the Harrapans did not have any army, the responsibility for this protection and the defense mechanism suggests the existence of a ruler, a government agency to manage the delivery of this service to its citizens. Archeological evidence of agricultural implements, irrigation and drainage systems confirmed the existence of advanced technology to support the day to day living style of this advanced civilization. These enormous achievements also imply a sociopolitical system to attain and maintain such a level of development. It is therefore not a conjecture to conclude that the Harrapan civilization was a stratified society.

This political structure could have been headed by a king-priest. Like most ancient societies, IVC also had a mother Goddess and guardian mother for each village. Evidence of IVC population's religious practices found goes back to 5500 BC. It may well be that the inhabitants of the two city-states Harrapa, Mohenjo-Daro and their governors worshipped a mother Goddess of fertility under a King-Priest by consent, not by force. This assumption gets traction in a statement of H. Kulke and D. Rothermund (2004: p. 17): "In both Harrapa and Mohenjo-Daro, archeologists found an acropolis raised on an artificial mound made of bricks, with large assembly halls and edifices constructed for religious cults. They added that in Mohenjo-Daro there was a Great Bath and to the east of this bath there was a big building (230x78 feet) which is thought to have been a palace of a king or of a high priest."

Several factors caused the collapse of the Indus Valley Civilization by 1300 BC. Since the beginning of the second millennium, the high cleanness and hygiene standards of the cities were declining. Through the lens of modern time non-compliance to zoning, multi-purpose business and residential location were mixed together. For example, it was not uncommon to find pottery kilns and metal furnace in the residential sector. Conceivably, the drain system could not be maintained properly. Dead bodies were buried in abandoned houses and streets adding to the insalubrity of the cities. Drinking water could have been contaminated which explains the rapid development of cholera and malaria mentioned earlier.

Climate change, manifested in a long global dry period, had negatively affected the vegetation of the region. This statement is made on the basis of soil samples from Harrapa. In the same vein, wood was used as the energy source for the firing of the huge number of baked bricks for residential construction, metalworking, pottery and faience.

Any civilization that had destroyed its environment did not survive. Hopefully, one-day humankind will exercise more respect for the (forest) ecosystems. The result is always the same. As an example, the fate of Easter Island located about 2000 miles west of Chile in the South Pacific Ocean can be used, From AD 1200 to 1700 the Rapa Nui, the aboriginal of Easter Island in Eastern Polynesia completely deforested their island by using the palm trees as rollers for moving the enormous statues they built in the memories of their ancestors. These massive creations usually weigh around 12.5 tons each with an average height of about 4 meters and 1.6-meters width at the base. According to the Bradshaw Foundation they were carved from the solidified volcanic ash of Rano Raraku volcano. Between 1200 and 1550, about 500 statues were moved from the quarries to their intended site set on a stone platform by a distance of up to 16 to 18 kilometers. Archeologists suggest that the motivation for this atrocious undertaking was the belief that these statues, face away from the sea, will protect the village.

Deforestation led to soil erosion and diminution of crop yield resulting in famine and even cannibalism. Today the Easter Island population is 5000, one-third of its original number before deforestation. Some of the statues were decapitated by angry Rapa Nui. The events that happened there make it an icon of environmental degradation and collapse. Easter Island will be remembered in history as the embodiment of resource negligence. The deforestation of the Dravidians homeland had led to a self-inflicted ecologic disaster shown in soil erosion with negative consequences on agriculture contributing to the demise of their civilization and the increasing presence of the Indo-Aryans.

Putting their migration dates even from before the Mature Harappan culture (2400-2200 BC) the Indo-Aryans arrived in India by three migration waves of different proportions to the North of India from Iran and Southern Russia. The last wave, the Vedic Aryans from Russian Turkestan occurred in 1400 BC.

The study of the social structure of (prehistoric India) must take into account not only the migration factor but also cultural and economic ramifications of this demographic change. The interaction of these factors between the prehistoric Indians and Indo Aryans created a shock between these two civilizations with a profound impact that can be felt until today in India.

It might be helpful to underline some of the Vedic Aryans cultural features* to get a better appreciation of this cultural shock between them and the Dravidians. Historically, the Vedic Aryans were light-skinned, primarily warrior nomadic people. Their main source of wealth was cattle which facilitated their mobility. They mastered the technology to make horse chariots, tools and weapons which they successfully used to conquer various tribes and communities in their journey towards India.

Their recreational activities consisted of gambling, chariot races, male fights and female dancers. They were united by shared cultural norms and language, the latter being an inter-branch of Sanskrit, Greek and Latin. They practiced Vedic Brahmanism in which Vishnu is a minor deity.

Scholars refer to the native Dravidian language as a language family in which Tamil was preponderant. Contrarily to the Indo Aryans, the Dravidians, as inferred earlier and based on archeological information from Harappa and Mohenjo-Daro sites, appeared to be peaceful people without an army. No trace of weapons was ever found on neither Harrapa nor Mohendo Daro. A unified Dravidian North-South language did not exist, rather a concept language family is more appropriate that is a group of languages related through descent from a common ancestral language or parental language, called the proto-language of that family. The prevailing theory is that speakers of Dravidian languages split into Northern, Central, and Southern ancestral languages somewhere around 1,500 BC. The Dravidians practiced a non-Vedic form of Hinduism in which, inter alias, Vishnu is the Supreme God.

The effect of these cultural differences was detrimental to the Dravidians. As reported by S. R. Ebenezer, the light-colored Aryans subjugated the Dravidians and the Indus Valley society were redefined in a caste system that is a form of social stratification wherein prestige, wealth and power are hierarchically arranged according to ethnic considerations and where upward mobility is impossible. Indeed, in Spanish and Portuguese the word "casta" means race, breed or lineage. In this inescapable four social class system, each of them is called varna in Brahminical or Hindu literature. The varnas are then divided into specialized sub-castes called jatis. Each jati is composed of a group deriving its livelihood primarily from a specific occupation.

1. The Brahmins (Priests). They consist of those engaged in scriptural education and teaching for the continuation of knowledge.

2. The Kshatriyas (Warriors and Princes). They take on all forms of public service including administration, maintenance of law and order and defense.

3. The Vaishyas (Landowners, Farmers, Tenants and Artisans). They engage in commercial activity as a businessman.

4. The Shudras (Commoners, Peasants, Servants). They work as semi-skilled and unskilled laborers.

The Untouchables. Mahatma Gandhi, the father of Modern India made the lowest caste a fifth lowly class with the name of Harijan or "Children of God". They cleaned sewers, disposed of dead animals etc. This signaled the beginning of a close stratification system in India. As illustrated in Figure 3.10, they are not considered part of the above four categories. Basically, the caste system divided the people into various sects who were responsible for different duties within the frameworks of society. The Vedic texts interpreted and taught by the Brahmins legitimized this social hierarchy including the endogenous marriage within each varna and jati. The Aryans' influence on the Indian social class system can still be felt until today.

Figure 3.10 Social Structure

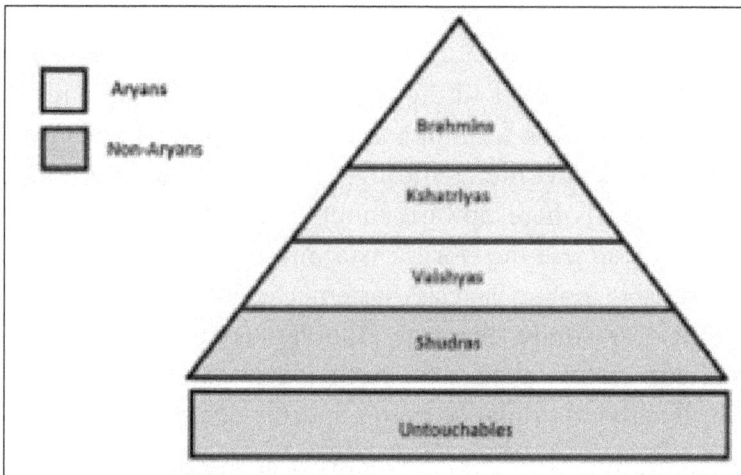

As can be seen, the caste system is a rigid hierarchy of classes that determines a person's occupation, economic potential and social status. Moreover, social mobility is impossible during one's lifetime. Under a divine seal, one must do good deeds and be reborn into a new caste level. However, history has revealed that social intercourse is inevitable particularly in a master-slave relationship in which the master assumed an absolute sexual right over his domestic slave women. A solution needed to be found for the children born between the "pure" Indo Aryans and the dark-skinned Dravidians and any admixture thereafter. As a recognition of the partial Aryans (Mulatto) descent they were admitted to the Shudras hence the difference between the first three upper layers Dwiji (born twice) and the fourth layer Awiji (born once). The untouchables are a detached class and a totally different matter.

It might be useful to further elaborate on the sociopolitical impact of this racial segregation. Over the course of a millennium, a large mixed-blood population emerged regardless of the stringent regulations in place to prevent that situation. However, the Indo- Aryans continued to assert their ethnocultural superiority solidified by many factors. They considered the Dravidians as sub-human species because of their dark skin color. Different religious ideologies, a language developed further the resentment towards the Dravidians. Finally, by setting some of the Dravidians in the lower and menial economic work occupational categories, like a self-fulfilling prophecy the Indo-Aryans rationalized their disdain by the concept of pollution. The Dravidians are unclean people which must be kept separate. Since the incumbents were locked in those positions for life, needless to say, that they were perceived as only capable of doing this type of work. As a corollary, any blood mixing with the Indo Aryans will make them weaker. This must have resonated well in Adolf Hitler's ears since he wrote in *Mein Kampf* "*No more than Nature desires the mating of weaker with stronger individuals, even less does she desire the blending of a higher with a lower race, since, if she did, her whole work of higher breeding, over perhaps hundreds of thousands of years, might be ruined with one blow. The historical experience offers countless proofs of this*". This quote shows with terrifying clarity that in every mingling of Aryan blood with that of lower peoples the result was the end of the cultured people. Socioeconomics struggles compounded with successive migration waves and religion imperative drove this system in that the high paying occupations became the monopoly of the first three layers with inter-generational transmission from the North to South of India. Over time, as part of a Sankritization process, Sanskrit was perceived as a refined or perfected manner of speaking, a marker of social class and educational attainment. Hinduism also got more traction particularly in the South with the assistance of Brahmin missionaries. As a result, Hinduism became the popular religion which in its essence is casteism. This ideology lasted until the accession to power of the emperor Ashoka (268 – 232 BC) of the Mauryan Dynasty who created the largest political empire in the Indian subcontinent and adopted the Buddhist religion. Then the Ashoka Empire met, inter alias, the selection criteria to review the primary state in India.

Emperor Ashoka the Great, the third ruler of the Indian Mauryan Empire, the largest ever entered history as a model of kingship in the Buddhist tradition. In 162 BC during the expansion of his Empire, Ashoka led a war against a feudal state named Kalinga (present-day Orissa) with the goal of annexing its territory that his grandfather had already attempted to do. Ashoka succeeded but at a great human cost. Some authors believe that the number of human casualties ranged between 100,000 to 300,000. Apparently, overpowered by remorse, Ashoka turned to Buddhism for spiritual peace and extended this religious ideology even beyond his kingdom.

In essence, Buddhism sustains the equality of every human being and, more importantly, the spirit of tolerance. In the Maurya's Empire, the largest political empire in the Indian subcontinent, compliance with his edicts to Buddhism was possible. An era of prosperity was achieved until the end of the third millennium BC. In the words of Amartya Sen "The Indian Emperor Ashoka in the third century BC, presented many political inscriptions in favor of tolerance and individual freedom, both as a part of state policy and in the relation of different people to each other". However, this is not to say that the social inequality of the preceding dynasties had disappeared. In the Northern and Western parts of the country, diffusion of the Indo Aryans culture and language took place in a master class (Arya Varna) interaction, which allowed for the absorption and acculturation of other groups. It may be helpful to remember that the Aryans did not erase the indigenous civilization of ancient India, which is speculatively identified with the Dravidian culture and language groups of south India. Nor did Aryan culture eradicate the many tribal traditions of India. The interrelations and interweaving of Aryan, Dravidian, and tribal cultures have created a tradition that has continued until today. Hindus in communities throughout the world reshape traditions in the context of their contemporary societies.

The relationship between the master-servant or slave has improved. This is not surprising considering the concept of respect and justice of Buddhism. Women were treated with respect but still considered subordinate to men. They were allowed to work and played important roles in many religious scriptures but upward vertical mobility was very rare.

The Ashoka empire collapsed with the murder of the emperor by his army general Pushiamitra Shunga in 322 BC. Some scholars believe that the size of the empire's territory made it difficult to control. It is not in the scope of this book to go through the 16 dynasties following dynasties leading to Babur the first emperor of the Mughal Dynasty in AD 1526. This decision can be justified by the importance of the Mughal dynasty period in Indian history. More specifically, the focus will be on the Mughal emperor Akbar, grandson of the first emperor; his son died accidentally in 1556.

By the beginning of the 17th century, Akbar was ruling over an empire of approximately 750,000 square miles stretching from northern Afghanistan in the northwest to central India's Deccan plateau in the South and the Assamese highlands in the northeast. By the same period, the empire had reached a degree of political stability and military dominance and cultural productivity which became the hallmark of the Mughals. The opulence and magnificence of the empire, the sophisticated decorative artisanal work were envied all over the world.

It is obvious that such wealth had attracted the attention of the European powers with a common goal to develop their economy by making profit from the lucrative spices, textiles and luxury goods of the Oriental market. Among them, the British East India Company (BEIC) formed in December 1600 followed by the Dutch East and West India companies respectively in March 1602 and March 1621 and the short-lived Portuguese East India Company in 1628-1633. Finally the French East India Company in 1664, Swedish East India for the purpose of conducting trade with China and the Far East. Except perhaps for the Dutch East India, colonization was not part of the corporate goal of any of these entities. After the death of Akbar, his son Salim Jehangir became the new emperor.

In 1623 the BEIC sought and obtained permission to build small factories on the Eastern and Western coast of India after the torture and execution of 10 British merchants on Ambon Island (present-day Makulu – Indonesia) by the Dutch competitor company. The BEIC's fortune grew rapidly and became a major corporate entity on the London financial market by the next two centuries. This growth led to a politico-economic process that set BEIC in a power trajectory never envisioned by its competitors.

Adam Smith defined political economy as a twofold process: a)the means to provide a plentiful revenue or subsistence for the people, or more properly to enable them to provide such a revenue or subsistence for themselves b) the means to supply the state or commonwealth with a revenue sufficient for the public services

After BEIC victories at the battle of Plassey (1757) and Buxar (1764) the company was given control of Bengal and more importantly the authority to collect tax revenue. One can read between the lines a major political authority in India. In addition, by the end of the 18th-century traders started developing systems of rules appropriate to India. BEIC made its profits through the management and control of the internal market and international trade, exploiting peasants and inflated expenses BEIC employees and management not even living in India. The 1757s can be considered the beginning of British imperialism in India. This new orientation largely explains BEIC's ascendance to the political command in India initiating the Raj administration. Indeed, subsequently, BEIC established its capital at Calcutta and in 1763 appointed Warren Hastings Governor-General of India consolidating British supremacy in this country. However, a movement in the opposing direction activated by a combination of many events started to emerge in Great Britain about the conduct of BEIC. The abuses and corruption of BEIC's employees in India, the anti-slavery movement, the 1789 Revolution in France pushed BEIC activities to the forefront. Governor-general Warren Hasting was impeached and replaced by Charles Cornwallis.

The political atmosphere in India did not improve. Since the first decade of the 18th century, no emperor was strong enough to maintain the integrity of the Mughal dynasty. The First War of Indias' Independence in 1857 marked the end of BEIC. Control of India was reverted to the Crown until the formal independence on June 15, 1947.

In summary, the imperialist and colonist* objectives that support the creation of BEIC can also be used to explain its demise both based on profit motives but by different means. On the one hand, BEIC's control over the land by eliminating all competitions had amassed an enormous fortune for its shareholders and the Crown at a minimal risk as a joint-stock company. The European market benefited from the exotic products and crafts of the Indian subcontinent. Later on, the construction of the factories, the tax collection and the setting of trading rules increased the liquidity of the company. BEIC's position has permitted Great Britain to take full advantage of the First Industrial Revolution by having a captive market to sell its textile and other products and at the same time a source of raw materials. On the other hand, these goodies were obtained at the detriment of the Indian lower classes. They became poorer by being unable to live on agricultural products because of the taxes and Great Britain's protection. If the period 1765-1947 is retained as the period of the British Raj, there were approximately 12 famines resulting in the death of more than 60 million people

According to the British economic historian Angus Maddison, India's share in world income fell from 22.6% in 1700 (Europe's share at that time was 23.3%) to 3.8% in 1952.

From a societal perspective, very little has been done by BEIC to maintain a national union in Egypt except for disapproving SATI* and the marriage of young boys and girls. BEIC supported the caste system. The first Governor-General of India, Warren Hastings directed the courts to base their judgments on the pertinent source to formalize caste law and to apply it more literally than presumably had been applied before. So the Mughal dynasty era and British colonialism reintroduced the caste system. Between 1860 and 1920 the British colonial system managed the labor force by the caste system. However, since India became independent in 1947, actions were taken by the Supreme Court of India to address this discrimination which is now illegal.

———————

Despite many religions, territorial expansion's wars, colonization, and famines India continues to attract the attention of the world. As a developing market economy, it is now the world's sixth world largest economy by nominal GDP (2.93 Trillion USD). The IMF Fiscal Monitor shows a Gini Index of .69 in 2016. However, according to the World Population Review report the Gini index has reached .83 in 2020. The disparity in income inequality can be explained by gender inequality and and unequal access to both sexes to work because of the sequel of the caste system. The poverty rate was 20 percent in 2020, a slight reduction from 2016 which stood at 21.1 percent.

India also has a history of cultural continuity. For millennia Hinduism has been the predominant religion and philosophical system of this country. In 2011 Hinduism was the religion of almost 80% of the Indian population, 14% adheres to Islam, while the remaining 6% adheres to other religions (Christianity, Jainism, Buddhism, Sikhism and various indigenous ethnically-bound faiths). But, as part of the social development profile, there are approximately 3,000** castes and 25,000** sub-castes in India, each related to a specific occupation based on religious, biological and socio-historical basis. The Untouchable lowest caste has been outlawed by the National Constitution of 1950. But the socioeconomic disparity continues to largely vary between the different castes. Indeed, as to per capita income in India, the caste with high income are the Brahmins followed by the Warriors. For example, according to Statista* in 2014 Jainism and Sikhism held the highest wealth index across the household. This means that social stratification and the sociopolitical system to meet god(s) imperative, drive economic inequality. Like in many developing countries, wealth concentration also remains an issue that need to be addressed.

Nonetheless, it is worth mentioning a few positive outcomes of the colonialism period. Among them a railway and road network ensuring the transportation of goods for interior and exterior trading; the abolition of the inhumane SATI; a court system to implement the rule of law and the press; the principle of political representation for the development of democracy; a bureaucracy to implement the government decisions.

The following statistics give some insights on the growth of India. Its share of the total merchandise and service global exports were respectively 1.6 and 3.5 percent in 2018. China stood at 12.8 for merchandise and 4.6 percent for service exports for the same period.

Although the population of India (1.37 billion) was almost similar to China's (1.43 billion) in 2019, major differences in politico-economic system make it inappropriate to draw further comparisons.

China

There are many narratives about the origin of Chinese civilization in traditional Chinese popular belief in China. According to historians like Sima Qian (145-86 BCE), there was once a great ruler named Huan-ti better known as the Yellow Emperor who emerged from the tribal system of pre-historic China to rule the region of Shandong between 2697-2597 BC. In this case, the Chinese people would be descendants of Huan- ti, the Yellow Emperor, a mythical figure whose reign spanned over two centuries in the third millennium BC. Until now the Yellow emperor plays an important role in Chinese nationalism.

In another narrative, according to the geochemist Sun Weidong the Chinese civilization would come from Egypt. Sun based his argument on the radiometric dating of Chinese bronzes which have chemical contents similar to Egyptian bronzes of the Shang Dynasty. He believes that the Hyksos, the prior inhabitants of Egypt, navigated to the coast of China after their expulsion from Egypt.

Be that as it may, China is one of the oldest civilizations in Asia succeeding the Majiyao culture. It was a group of Neolithic communities who lived primarily in the upper Yellow River region in China. This culture existed from 3300 to 2000 BC. China is a multi-ethnical country with Han forming the majority of the population and for that matter the whole world (18% of the global population). The Han ethnic group came from a large tribe 3000 years ago from the Northern and the Central Plain of China. The four major non-Han ethnic groups are the Manchus, the Mongols, the Hui and the Zang.

As mentioned earlier, from a cultural perspective *it may be* possible that Indus Valley civilization exerted some influence on the beginning of urbanization in China. Feudalism is another common point between the old world civilizations. As you will see in Part V feudalism* occurred in the European medieval period before the emergence of the modern states. However, it also happened in most early empires but with substantial differences in Mesopotamia, China, Indus Valley and Egypt. It is a decentralized form of government in which a monarch or lord divides and allocates lands called a *fief* to fighters in exchange for military services. The person who accepted the land becomes a *vassal* and the man who gave the land became the lord of the recipient. This system arose from the aristocracy's lack of confidence in the monarch to maintain security over his territory.

The existence of the Xia dynasty is still unconfirmed. However, it is well documented that the following Shang dynasty was overthrown by King Wenwang father of Ji Fa the founding father of the Zhou dynasty. Education, philosophy mainly Confucianism, technology were the priorities of this dynasty. In line with the selection criteria enunciated at the onset for the review of inequality in the primary states, the Qin Dynasty was selected for analysis in the following pages.

Qin, formally Qin Shi Huang, terminated the 800 year Zhou Dynasty with the capture of the city of Chengzhou and the last Zhou ruler. Qin put in place an administration and social structure that lasted more than his dynasty. The self-proclaimed first emperor of China, Qin Shi Huang founder of the Qin dynasty (221-207 BC) is known as the unifier of the land. He extended his kingdom from the North to the South and became the strongest of the seven kingdoms. More importantly, however, are the socio-economic reforms that he accomplished and Qin's formidable discipline in this process. Agriculture and trade were the main sources of revenue for the state treasury to sustain the army and the empire.

What were the social implications of the reforms that Qin introduced?

He replaced the Fengjian, a social structure and decentralized government incorporating feudalism, one of the causes of the Zhou's downfall, by a prefectural system composed of thirty-six prefects led by the emperor himself thereby eliminating dissension between the local officials and reducing the power of the nobles. In addition, by allocating lands to his generals on a non-hereditary he increased his commanding position on the army.

Qin Shi Huang created a centralized government and a stratified society seating at the top of the pyramid. Through his administrative reforms, the emperor became an autocrat accountable to himself and set up a system robust and resilient enough to sustain a stable economy and to maintain a strong army. Government officials which include politicians and military commanders (politician recipients of large tract of lands* from the emperor) form the second layer. Trading and bartering are carried out by the merchants in a beneficial relation-ship with the artisans and craftsmen. The last two layers, the farmers, peasants, servants and slaves form the largest proportion of the popu-lation. Slaves were captives from previous conquest and convicts for misbehavior against the ruler and unrecognized migrants. There were at least two million of them used in the initial construction phase of the Great Wall, road building, irrigation, palaces and the Cotta Mausoleum. In this society power, prestige and property are inversely proportional from bottom to top. In this structure, people treat each other in a different way depending on the social stratum they belong to, conceivably more respectfully from the bottom up. In the Qin dynasty, some indication of class struggle had been reported. For example, the merchants became rich by trading a variety of commodities such as tea, salt, rice, porcelain, gold, silk and imported and products but still remained low in status. In the Qin Dynasty, merchants could not wear silk although they were rich enough to buy countless of them. This situation has lasted until the fourth century BC. It is a fact that some friction existed between farmers and soldiers. Although the former occupied a higher class than the latter they were treated badly by the soldiers. My assessment of the plausibility of this situation rests on the key military characteristic of the Qin empire. He has built a formidable army which has extended his control over the largest population in China's history. Agriculture then was a priority enabling to feed both the army and the population, thereby maintaining peace and security on the territory. Trading and the collection of duties, taxes became secondary and require a minimum secured environment with the understanding that money or currency is necessary to support the sovereignty of a government.

Those many transactions could be considered the founding basis for the Silk Road trade. On the one hand, the army can be mobilized at the whim of the emperor, therefore the political usefulness of this entity to the state is a fait accompli. On the other hand, the merchants, although difficult, can escape the call by hiding. Hence the perception, at least at that time, that merchants regardless of their business acumen were regarded as unproductive, unreliable, building their fortune on the work of others. In other words, merchants were seen as a social disturbance for their excessive accumulation of wealth or erratic fluctuation of prices despite their economic usefulness.

It so appears that for the most part of Chinese history a merchant can be rich and still low in status. In many subsequent dynasties, merchants' children could not even reach the government bureaucracy, unless they have successfully passed the Chinese Imperial examinations widely used since the Tang dynasty (618-907 CE). That said, daughters of merchants could reach a higher social status level by marrying a man of that level. This leads to a brief review to determine the extent of social mobility in the Qin Shi Huang Empire. Simply defined, upward mobility is the possibility of moving to a social stratum of higher socioeconomic, power and prestige status. Was upward mobility possible? In other words, was this move compatible with Qin's administration ideology?

This a daunting task in view of the fact that most of the pertinent information are no longer available since many documents are either not readable or simply lost with the passage of time. However, it is known that early in his administration Qin Shi Huang adopted the Legalism* reversing the Confucianism* ideology of the preceding Zhou Empire based on the strong advice of the statesman Li Si. It becomes then more logical to address first the second question. On the one hand, legalism encompasses a powerful state controlled by a system of laws prescribing punishment and rewards for specific human behaviors in order to subject everyone to the power of the ruler. The legalism rationale is that the individualism of human beings blurs their views of social harmony and it can only be achieved through strong state control and absolute obedience to authority. Legalists aim at developing a rich state and a powerful army composed of competent and clever people through a selection system based on meritocracy. In "The Book of Lord Shang Yang" pp. 34-36 one can read that legalism at its heart was the replacement of erstwhile aristocratic ranks with the new system of twenty (initially fewer) ranks of merit for which most *males* were eligible regardless of pedigree or economic status

Confucius (551 BC-479 BC) is known by the record of his ideas and teachings reported by the philosopher himself in Analects, by the famous blind historian Zuo Qiuming circa 400 BC in *Zuozhuan* and by the Confucian's follower philosopher Mencius. Confucianism is often characterized as a system of social and ethical philosophy to establish the social values, institutions, and transcendent ideals of traditional Chinese society. In Confucianism man is the center of the universe: man cannot live alone but with other human beings. For human beings, the ultimate goal is individual happiness. The necessary condition to achieve happiness is through peace.

Confucianism revolves around seven main virtues: filial piety and charity, honesty and uprightness, loyalty, consciousness and consideration for others, knowledge, faithfulness and integrity. I will briefly consider a few of them. Filial piety establishes the due respect from child to parent, minister to ruler, wife to husband, younger to older brother, friend to friend. While important for the good functioning of a society, some scholars also see this chain of respect and obedience as an acceptance of the established social structure. Everyone should live up to the meaning of his title.

Knowledge in this case is a synonym to education where correct behavior, good manners, correct speaking can be learned, assuming that access to education is available to all. Consideration for others is among those virtues in which humaneness and compassion are expressed and condensed in the "what you do not wish for yourself, do not do to others". It is obvious that Confucius did not support physical punishments because of their counter-productiveness in governing people. He would instead opt for moral suasion to develop a sense of shame and remorse in the guilty person.

In contrast, Shang Yang (390 BC – 338 BC) in a rebuttal of his conservative opponent claiming that "one who imitates antiquity does not err" Shang Yang (390 BC – 338 BC) answered: "Antiquity and its paragon are not disparaged, but their model was appropriate for their time only and cannot be followed today. Hence, I say: there is no single way to order a generation; to benefit the state, one needs not to imitate antiquity. Simply put, there can be no unified model of the past. The lesson to be learned from the paragons' successes – if there is one – is to be flexible and adaptive" (Book of Lord Shan Yang - Page 89).

Legalism is a utilitarian philosophy aiming to maintain a wealthy state with a strong army. At the core of this philosophy is the assumption that humans are irreversibly selfish, covetous and need to be controlled using laws in order to prevent chaos. Through a system of reward and punishment for obedience and defiance to the law, people's behavior would become predictable thereby making easier the responsibilities of the ruler. Finally, the law is the supreme authority. Neither the emperor nor the army personifies the law. In other words, it is the position of the ruler, not the ruler himself, that holds the power.

No one could argue about flexibility and adaptiveness. Early in the Qin empire legalists philosophers and politicians Han Feizi (280-233BC) and Li Si (280-208 BC) convinced the emperor to choose the legalism ideology. This choice can be explained by the prevailing political and socio-economic environment: Turbulent period in which the six other states were fighting for power resulting in Qin supremacy – A population including a large army to feed resulting in the agrarian reform – irrigation, road building projects to be undertaken – border security to enforce. This is a long agenda like any new government. Law and order were of utmost importance.

However, the legalist ideology, implemented in laws covering every aspect of human affairs seems unjustifiable. People were sentenced to death for unknowingly breaking the law. Conceivably, more officials were needed to carry out the Qin's administration agenda efficiently i-e the civil ministers, the chamberlains to manage the palace bureaucracy and the district officers and clerks.

Meritocracy was the key principle for upward social mobility. But apply "rule for all, select and advance the virtuous and capable ones" could be a challenge because of the weakness and selfishness of human nature when dealing with non-measurable selection criteria. In a cogent paper Yuri Pines*has reviewed this complex challenge and credited Qin Shi Yang for establishing an objective method for promoting the best candidates. He concluded that intellectuals of the elite based on their abilities, servant men could reasonably expect promotion in the bureaucracy due to their military performance. In his assessment, even a bondservant could receive a rank of merit in exchange for his military achievements. Qin's empire became a mobile society in which pedigree played no role in determining one's status. In my assessment, the most practical way to interpret this last statement is that vertical upward mobility, except within the army, is confined within a particular layer. For instance, a merchant or artisan can become richer or more skillful over time and become more respectable. An educated officer drafted from the army because of his performance may become a government official. I suspect that it would have been difficult for a farmer to join the army because farming was a priority for the empire to sustain the army. In fact, slaves were given to farmers having met their quota to increase their efficiency. The hard reality was without good performance in the military services, the possibility of upward mobility remained slim.

A review of social mobility in ancient China would be incomplete without addressing the situation of women. Even in the absence of demographic data, it is safe to assume that they constituted a great proportion of the population. I have deliberately written in italics the words male and social mobility to emphasize their absence in this discourse. Surely, women were sometimes part of the labor force in agriculture, artisanal work particularly tending silkworms and weaving silk cloth. However, not a single laudatory strategy about them going up in the social ladder except marrying a man of a higher class.

As patriarchal replaced society matriarchal system, women had no rights whatsoever. To put this exclusion in perspective, consider for instance the denial of acquiring property or holding office. In other words, they were excluded from all political, economic and social activities. A woman must subservient to her father, older brother and if married to her husband and father-in-law. If her husband died, she cannot remarry. Those attributes fit well in Confucius's idea of family morality; the core of women's role was obedience and the key of women's status was obedience. I could not find specific data on this gender differential treatment but conceivably it led to a substantial social cost in the Qin dynasty taking into account in the frequency of war led to more widows. Fortunately, women social status started to improve since the Second Century A.D. with the Taoist movement of the assertion of women's rights.

Qin Shi Huang occupies an important position in China's history for the following achievements

1. Unification of China by conquering the remaining seven warring states. (See Note in Appendix I)

2. Agricultural reform so that more people can be fed by redistributing all lands previously owned by the nobles to his generals but on a non-hereditary vassal basis. One of the main reasons for this distribution, in addition to a recognition of their performance in war, was to eliminate the power of the preceding patrician elite. This is rather prophetic for two reasons. First, the fall of the succeeding Han empire can partly be attributed to the fight for power between the strongest armies. Second, the army provided by the nobles and vassals of medieval Western Europe has imbalanced the power of the Kings. In the words of the politician and diplomat Niccolò Machiavelli "The Kings lack the power since they cannot look for support from attached and faithful troops". Feudalism caused peasants to revolt by creating a gap between rich and poor leading to social unrest.

3. Dujiangyan Irrigation System through which Sichuan, a province in southwest China, became the most productive area in China.

4. Infrastructural work i-e roads and canals to improve transportation and initiation of the Great Wall construction by forced to prevent raids from nomads to the Northern border of the empire.

5. A standardized calligraphy writing system, a code of law, weights and measures and a currency (a round coin with a square hole) across the country.

6. Qin's army in Terracotta: An estimated 8,000 life-size terracotta figures They were created to serve the emperor in the afterlife and include a mix of chariots, cavalry, armored soldiers and archers.

The road to modern China cannot be analyzed without even briefly examining the 1911-1949 period. It has been a turning point in China's political history.

The two hundred and sixty-seven years of the imperial dynasty of China ended with the Qing dynasty (1644-1911/12). This radical change to overthrow a two-thousand year monarchic system can be explained by several factors and events which had caused profound dissatisfaction. For exanple, the Monarch's failure to modernize the state weakened its abilities to withstand foreign powers. As a result, the territorial integrity was affected by the two opium wars with the concession of Hong Kong to the British Government and an additional 99-year lease according to the Second Convention of Peking in July 1/1998. Furthermore, after the Sino-Japanese Imperial, China lost Taiwan and part of Manchuria.

But there is also an ethnic issue that should not be underestimated. According to the Hoover Institution, the 1911 Revolution was also triggered by the resentment of the Han people (98% of the population) towards the Manchu ethnic minority which dominated the Qing dynasty, the second time in China's entire political history.

Political events rarely emerge in isolation. It is worth mentioning some other important events preceding the 1949 Revolution. On January 1/1912, the Nationalist Party or Kuomintang (KMT) replaced the Qing dynasty with the People's Republic of China headed by Dr. Sun Yat-sen, the provisional president, succeeded three months later by a series of short term governments until 1928. In the meantime, one important military and political figure, Chiang Kai-shek, joined the KMT in 1918 and became its leader in 1925. In 1921 Mao Zedong became the leader of the Communist Party of China (CPC).

In 1927 Chiang Kai-shek established a nationalist* government in Nanking, the capital of Jiangsu province of the Republic of China. He undertook some radical changes with profound consequences and had differentiated him from other leaders: He purged the KMT from the communists and confronted the Japanese aggression. A three-year civil war broke between the communists and nationalists which Mao Zedong wan.

The 1949 Revolution led by Mao Zedong resulted in the creation of the People's Republic of China with Beijing as the capital; Nanking had been the capital of the former *Republic of China* of Chiang Kai-shek. 600,000 Nationalist troops and about two million Nationalist-sympathizer refugees retreated to the island of Taiwan officially called the Republic of China. Chiang Kai-shek ruled over Taiwan until his death in 1975. The 1949 Revolution led by Mao Zedong resulted in the creation of the People's Republic of China. Chiang Kai-shek, 600,000 Nationalist troops, and about two million Nationalist-sympathizer refugees retreated to the island of Taiwan. Chiang Kai-shek ruled over Taiwan until his death in 1975.

The foregoing reflects the summary of historical events that have led to the creation of modern China (*People Republic of China*) and Taiwan (Republic of China) shaped by two leaders of different political at the onset. Internationally, the turn of events seems to have favored the official recognition of the former while the latter had managed to achieve the well-being of its people from a western perspective of democracy and freedom.

For the sake of consistency with the review of the other primary states, I have compiled a few statistics which talk for themselves for both China and Taiwan. They have evolved to become powerful trade partners to most developed countries. The productivity of modern China by, inter alias, incremental reforms and institutional complementarities, has substantially increased (Yuen Y. Ang 2016: pp.74-88). China is now far away from the Great Leap Forward of Mao Zedong. It is noteworthy to mention the contribution of Deng Xiaoping's contribution (1976-1989) in China's modernization process for combining socialist ideology with free enterprise.

China GDP per capita in 2018 was $17,936 - Taiwan GDP per capita in 2018 was $24,807

China Gini index 2008-2018 scored 46.8 - Taiwan Gini index 2008-2018 was 33.8

According to the World Bank, more than 850 million Chinese people have been lifted out of extreme poverty; China's poverty rate fell from 88 percent in 1981 to 0.7 percent in 2015, as measured by the percentage of people living on the equivalent of US$1.90 or less per day in 2011 purchasing price parity terms. As at the end of 2018, the number of people living below China's national poverty line of 2,300 yuan per year (in 2010 constant prices) is 16.6 million which translates to 1.7% of the population with hopes of totally eradicating poverty by 2020. To deliver the goal of eliminating poverty by 2020, China needs to lift around 8.3 million rural residents out of poverty each year starting now until 2020. This goal was achieved on November 23rd, 2020.

Extreme poverty has almost been eradicated in Taiwan, with less than 1 percent of the population (129,968 people or 56,720 households) considered as poor or belonging to the low-income bracket.

China- According to the 2017 report of the World Economic Forum, China now ranks 100th out of 144 countries for gender parity, falling for nine consecutive years since 2008, when it ranked 57th. The country also ranked 105th in female representation among legislators, senior officials and managers. The Party Congress, just concluded, was marked by a striking absence of females in top political posts. According to the World Bank collection of development indicators, compiled from officially recognized sources, the female population in China was reported at 48.47 % in 2016.

In this context, there is another fact worth underlining. China's economy had shown a double-digit percentage growth in the first decade of the 21st century. Even the dismal 6% 2019 performance could be considered acceptable considering that the central bank forecast for the US economy is 2.2%. But the issue of wealth distribution in China's society has lately attracted a lot of attention from a gender parity perspective. Although female labor participation was 60.4% in 2019, far higher than the USA and Canada (~47%), differential treatment of women seems to be growing. Gender inequalities in the distribution of property are rampant. Perhaps this systemic discrimination is a revival of the Confucius philosophy mentioned in the Qin dynasty in which the patriarchal replaced the matriarchal system of the previous dynasty.

A case in point is the situation of women in the conversion of farmland for development as a result of economic development. In a socialist market economy, rural land ownership is vested in rural collective economic organization. In most locations, the collective owner is represented by the Committee. The challenge is the low participation of women at the decision-making level of these committees which leads to an asset gap between men and women for generations (Gail Hershatter 2007)

Taiwan- The Republic of China (ROC) has a relatively low level of gender inequality, ranking 5th worldwide with a Gender Inequality Index of 0.052. Tsai Ing-wen Taiwanese politician and professor is president of the Republic of China since May 20/2016 and the second president of the Democratic Progressive Party (DPP). From the beginning of this millennium to now, 48 cabinet positions have been occupied by women in the ROC.

China-The People's Republic of China is a socialist republic with a one-party system, the Communist Party of China.

Taiwan- There are hundreds of officially registered political parties in Taiwan. However, the Democratic Progressive Party founded in 1986 is one of the major political parties in Taiwan along with the historical dominant Kuomintang (KMT).

Endnotes

3a. After the fall of the Ottoman Empire the name of the city was changed to Istanbul.

3b. The Epic of Gilgamesh stands as the oldest piece of literary work on the planet.

3c. Hashemite: A member of a princely Arab family claiming direct descent from the prophet Muhammad.

3d. Sylvia Black PhD. Valley of Dry Bones

3e. Shia and Sunni constitute the two major branches of Islam. Shi'ites, the adherents of Shia, believe that God chose Ali ibn Abi Talib cousin and son-in-law of Muhammad to be the next successor. The Sunnis believe that Abu Bakr was the proper successor of Muhammad. Abu Bakr was chief advisor to the Prophet Muhammad. After Muhammad's death, he was elected leader of the Muslim community.

Islam is the official state religion in the Republic of Iraq, but the constitution guarantees freedom of religion. Shia Islam, the main religion in Iraq, is practiced by 64% of the population, while Sunni Islam is followed by 33% of the people. Iraqi Kurds are 85% Sunni – 15% Shia Feyli (Mesopotamia dialect of Southern Kurdish) Kurds. According to the CIA World Factbook about Iran, approximately 90–95% of Iranians associate themselves with the Shia branch of Islam, the official state religion, and about 5–10% with the Sunni and Sufi of Islam.

The largest religious group in Syria is Sunni Muslims, who make up about 60% of the population, of whom Arabic-speaking Sunnis form the majority, followed by the Kurds, Turkmens/Turkomans, Circassians (Northwest Caucasian nation natives to Circassia) and Palestinians.

In a poll conducted by Sabanci University in Tukey, 98.3% of Turks identified themselves as Muslims. Most Muslims in Turkey are Sunnis forming about 80.5% Shia denominations in total constitute about 16.5% of the Muslim population. Demographically, Turkish people make up 75% of Turkey's population while Kurdish people make up 18%. Other ethnic groups make up the remaining 7%.

3f. The Kurdistan Workers' Party (KWP) is a far-left militant political organization based in Turkey and Iraq.

3g. In this study the authors defined Middle East as encompassing the countries from Egypt to Iran and from Turkey to the Persian Gulf countries (Bahrain, Iraq, Kuwait, Oman, Qatar, Saudi Arabia, the United Arab Emirates (UAE)) and Egypt.

3h. As per Chart 3.4, the Middle East is the most unequal region in the world. (https://wid.world/document/alvaredoassouadpiketty-middleeast-wid-worldwp201715/)3i. The region of the Middle East and Northern Africa (MENA) is defined as encompassing: Algeria, Bahrain, Egypt, Iran, Iraq, Israel, Jordan, Kuwait, Lebanon, Libya, Morocco, Oman, Qatar, Saudi Arabia, Syria, Tunisia, Turkey, United Arab Emirates and Yemen (including North and South Yemen).

3j. Estimates of "directly-related" deaths: Accountings of the number of deaths resulting directly from an episode of political violence are difficult to determine and often vary widely. This difficulty is especially problematic as the distinction between combatants and non-combatants has grown increasingly obscure as "less formal" civil conflict interactions in less institutionalized societal systems predominate in the contemporary era. Such estimates of "battle-related deaths" should be regarded simply as estimates of the general magnitude of the violence. The numbers listed here reflect the median or mean of often widely disparate estimates listed in the various sources and are provided solely as a reference point. Casualties among non-combatants directly related to the violent conflict are inconsistently estimated (if at all) in the various source. Far more problematic than "battle-related deaths" for societal systems are the much larger numbers of persons directly and indirectly, physically and psychologically, distorted and disturbed by violence during episodes of armed conflict.

3k. Quantitative output of certain procedures that are necessary conditions for following the democratic principle.

3L. Palestine, the White Paper stated: "in the eyes of the law shall be Palestinian," but the Jewish community existing there – "a community, now numbering 80,000" – was to be internationally recognized as the Jewish National Home in Palestine" and its right to exist "should be internationally guaranteed" (A. Axelrod 2014 p.61).

3m. For the sake of clarification The Nile River flows from south to north. Therefore, the upper Nile is south of the lower Nile. Upper and Lower Egypt were named because they were on the upper and lower Nile, respectively. So, Upper Egypt is south of Lower Egypt because the upper Nile is south of the lower Nile.

3n. The length, strength, color of Egyptian cotton are characteristics of great value, while the uniformity of fiber due to the quality of growth, renders them, in manufacturing processes subject to less waste than any other kind. Egypt's cotton production in 1919 was 1.1 million 500-pound bales which represent 90% of Egypt's export. Egypt supply 30% of UK Cotton needs. (Cotton Production and Distribution. Department of Commerce. Bureau of the Census – page 82, bulletin 135. Washington Government and Printing Office. Washington Government and Printing Office).

3O. The Dinshaway incident was a clash between the officers of the British army and the Egyptians in Dinshaway village of Egypt. Though there were few injuries and casualties, the British officers' response was out of proportion. This incident is commemorated until today by the Dinshaway Museum (oxfordreference.com)

3p. For a detailed account of the historical events affecting the peasant class before the emergence of the urban middle class, see Social Change in the Nineteenth century: https://countrystudies.us/Egypt/23.htm. The US Library of Congress

3q. Indo–Aryans are natives of the Indian subcontinent and a diverse Indo-European-speaking ethnolinguistic group of speakers of Indo-Aryan languages. They split around 1800-1600 BC from the Iranians where after the Indo Aryans migrated into Anatolia, what is today as Afghanistan, Bangladesh, India, Pakistan and Nepal. The Iranians moved into Iran both populations bringing with them the Indo Iranian languages.

3r. Sati was a former practice in India whereby a widow put herself to her husband's funeral pyre.

3s. I have provided in the New World section a definition of colonialism and imperialism but in the meantime, it is appropriate to underline that, inter alias, the absence of permanent settlement differentiates colonialism from imperialism. Colonial imperialism is more appropriate to describe England's commercial and political relations with India that is imperialism from 1608-1765 and colonialism during the Raj period from 1767-1947.

3t. Gini index is a measure of income or wealth distribution in a society. Named after its inventor, the Italian sociologist Corrado Gini, the scores range from 0 for complete equality where all households have the same income or wealth to 1 for complete concentration where one household has all the income or wealth.

3u. Both Confucianism and Legalism in China aimed at a better and stable society, although fundamentally different particularly from a humane and moral viewpoint but with some common grounds in many respects such as education, respect of the social order. Legalism suits well to a totalitarian regime which has allowed Qin Shi Huang to unify China at that time and to create a solid administrative structure for the following dynasties but the strict political regime has proven not viable in the long run.

3v. The 1919 Treaty of Versailles, legalizing the end of World War I, recognized the Japanese claims to former German rights in the Shandong peninsula of China. This territorial attribution raised an outpouring of nationalistic sentiment.

3w. Carbon dating is a specific method of radiometric dating that uses the decay of C14. It works best with material less than 50 000 years old. Depending on sample, lab and method, accuracy might be as much as about ±60 years. Source: Reddit.com.

3x. The Abaza family, is an Egyptian family of Circassian origin that has had an influence in the late 18th century to modern times. It is known for having produced the largest number of nobles under the Muhammad Ali dynasty from the 19th to the mid-20th Century.

PART IV
Inequality in the New World

Introduction

Modern state global colonialism and imperialism began in the 15th century with the Age of Discovery. This was spearheaded by Portuguese sailors who explored the coasts of Africa then the Spanish colonization of Meso and South America. Subsequently, the French, the Dutch and the British followed suit in the rest of the world. By the 20th century much of Africa had been colonized by the major European powers— the United Kingdom, France, Netherlands, Germany, Belgium, Spain, Portugal, and Italy. But first, I thought appropriate to introduce the colonization of the new world with the following anecdote.

"Watch out for these guys; they've come to steal your land."

As the story goes, when NASA was preparing for the Apollo lunar mission, some training took place on a Navajo Indian reservation by the potential astronauts. One day, a Navajo elder and his son were herding sheep and came across the space crew. The old man, who only spoke Navajo, asked a question, which the son translated: "What are the guys in the big suits doing?" A member of the crew said they were practicing for their trip to the moon. Translated to the old man, he became quite excited and asked if he could send a message to the moon by the astronauts. Recognizing a promotional opportunity for the spin-doctors, the NASA folks got hold of a tape recorder. After the old man recorded his message, they asked the son to translate. He refused. So the NASA folks brought the tape to the reservation, where the rest of the tribe listened and laughed, but refused to translate the elder's message to the moon. Finally, NASA called an official government translator. He laughed and reported that the moon message said: "Watch out for these guys; they've come to steal your land."

My intent for sharing this anecdote is to emphasize that human history often changed direction which led to unpredictable circumstances. During the Age of Discovery and colonization, decisions were made that affected many societies' evolutionary trajectory, some for the worst - some for the better. With the wisdom of hindsight, historians sometimes wonder whether those changes were inevitable.

I will consider two primary states in the New World namely Mexico in Mesoamerica and Peru in South America. I then remain consistent with the pre-established framework of studying six primary states including the four previously covered in the Old World.

The New World's study is preceded by the analysis of Hispaniola Where Christopher Columbus established the first European colony with the related extractive economic institutions for the benefit of the Spanish Crown. The colonization of Hispaniola provides an insight in to the colonist motives as evidenced by Columbus's behavior towards the natives. In addition, I thought it appropriate to provide an overview of the sociopolitical environment before considering Hispaniola.

As mentioned earlier, modern-state global colonialism and imperialism, began in the 15th century. As is often the case between competing nations, conflicts emerged between colonists about the control of their colonized areas. For example, at the beginning of the 17th century, the French and British settlers began to occupy the western part of Hispaniola threatening Spain's ownership of the island. It took a treaty to end this conflict. By The Treaty of Ryswick Spain ceded the western third of the island to France before Haiti became an independent country in 1804.

Christopher Columbus's proposal to sail west to find a new maritime route to India for commodities was originally rejected by Portugal, England* and the cities of Genoa and Venice. By the mid-1400s aggressive Portuguese sailors had already navigated the west coast of Africa and established coastal ports in Congo, the western coast of India and Brazil. But, Spain's religiosity and its competition with Portugal and the imperative of necessities convinced the Spanish monarchs to sponsor Columbus's expedition. More specifically, their real motives were wealth and glory in the land of gold and spices in the Indian Ocean including the dissemination of Christianity.

In Part II, I described the influence of religion on the political sphere. Re-emphasizing religion's role in the discovery of the New and its implication in the Spanish colonization of America might be useful.

A large Jewish and Muslim population changed medieval Spain's ethnic profile. This population had a profound effect on the country's art, architecture, literature and particularly the economy. Jewish intellectuals made substantial contributions to many spheres of activity including medicine, engineering, bureaucracy and trade. But the religious zeal of medieval Spain had wiped out this contribution from Spaniards' memory. By AD 732 Islam had spread throughout the Middle East and into Europe. There was an 800-year long campaign of violence by Spain and Portugal against the Muslims, known as the Crusades to reconquer the lost territory in the Middle East from Turkey to the Sinai Peninsula. In Spain, the struggle continued with the expulsion of the Muslims by the end of the 13th century. But the wind of religiosity blew even stronger and subsequently turned on the Jews who were persecuted in the Pogrom* of 1391. This hostility stemmed from the Spanish conviction that the Jews had caused the Black Death which killed one-third of Europe's population although there was no evidence to that claim.

The inquisition was an important religious and political event during the 13th-17th century period. The Spanish Inquisition officially started in 1481 with the transfer of its implementation from the Pope to the Crown. As a result, Jews had the choice of either converting to Catholicism or death. But even converted, Spaniards believed that the Jews' conversion was just a cover and they were suspected of heresy. Between 1481 and 1681, thousands of people were put to death by hanging or being burned alive. This religious intolerance continued into the colonization period. The religious zeal of the Catholic nations of Spain and Portugal motivated the colonists to convert Native Americans to Christianity as part of the movement to global dominance of Christianism. A quote from Columbus's journal about the inhabitants of Hispaniola during his first voyage is consistent with this objective: "...They should be good servants and intelligent, for I observed that they quickly took in what was said to them, and I believe that they that they would easily be made Christians, as it appeared to me that they had no religion".

In March 1493 Columbus returned to Spain from the first expedition and, in addition to the kidnapped natives, he also displayed to the court the gold he had found and some exotic fruits, tobacco plants and chili pepper. In the background, the political work was already done. The Spanish monarchs had sought and obtained from Pope Alexander VI exclusive title to Columbus's findings. Spain, like Portugal, thus became engaged in the golden age of colonization.

This major historical development has been long debated by many scholars. In the words of R. J. Horvath quoting Strausz-Hupe and H. W. Hazard "Although colonialism ranks with the most influential processes in human history, Western scholars have not really come to grips with the phenomenon. Academic establishment possesses no widely accepted theory of colonialism, nor does any substantial agreement exist upon what colonialism is". As one of the main instruments of state formation, colonialism existed in the Greek, Roman and Moors empires but some of its parameters such as technological development and the extraction strategies changed over time. For example, medieval Europe with its fast sailing ships were able to conquer distant countries in the New World. A further issue complicating a standard definition of colonialism arises when imperialism is factored in. As a result, the focus is often on the implications of colonialism rather than its meaning. Nevertheless, colonialism is an emotionally charged word from either a (former) colonizer or colonized standpoint. Hence the need for an approach based on a flexible framework that will survive the test of space and time.

For the purpose of this book, I will use the following definition: Colonialism is a form of domination of a country's inhabitants and territory (the colonized) for the purpose of economically exploiting them for the benefit of another country (the colonizer) and extending its theological or cultural dominance. This definition will also be used to assess the legacy of colonialism. With respect to the relationship between colonialism and imperialism, Ronald J. Horvath suggests that the presence or absence of a permanent settlement in the colony differs them. Indeed this distinction is evident in many countries. For example, permanent settlers and settlements of the colonizer were often established in the New World. However, most of Africa and Asia were imperialized - they were dominated without settlers. The distinction between colonialism and imperialism also sustains different types of relationships between the colonizer and the colonized from resource exhaustion, assimilation, extermination or something in between called relative equilibrium.

On the basis of "convoluted" calculations, he sailed westward from the Spanish port of Palos on August 3/1492 hoping to reach the land of gold, spices and pearls in Asia because of the control of the Black Sea by the Ottoman Turkish Empire. The strategic position of the Bosphorus Strait gave control of vast quantities of wealth and power by whoever controlled the Black Sea. In the following map, the square illustrates the trade's blockade by the Ottoman Empire

Map 4.1 Silk Road Main Route in Medieval Time

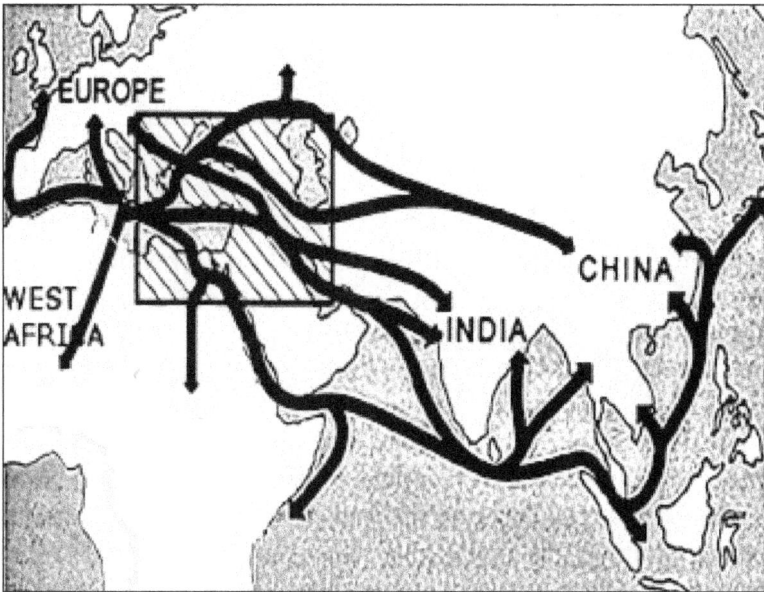

Source: globalsecurity.org/military/world/china/silk-road-medieval.htm

Three months after Columbus left Spain he successively discovered the Bahamas, Cuba and Hispaniola (now Haiti and the Dominican Republic) where he stayed. The first contact with the inhabitants of

Hispaniola was pleasant. The local people brought food and Columbus and his crew reciprocated with glass beads and hawks' bells planned for this kind of encounter. This kindness led Columbus to write in his diary "they traded with us and gave us everything they had, with goodwill... they took great delight in pleasing us. They are very gentle and without knowledge of what is evil; nor do they murder or steal. Your highness may believe that in all the world there can be no better people. They love their neighbors as themselves, and they have the sweetest talk in the world, and are gentle and always laughing."

But Columbus's assessment veiled the long development of a civilization that had existed for thousands of years. The Taino were a subgroup of the Arawak populating the Caribbean Greater Antilles having been driven out by the Caribs who retained supremacy in the Lesser Antilles. Both the Caribs and the Tainos came from the South American mainland. As Columbus had experienced, the ferocious Caribs' warriors constantly raided the neighboring islands for slaves and women.

The Taíno were agile swimmers and mastered the technology of building large canoes capable of transporting heavy cargo for trade purposes. It meant that the Taino interacted and traded with the other Greater Antilles populations.

In a publication by Durán Berríos, the religious beliefs of the Taíno were described as polytheistic (This publication seems no longer available). Like most ancient civilizations, they believed in an afterlife and that deities affected human activities. Religious ceremonies led by the behique (religious leader) and the cacique (political-religious leader) were held at the Batey* or at the cacique's home.

Chiefdom, the usual sociopolitical predecessor of state and empire, existed in Hispaniola at the time of Columbus's arrival. The territory was clearly divided into five chiefdoms or cacicazgos, each headed by a paramount chief or cacique. These were: Marién (Guaganagarix), Maguá (Guarionex) Higüey (Cotubanama) Maguana (Caonabo) and Jaragua also called Xaragua (Bohecchio). [Cacique's name in bracket]

Figure 4.2 The Five Chiefdoms of Hispaniola

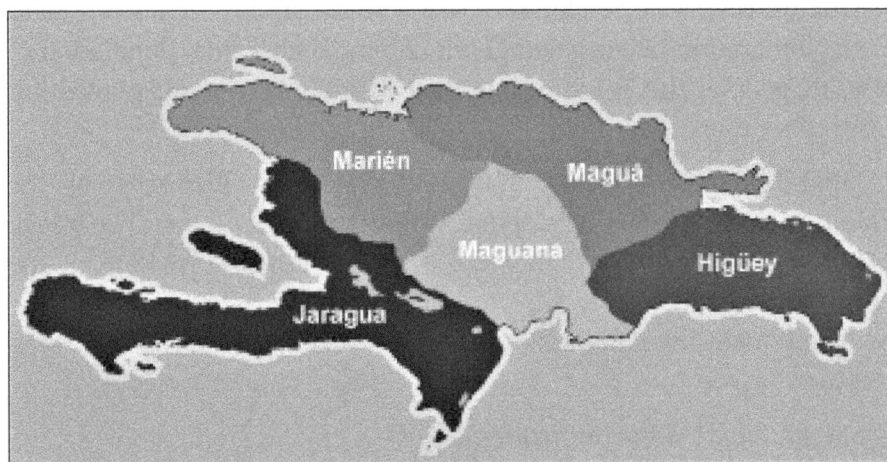

This map could be a consolidation of other maps since other sources mention a myriad of different chiefdoms. In fact, some authors posit that hundreds of chiefdoms existed in Hispaniola. Although I acknowledge the difference between geographical demarcation and political division (J. S. Badillo (2003) I will focus on five chiefdoms as shown in the above map and in the note section of Appendix II. In this respect, I have identified the chiefdom of Ciguayo of the Samana peninsula protrudes the chiefdom of Maguá ruled by the cacique Mayobanex. This distinction is important for the understanding of inter-chiefdom chieftaincy's marriage. Each cacicazgo (Chieftaincy) may include 70 to 100 communities which in turn accommodated hundreds of residents each. There appears to be an inconsistency between Hispaniola's population size range and the number of caciques. It would suggest a population range by cacique of 60,000-80,000 which is far above the theoretical 10,000 limit for a single chiefdom. Beyond this threshold, it becomes difficult to manage the chiefdom. This theory got some traction when the number of chiefdoms of Cuba and Puerto Rico are proportioned with their populations, respectively 100,000 and 30,000-60,000. The largest Antilles had 29 chiefdoms with 3,448 people per chiefdom. In the same vein, Puerto Rico had 21 Chiefdoms with 2847 people per chiefdom. It is possible that there were only five chiefdoms in Hispaniola but many more tribal societies living here and there and between them. This latter alternative seems more plausible. The five chiefdoms would represent an agglomeration of many simple chiefdoms with a total population of 300,000 people. This is more consistent with the Hispaniola population from other sources.

The following pyramid illustrates the social hierarchy of the Taino society when Christopher Columbus arrived in Hispaniola. The Taínos were divided into three social classes consisting of the noblemen which include the cacique, the bohique or priest and the medicine man, the Nitainos or sub-chiefs and the Naborias (Working class).

Figure 4.3 Taino Political Structure

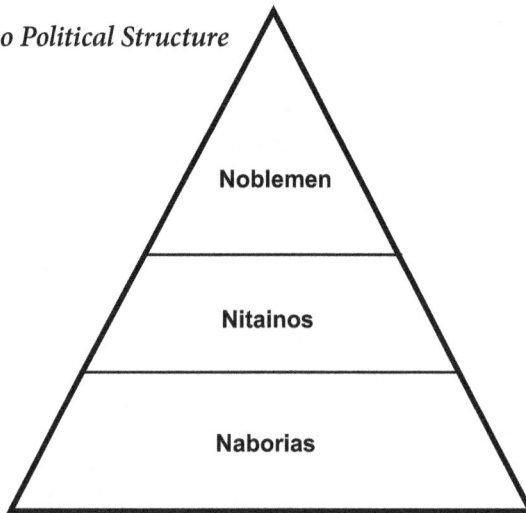

The Taíno Indians in Hispaniola lived in organized, hierarchically arranged kingdoms. The cacique, supreme authority of the chiefdom, had responsibility for assuring the well-being of the Taíno society in all aspects of their life. They controlled the collection and distribution of food, trade goods, and community festivals. They functioned as the spiritual leader who contacted the supernatural through hallucinogenic trances by inhaling cohoba, ground seeds of the cojobana tree using a Y-shaped pipe. The Nitaino were the sub-chiefs who were part or part of the elite, the equivalent of nobles in the European context. They assisted the cacique in large enterprises such as the collection and distribution of food, trading of prestige goods all key characteristics of a chiefdom polity. The Nitaíno and the Bohique represented the elite. At the bottom was the Naboria. These were the workers at bottom of the pyramid represented the workers, the largest portion of the population who were involved in fishing, farming, building and artwork. The Taíno chiefdoms were a classless but ranked society consisting of the nobles, the nitainos and the workers.

But did inequality exist in Taíno society?

As stated in Part II, a chiefdom is an autonomous political unit comprised of a number of villages or communities under the permanent control of a paramount chief (R. L. Carneiro 1981: p.45). Chiefdoms are characterized by permanent and institutionalized forms of political leadership (the chief), centralized decision-making, economic interdependence, and social hierarchy. Surplus or overproduction of goods by force is characteristic of the chiefdom polity. Paid in the form of tribute to the cacique, the goods are given to the paramount chief allowed him to maintain a lavish lifestyle inherent to his rank. In return, the producers were protected from outside enemies.

The tributes were more visible in Hispaniola because of the Conuco* system. It was created by the Taíno to feed just themselves and not to have any surplus. Twenty persons working six hours a day for one month will make planting of such Conuco provide bread for 300 people for two years" (J. F. Richards 2003: pp. 248-250). Note that bread means cassava made from yucca. Whatever excess was produced went to the cacique who could keep the excess product, trade it for goods for himself or give it to high officials to ensure their loyalty. This dynamic was not unique to Hispaniola. It was also observed in Hawaiian chiefdoms, self-sufficient communities (T. Earle 1977: pp.213-229). There again, the paramount chief did not redistribute staple goods but trade them for prestige goods to give to his followers to help him maintain his authority. This fact confirms that inequality existed even in the Taíno society driven as always by the thirst for power, prestige and wealth.

This absence of surplus had incited some authors to posit that the Taíno's chiefdom polity was not a true chiefdom but rather an intermediate polity between the tribe and chiefdom. I disagree. I think it was a polity on the way to become a state potentially like the Natufian. The Taínos traded with others in the Greater Antilles, had a centralized decision-making system and was technically capable of producing a surplus.

From a gender parity perspective, the role women in the Taíno society is worth mentioning. Although polygamy was common, women participated in all walks of life even cacica. Women fished, farmed and drove out invaders. The Taino were a matrilineal society - a kinship system in which ancestral descent is traced through maternal lines.

In Hispaniola, the succession and inheritance to the cacique or any of the elite class positions were complex considering the social interaction between the various chiefdoms. This complexity arose from the intermarriage of caciques of different chiefdoms and other strategies for power consolidation. The chiefdoms of Maguana and Jaragua were the most influential of the remaining three not because of the size of their combined territories but of the bloodline uniting these chiefdoms. Anacaona, wife of the Maguana cacique Caonabo was Boheccio's sister. After Caonabo's execution for destroying the La Navidad settlement, Anacaona became cacica of Maguana. These alliances also give an insight into the cacique's power. As mentioned in Part II, chiefdom as a political organization is unstable because of the internal strife within component tribes and external competing forces. These alliances were a strategy to counteract internal strife and protection against outside invaders rooted in the tribe tradition.

Marriage as a mechanism of political alliance was not a new phenomenon. It had occurred in more advanced societies around the globe. In 1346 Sultan Orhan Gazi of the nascent Ottoman Empire married Theodora Kantakouzene, daughter of John VI Kantakouzenos, Emperor of Byzantium. In the land of the colonist, less than 7000 kilometers from Hispaniola, the marriage of Ferdinand II of Aragon to Isabella of Castile on October 19/1469 consolidated the political power of Spain in the Iberian Peninsula. After all, it seems that the Taino caciques were just as politically astute as the Spaniards.

Other than marriage, another strategy for cementing a relationship was the manipulation of the line of descent of one cacique in the other by areito. A case in point is Guarionex (cacique of Maguá) and Mayobanex (cacique of Ciguaho) in the Samana Peninsula, two neighboring chiefdoms. Areíto was a public ceremony to honor the heroic deeds of Taíno ancestors, chiefs, and gods. It was held at times of importance such as marriage or death, after a disaster, or to give thanks to the gods and ancestors. This high-profile event is the exclusive responsibility of the cacique for organized the ceremony in designated spaces usually public plaza or dance ground outside the cacique's house. Guarionex gifted his honorific role at an areito to Mayobanex. So doing, he incorporated Mayobanex in his line of descent. It worked. When Guarionex escaped the hard labor conditions imposed by the Spaniards, he sought and obtained refuge in Mayobanex chiefdom despite the opposition of his subordinates. The areito ritual created a bond he had to honor. This astute strategy guaranteed his loyalty. His motives for not giving up Guarionex were reported by the priest and chronicler Bartolome de Las Casas: "Tell the Christians that Guarionex is a good and honorable man. He has done evil to no one – that is a public and known fact. For this reason, he is worthy of a heartfelt help in his humiliation and flight, worthy of support and protection. But the Spaniards are evil men and tyrants. *They come for one reason, to seize land not theirs.* They know only how to spill the blood of people who never provoked them. Instead, I intend to try with all the power I have, my people have, to smash and drive out the Christians from this land (Bartolomeo de Las Casas 1995: p.83)". The sentence in italics confirms the veracity of the opening anecdote of Part IV and reflects the spirit of colonialism under the banner of evangelism. This behavior was seen with the Aztecs and the Incas. Eventually, the Spaniards conquered the Mayobanex chiefdom. Guarionex drowned himself on his way to Spain and Mayobanex died in prison and his chiefdom community enslaved.

The intermarriage of caciques of different chiefdom and the manipulation of the line of descent and the areyto strategy had an enormous impact on the structure of the Taíno society. In "Taíno Elite Integration and Societal Complexity on Hispaniola S. Wilson states "one implication of a system in which it is politically advantageous to have ties of kinship with the rulers of other surrounding political units is that the stratum of society involved in the process will possess ancestral lines not shared (initially) by the other strata of the society". Just as tribes are based on the deep-seated human instinct of looking out for one's family, this social setting carried the potential for creating a disjunction between the elite and consequently with the commoners. As part of the political consolidation process, social stratification increases before being institutionalized as a state polity. This could have been the next political evolution of the Taíno's society had the Spanish invasion not taken place.

On Christmas Eve of 1492 Columbus left Hispaniola for Spain aboard the Santa Marina along with the Pinta and the La Niña anxious to deliver the news that he had discovered a western route to the Orient and to display the wealth potential of Hispaniola. Unfortunately, a few miles out the *Santa María* drifted onto a bank and foundered. With the assistance of the Taíno, his crew dismantled the ship and he ordered them to build a small fortress with the materials onshore. He called the fortress La Navidad (Christmas), the first settlement built by a colonizer and an important event reflecting the imperialism aspect of Spain. Three weeks later in January 1493, Columbus finally set sail aboard the *Niña*, leaving behind 39 sailors charged with the specific duty of amassing gold.

For his first return trip to Spain Columbus kidnapped between ten and twenty Tainos of which only eight survived. He also brought a small amount of gold and a selection of native birds and plants to illustrate the richness and peculiarity of the New World to King Ferdinand II and Queen Isabella. In the words of Carroll and Noble ...."To Columbus, it was literally inconceivable that he had found previously unknown lands. Like other Europeans of his time, he believed firmly in the completeness of human knowledge. What he saw, therefore, he incorporated into his existing worldview, and the Native Americans thereby became, to the satisfaction of most Europeans, simply Indians."

The discovery of the New World and its inhabitants had shaken the belief system of Europeans. There was no reference in Christian theology or Western cosmology that supported such a discovery. The very definition of the frontier between the known and unknown implied its movability and ephemerality. Fast forward to our current time, I foresee the same social shock if one day *Homo sapiens* is officially exposed to the presence of an alien from outer space.

Did Columbus accurately describe where the New World was? Certainly not. So much was at stake politically that he retreated to the much comfortable zone of projection and promises to his creditors. He knew that the islands he'd discovered were not in the Indian Ocean. To conceal the truth Columbus made his crew including the expert cartographer Juan de la Cosa, swear that Cuba was a very long peninsula instead of an island. However, Juan de la Cosa had shown Cuba as an Island in his early 1500 map (Bergreen 2011 p. 175). Columbus's misrepresentation was a lie. But the truth was out there. This secret could not last long. Shortly thereafter, motivated by the fear of humiliation he revealed that Cuba was an island. This incident demonstrates Columbus's manipulative character.

An assessment of Columbus's motives can be summarized in three words power, prestige and wealth disguised as glory, gold, and goods despite his deep religious beliefs. In October 1492, Columbus wrote in his journal, "With fifty men they can all be subjugated and made to do what is required of them". In his own manuscript published in 1493, he stated: "There I found very many Islands, filled with innumerable people, and I have taken possession of them all for their Highnesses done by proclamation and with the royal standard unfurled, and no opposition was offered to me". Believing in a single religion, members of the then Spanish Christian Church viewed Taíno as suitable for conversion to the true faith, and if not, worthy only of death or enslavement. Such an attitude characterized the Spaniards' relations with the Hispaniola residents.

While Columbus was in Spain, the 39 men of La Navidad went on a rampage, stealing the Taínos' gold and precious objects and abusing the native women. The courageous Caonabo, cacique of a neighboring chiefdom did not tolerate these actions. He set fire to the fortress, forcing Columbus's men to the sea. Eight were drowned, three were killed onshore and the rest ran away with their women and the stolen gold. Greed caused the destruction of La Navidad settlement.

Columbus returned to Hispaniola in November 1493 with 17 ships and 1,200 men to enlarge the settlement. But he found La Navidad burned to the ground with no inhabitants and no gold. The military power of the conquistadors was no match for the Taínos. Caonabo was arrested and the rest of the cacique's chiefdom enslaved. Columbus then ordered the building of another settlement La Isabella, on the eastern side of the island. This marked the beginning of the Spanish imperialism marked by the Taino's extermination by forced labor.

Population figures of ancient societies are generally imprecise. Recently, historians have estimated the pre-Columbus population of Hispaniola at more than a million people. But I estimate it at 300,000 based on the robust arguments of the historian Laurence Bergreen* and the demographer Massimo Livi-Bacci. The combination of the repartition of the workforce between agriculture, mining for gold and personal servants to the conquistadores seems to support this population number. Equally debated, however, is the chronology of the Taíno destruction*. Regardless of the initial population size, three decades following the arrival of Columbus, the population of Hispaniola was reduced to a few hundred and by 1550 none of the original Taíno were alive on the island. They were gone, so was their language. Some mestizos (children of Spaniards and Taino women) survived and they intermarried with people of Puerto Ricans and descendants of West African slaves. A 2003 mitochondrial DNA study under the Taíno genome project determined that 62% of people in Puerto Rico have direct-line maternal ancestry to Taíno/Arawakan ancestors; hence the conceptual roots of living Taino. Spain's original goal was to find an alternate source of commodities and precious metals!

The goodwill of the first peaceful encounter with the native in the first voyage to Hispaniola did not last long. The kidnap of eight to twenty "Indies" the death of the sailors left on the island before returning to Spain and the destruction of La Navidad permanently soured the relationship. As a result, the Spanish imposed harsh living conditions, sanctioned by *repartimiento** on the Taíno. Shortly after his return to Hispaniola from Spain, Columbus ordered all miners to provide approximately 85 grams of gold dust to the Spanish every three months. Sanctioned by *encomienda** the tribute to be paid by farmers was 25 kilograms of cotton. This forced farmers to switch from subsistence farming to cotton while still having to feed themselves and their families. Then there was an additional tribute to Adelanto, the leader of the Spanish forces loyal to Columbus's family. The motivation of the Spaniards became clear - a thirst for precious metals.

As part of the *encomienda* system, the places of work were sometimes moved to other locations on the island which implicitly led to a disruption of the family bonding. Exaggeration or not, thousands of Tainos desperately retreated to the mountains, apparently some committed suicide by poisoning themselves or jumping off a cliff. In the words of Livi-Bacci (2012 p. 48): "These general causes had a profound impact on the demography of the Tainos. Unions were more difficult and precarious; fertility declined. In 1514 children below 14 made up only 10% of the total population, a situation consistent with a rapidly declining population".

Christopher Columbus brought horses, cows, pigs, dogs, cats and a few plants including wheat, barley and sugar cane. The wheat and barley did not thrive in the climate, but the other plants and animals did and they are still part of the fauna and flora of the island. The diet of the Tainos consisted mainly of fish, cassava, turtle, water birds and some rodents. There were no large mammals in Hispaniola prior to the arrival of the Spaniards. No direct archaeological evidence of sloth-human interactions has been found so far. Contact with the Spaniards and the introduction of new types of animals brought pathogens to the island against which the Taínos had no immunity. These include smallpox, measles, influenza, and typhus. Disease, mainly smallpox, a pathogen carried by a pig, killed 95% of the Taíno population after 1518.

By the time of his fourth voyage to Hispaniola in June 1502, Christopher Columbus had lost his prestige in Spain. Words about the harsh treatment of the Taínos and the hanging of some of his crew for disobeying him had reached Spain. To his detriment, Portuguese explorer Vasco da Gama discovered a sea route to India in May 1498. In Hispaniola, the situation was not better. He had to deal with discontented settlers for whom the reality of the land did not match their expectations. After an investigation by Francisco de Bobadilla, a special envoy of the Spanish king, Columbus was sent back to Spain, lost his governorship for mismanagement and was replaced by Nicolas de Ovando, a Spanish nobleman and former soldier, Columbus returned to Hispaniola on June 1502 accompanied by his brother and son. However, he was denied entry by the new governor. He returned to Spain and died in Valladolid on May 20/1506 still protesting that he has discovered a new route to the land of spice in the Far East.

There lingers a recurring question. Was Columbus a Hero or a Villain?

The answer is complicated. However, the question can be answered if I separate the man from his action. I believe that it is fair to venerate Columbus for his stamina and exceptional expertise in navigation, with the caveat that the Vikings arrived in America in the 11th century well before Columbus.

Sir Winston Churchill, one of the great politicians of the preceding century said "History will be kind to me because I intend to write it." Indeed, he will always be remembered as a clever strategist during the Second World War and a peacemaker initiator in the Cold War period. Of importance, his actions were consistent with his beliefs.

I feel obliged to speak about Columbus's legacy to show that no public figure can avoid the verdict of history. Christopher Columbus was an educated man. As an autodidact, he learned Spanish, Portuguese, Greek, Latin and Italian. And, although uncommon for a Genovese he could only write in the Italian language. He was well versed in mathematics, cartography, and navigation. At the age of 22, he was a seaman who had logged in many trips to the East Indies. Later because of his courage, tenacity and leadership, he obtained financing for the four voyages to Hispaniola. Columbus had a profound Catholic faith and a thirst for wealth and prestige which made him a perfect match for the Catholic monarchs of Spain in their rivalry with Portugal. However, there is a disconnect or even a contradiction between the writings of this devout Christian and his actions. It was he, not the monarchs, who authorized the calamities inflicted on the Taínos. His revenge for the destruction of La Navidad, the enforcement of *encomienda* (a main cause of the extermination of the Tainos), the arrest of Caonabo, the public hanging of the *Cacica* Anacaona, the enslavement of the cacique' members are historical facts that cannot be denied. Monuments to Columbus erected in most Latin American countries ensure he will never be forgotten. As to whether he should be venerated will remain a matter of debate.

Colonization of Mexico

In April 1519 Hernando Cortés stepped ashore on the beach of Chal-chihuecan on the eastern gulf coast of Mexico in present-day Vera Cruz. He arrived with a fleet of 11 ships, 508 soldiers, about 100 sailors, and 16 horses. Eager to follow the steps of Columbus, he sought to appropriate land for the Spanish crown, convert native inhabitants to Catholicism, and acquire precious metals and spices for Spain (Altman, Cline Pescador 2003: p.53). However, in Mexico, he encountered a civilization that was culturally and politically different from the Taino of Hispaniola and Cuba where he respectively occupied the positions of notary and clerk of the treasurer.

As reported by the Spanish soldier and author Bernal Diaz del Castillo who accompanied Cortés to Mexico: "on reaching the market place, the largest being at Tlatelolco in Tenochtitlan ran by professional merchants known as *pochteca,* we (Spanish conquerors) were astounded at the great number of people and the quantity of merchandise and at the good order and control that was maintained, for we had never seen such a thing before…". The richness and sophistication of Aztec culture was obvious from the onset. Mexico population was estimated at 16.8 million (Massino Livi-Bacci 2012: p.41)

In Mesoamerica, the Aztecs are one of the most documented civilizations. It flourished in the post-classic period from 1300 to 1521. A large body of literature is available based on indigenous writings, eye witness accounts by Spanish conquerors such as Bernal Dias del Castillo, archeological fieldwork carried out in Mexico City particularly Templo Mayo and the twelve-volume Florentine Codex of the Franciscan Friar Bernardino de Sahagún and other codices. The following is a brief summary of the Aztecs centered on main historical events relevant to the scope of this book particularly in the late post-classic period AD 1250-1521.

Figure 4.4 Map of Ancient Mexico

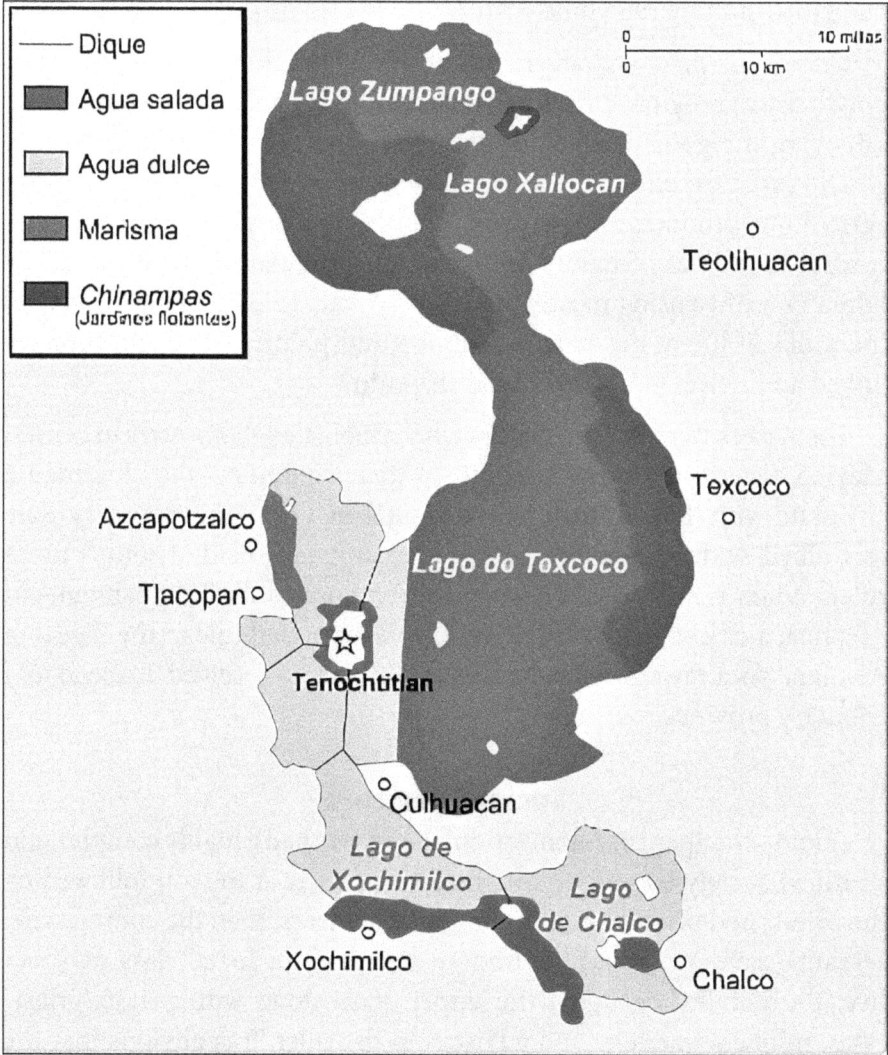

The Aztecs or Mexica, a Nahuatl* speaking people, probably originated from a nomadic tribe in Aztlan in northern Mexico. To be more correct Aztlan may also include other people from this mystical place in Northern Central Mexico. The original language of the Aztecs was a pictographic script that used representational drawings, similarly to cuneiform and hieroglyphic writing which also used drawings.

One of the main characteristics of the Aztecs is their adherence to a polytheistic* religion, a firm belief that an order must be maintained by satisfying the gods particularly the main god Huitzilopochtli, the sun god, to avoid the end of the world. Like most ancients societies living on agricultural products for existence, they believe many gods and goddesses control the forces of nature and they must be constantly appeased by human sacrifice using mostly prisoners of war. This belief permeated all the walks of life of the Aztecs. Religion and politics became intimately linked and reflected in their social structure.

The Aztecs were fierce warriors who established themselves in central Mexico. Overtime on the strength of their conquests, they founded a city-state with Tenochtitlan as the capital in 1325. This new city-state was allied with Azpotzalco, a Tepanec city, and paid "tribute" to its ruler. When war erupted between the Tepanecs and the inhabitants of Alcohua, a city of Texcoco, the Aztecs played a vital role in the defeat of Alcohua. As a reward for their loyalty, the Aztecs received Texcoco as a tributary province.

Social Structure

Prior to the Spanish colonization, the Aztecs had a highly complex and stratified society composed of a hereditary ruler at the top followed by the priests and priestesses, the council of advisors, then the commoners; servants slaves occupied the bottom tier. From a social class perspective, the nobility occupied the upper class along with priests/priestesses, military warriors, and advisors to the ruler. It is obvious that the nobles ran the government through their networks. They also reaped the greatest rewards from the expansion of the empire. The middle class was the largest group in Aztec society and consisted of accountants, lawmakers, merchants, quarry and feather workers, potters, weavers, sculptors, painters, goldsmiths, and silversmiths.

Commoners were those who worked on state or privately owned plantations and functioned primarily as agricultural laborers. They did not own property but were permitted to live on a plantation or estate if they worked the fields and contributed a (probably significant) percentage of their crop to the owner. Servants were people who, although the nobility owned them, were not considered to be property the way a slave was. They were free to marry and their children were born free. They could also own property, slaves, and even their own servants. However, they could be sold just as easily as slaves unless the owner had a written document freeing them from their bondage. They were also allowed to have businesses or make trades of their own to support their families and themselves.

Slaves constituted the lowest class in the social hierarchy. In most cases, slaves were prisoners of war acquired during the expansion of the Aztec Empire. However, Franciscan friar Diego Durán reported other situations which may have led to slavery including voluntary enslavement for failure to repay a debt or a tribute, stealing, or murder. Slaves were owned by the nobility and those of the merchant class who had amassed some wealth. Unlike servants, they were considered property and could be sold and resold. A slave was the legal property of his master who could do whatever he wanted with them within limits because slaves had certain rights. If they chose to marry, they could with their master's permission. Any children they had were also slaves unless one's spouse was free i.e., not a slave. Slaves could buy their freedom or a master could write a letter releasing the slave from bondage.

Another notable feature of the Aztec civilization was their judicial system. They had a three-level court, similar to the common judicial system of most democratic countries: local courts, the *Teccalco* court in Tenochtitlan, and the high court at the Emperor's palace. A court of appeal in the city of Texcoco was made up of twelve judges and sat every 12 days. The king of Texcoco presided over the most difficult cases. No case could last for more than 80 days. Judges sat from sunrise to sunset and were put to death if they took a bribe. The rule of law prevailed to protect the class system and its citizens. The Aztecs were not as primitive as the Spanish conquerors thought!

Was upward mobility possible in Aztec society? It seems that it was possible for someone from the lower class to join the upper class on the basis of his military achievement or marriage. This was evident during the reign of the emperor Montezuma I.

With respect to gender imbalance, the situation was more complicated. Mythology and evolutionary events played an important role in the emergence of male dominance in Aztec society. The reported mythological conflict between the gods Huitzilopochtli and his sister Malinalxoch and events that took place between AD 1248 to 1345 led to a class of priest warriors. Initially, women had equal rights. They could be priestesses, producers, or vendors and royal blood ran through the female line. Women may also have played leading political roles before the state was centralized. After the defeat of the Tepanecs, facilitated by an alliance of the Aztecs with the Acolhuans of Texcoco, a male descendant of the king had succeeded the ruler. This signaled the beginning of gender discrimination. As June Nash put it "women did not seem to be losing their importance in the domestic economy during the rise of the military dynasty, they were not becoming a part of the new predatory economy of war and tribute".

Traditionally girls were educated for housekeeping and boys for military services. This exclusion from the military prevented women from accessing the wealth and prestige of the war economy. Therefore, inequality existed in Aztec society from the social evolutionary complexity as it did in other ancient societies. In less than three hundred years, the Aztec egalitarian social structure became a predatory empire marked by social stratification.

The Aztec Empire was an informal empire because it did not invoke supreme authority over conquered lands; it only expected tributes to be paid. The informal nature was seen by the fact that local rulers were usually restored to their positions once their city-state was conquered and the Aztecs did not interfere in local affairs as long as they received a tribute. The title 'emperor' did not have the same connotation it did in other civilizations.

Between the 14th and 15th centuries, approximately 50 city-states were formed in the north and central Mexico each headed by a hereditary ruler. As a result of military conquests, inter-marriage, intimidation and diplomacy for territorial expansion, wealth and power, three city-states dominated the Valley of Mexico: Texcoco, Tlacopan and Tenochtitlan as shown in the above map. In 1428, the Tepanecs were defeated in a war between the city-states of Texcoco and Azcapotzalco due to an alliance of Texcoco and Tenochtitlan. The conquest of other city-states and surrounding territories continued with Tenochtitlan gradually occupying a dominant position. In 1430 the three remaining cities formed an alliance known as the Triple Alliance, the highest level of political organization in post-classic central Mexico. The first order of the day was the drafting of a treaty for the division of wealth. Land acquired from the conquests was to be jointly held by the three cities. Tribute was to be divided: two-fifths each went to Tenochtitlan and Texcoco, and one-fifth went to Tlacopan. Each of the three kings of the alliance assumed the title of Emperor in turn, but Montezuma I emperor of Tenochtitlan, dominated. It should be noted that the city-state of Tlaxcala in central Mexico was never conquered by the Aztecs.

This Triple Alliance treaty gave insight into the motivation of the nobility. As part of imperial reform, uncooperative kings were replaced with puppet rulers loyal to the Tenochtitlan emperor. A new imperial *tribute system* established Mexica tribute collectors who taxed the population directly, bypassing the authority of local dynasties. Nezahualcoyotl, the warrior and ruler of the city-state* of Texcoco, instituted a policy in the Acolhua lands of granting subject kings tributary holdings in lands far from their capitals. This was done as an incentive for cooperation with the empire; if a city's king rebelled, he lost the tribute he received from foreign lands. Some rebellious kings were replaced or appointed governors rather than dynastic rulers. The coercive force was not the instrument binding the Triple Alliance. Instead, it was the interest of the nobility in collecting tributes from the commoners (M. E. Smith 1986: pp 70-91).

For the sake of clarification, a tribute is not synonymous with tax, particularly in the Aztec context. In fact, in Part II dealing with the chiefdom polity, I associated the surplus paid to the chief as a land tax. In "Aztecs Paid Tax, Not Tribute" the Ethnologist, Michael E Smith suggests that "tax is more appropriate than tribute. There is a difference between tribute and tax. Tribute can be seen as variable levies exacted at irregular intervals while taxes "when compared to tributes and tariffs, stand out as steady and regular disbursements. Their payment is based on the calendar, not on particular events or on the arrival of certain commodities. In contrast to tributes, taxes are normally recurrent, predictable, routinized and based on statutory obligation".

Montezuma I, emperor of Tenochtitlan issued new laws that further separated nobles from commoners. By royal decree, a religiously supervised school was built in every neighborhood. Commoner neighborhoods had a separate school where they received basic religious instruction and military training. A second, more prestigious type of school served children of the nobility, as well as commoners of high standing seeking to become priests or artisans. Moctezuma I also created a new title of "eagle-noble" (Lockhart 2005 pp109-111). This title could be conferred on commoners and was a form of non-hereditary lesser nobility awarded for outstanding military or civil service. In rare cases, commoners who received this title could marry into royal families and become kings. Needless to say, the possibility of a commoner becoming a noble was tolerated but not warmly accepted by the elite. The non-hereditary provision embedded in this title probably provided some consolation to the nobles.

I have mentioned that the Aztec Empire's religion was polytheistic. While the imperial cult was that of Huitzilopochtli, conquered provinces were allowed to keep their own gods and goddesses provided the imperial god figured in their local pantheons. As part of Montezuma I's reforms, he instituted what is called the Flower War. It was a strategy of taking prisoners of war for the purpose of sacrificing them to the gods. Because Tenochtitlan was constantly at war as it extended its kingdom, this strategy ensured a steady supply of healthy sacrifices!

As the campaign of extension went on and the empire grew, the flow of provincial tributes increased considerably in return for military protection and political stability and protection and economic integration across the network of diverse lands and peoples who had significant local autonomy. At the height of the empire's power, tax was extracted from 371 cities-states across 38 provinces and the Aztec Empire covered an area of approximately 200,000 square kilometers. Although not publicly expressed, a sense of discontentment was fermenting in the conquered population. And the tax remittances were severely affected by a prolonged drought (1450 to 1454) in the Valley of Mexico.

When Montezuma II accessed power in 1502, he continued the consolidation and reforms initiated by his predecessor. However, he abolished the possibility for the commoner to advance to mobility. After his death, on June 29, 1520, his younger brother Cuitlahuac became the next emperor. He died of smallpox in October 1520 and was succeeded by his nephew, Cuauhtémoc. The Spanish army forces led by Hernando Cortés who, in alliance with the discontents of the Aztec rules particularly the Tlaxcalans, conquered Tenochtitlan (present-day Mexico City) successfully on August 13, 1521, ten months after La Noche Triste* (The Night of Sorrows)* event.

It is unclear why Cuauhtémoc, the last Aztec emperor, was hanged. Some argued it was for his refusal to reveal the location of hidden Aztec treasure. Others alleged that Cortés ordered the execution because Cuauhtémoc refused to denounce his co-conspirators in the plot to oust Cortés. The Aztec civilization ceased to exist in 1521 and politically became a colony of Spain.

He then razed Tenochtitlan including the temple to the main god Huitzilopochtli, the patron of the Mexica tribe to build a new city, currently Mexico ending the Aztec civilization. No more ritualized killings or religious festivals removing thereby one of the main impediments to the Christianization of the Aztecs. This was the beginning of the spiritual conquest of Mexico starting with Tlaxcala, the ally of Cortés in the military conquest of Tenochtitlan. The city-state of Tlaxcala converted immediately to Christianity.

The appointment of Antonio de Mendoza, the first Viceroy to New Spain in 1532 was intended to curb Cortés's insubordination and power drives and greed. Eight years later Cortés returned to Spain where he died on December 2[nd,] 1547. Charles V then invoked more control over its colony by prohibiting slavery, (unless the converted returned to their old religion), repartimientos and claiming all indigenous people as his own subjects by laws. However, this was not sufficient to uproot the inequality in New Spain's social structure. If a caste system is a class structure that is determined by birth, the New Spain government officials reflected this definition. The best positions went to the Spaniards.

New Spain was a multi-ethnic society made up of the Spaniards, the Criollos (people born from "pure" Spaniards in New Spain - not to be confused with Creoles) the native Indians, the Africans, the Mestizos (people born from "pure" Spaniards and native Indians or any other race), the Moriscos (A minority of Muslims converted to Christianism) and a few hundred Crypto-Jews*. Given the large number of single men and women who came to Mexico in the Pre and Post conquest periods, mestizos likely formed the majority of the population. From this perspective, one could see a caste system composed of an elite class of "pure" Spaniards, followed by the Criollos and the Mestizos thereafter; the native Indians being at the bottom. As a general rule only Spaniards born in Spain could be appointed to the position of Audiencias (Judges) and Alcades (Magistrates or Mayors) The ramifications of this systemic discrimination carried enormous consequences considering that in 1571 there were 25 municipalities created by the crown and 82 by 1624; hence one of the sources of the popular discontent leading to the revolution of 1810.

Cortés used the city-states administrative structure on which the Aztec Empire was built to rule the indigenous populations via their local nobles. Those nobles pledged loyalty to the Spanish crown and converted, at least nominally, to Christianity, and in return were recognized as nobles by the Spanish crown. They acted as intermediaries to convey tribute and mobilize labor for their new overlords, facilitating the establishment of Spanish colonial rule. The honorific title of noble was converted to Don for man and Dona for woman. Cortés introduced the encomienda system with the exception that the indigenous were not slaves or removed from their home community but they still worked in harsh labor conditions in farming and mining. In the 1520s, slaves from Africa arrived in Mexico to increase the workforce. Slavery has existed in Spain since the 15th century.

During the 16th century, 240,000 Spanish soldiers came to Mexico followed by an additional 450,000 in the next century. This latter group included commoners, aristocrats from Spain and a few Canarians (inhabitants of the Canary Islands). This migration played an enormous role in the economic development of New Spain. As the majority were single man and woman, miscegenation took place leading to many mestizos

Based on the definition of colonialism mentioned earlier, assimilation characterized the colonization of Mexico in terms of the relationship between the colonizers and the colonized. Indeed, today while Spanish is spoken by the great majority of the Mexican population, Nahuatl, the original language of the Aztec is still spoken by 1.5 million of Mexican and Mixtec by another 500,000 thousand people. The Mixtec are indigenous Mesoamerican peoples inhabiting the modern-day Mexican state of Oaxaca, Guerrero and Puebla in a region known as La Mixteca. But more importantly, this migration played an enormous role in New Spain's economic development during the Colonial period.

Although the transition process from the conquest to the prosperity of New Spain remains unclear, there is, however, enough evidence to assert that the hegemony of Mexico City, formerly Tenochtitlan, played a fundamental role in the reorganization and socio-economic development of the newly conquered Spain country until the mid1500s. The establishment of the institution's town council, mayor and court by Governor Hernando Cortés , the appointment of Treasury officials, viceroy, Antonio de Mendoza by the Crown illustrates a few systems in place for an orderly administration of Mexico. But, while the Crown policies were implemented, it did not take long for government and royal officials, magistrates, even the archbishop of Mexico to personally invest in various sectors of the local economy leading to political struggles and infighting. You may know the old saying "who has the land, has the gold" some accommodation satisfying the financial appetite of all parties involved had to be reached. In 1535 the authority to made grants was removed from the mayoral to the viceroy and the judges followed by increased restrictions on holding and perpetuation of encomienda, the right to demand tribute and forced labor from the Indian inhabitants of an area. In order to put the landholding issue in perspective, half of the 506 encomienda holding network lived in Mexico City (I. Altman 1991: p 479), (R. Himmerich 1996). It was the main economic and political institution in New Spain. The evidence points to a concentration of wealth in the New Spain upper class. The rich encomienda holders were able to solidify their position by diversifying their investments in many sectors of the economy such as sugar cane, textiles and mining.

Gold mining was the first and most sought-after economic activity of the Spaniards. This was probably due to the modest capital investment required and the readily available Indian labor force. Ida Altman reports that Indian slaves were sold for three to five pesos or even less. A basic mining work unit encompassed a managerial administrative staff, a Spanish miner supported by an attendant /helper and a black slave; the mining operation being carried out by a group of 40 to 100 Indian slaves or encomienda workers. But with the mining of silver at Zatecacas in northern Mexico and Taxco in the south between 1530 and 1550, the gold rush had slowed down due to a combination of many factors among them, increased labor cost due to high Indians' mortality and more scrutiny of encomienda illegal operations. Historically, the Aztecs of Taxco had developed an expertise in silver and various gifts to their gods were made of silver.

The second category of economic activity was fulfilled by the merchants. A small minority of them resides in Mexico City. According to I. Altman, 56 merchants were recorded for 1525 and 1527-1528, and 107 for the period 1536-1538. They worked in partnership and maintained representatives in towns or provinces. They were involved mostly in European cloth and clothing, wine, oil and black slaves, importing merchandise and wholesaling to other merchants. The delivery of merchandise throughout New Spain was made by Indian carriers, muleteers preceding transportation by wagon roads. There is also evidence of commercial activity in this latter period between Mexico and Peru trading tools, hardware, horses and silver.

Table 4.5 Artisans in Mexico City (1525-1555)

Clothing Trades	131	Leatherworking Trades	54
Metalworkers	71	Silversmiths	52
Construction Trades	32	Barbers – Surgeons – Pharmacists	39

Consolidation from: Actas de cabildo de la Ciudad de Mexico, Vol. I-IV (Mexico City, 1889); A. Millares Carlo and J. I. Mantecon, Indice y extractos de los protocolos del Archivo de Notarias Mexico, D. F. (Mexico City, 1945-46)

Such an effervescent economy incited the development not only of other trades such as residential and commercial building construction, blacksmiths, silversmiths, metalworkers but also in liberal professions, medical doctors, surgeons, pharmacists, lawyers and the need to regulate their practices. As one can expect, infringement in someone else field of expertise or areas of activity was likely to emerge. As a result, there were more lawyers than medical doctors. In fact, Altman reported there were three times more of the former than the latter.

It is now possible to describe the structure of the Colonial Aztec society keeping in mind that Cortés kept the politico-administrative structure of The Triple Alliance in which Tenochtitlan played a central role. The new social structure of New Spain consisted of an upper class, a middle class followed by a lower class. The upper class encompassed the Governor, the Viceroy, the archbishop, the city rulers and the judges, the professionals, the wealthy encomienda holders; the middle class was composed of the merchants, traders and artisans; the lower class consisted of Indians and the slaves. I will come back to this point on the next page. It should be noted that Indian slavery was abolished in 1542 but persisted until the 1550s. Nonetheless, slavery of Black Africans continued. A similar situation occurred with repartimiento; although abolished in 1601 its practice continued until 1633. More than one hundred years thereafter the encomienda system was abolished by royal decree in 1720. I suspect that the amount of wealth derived from these systems was too great to be abandoned overnight.

Considering that the New Spain Governor built his bureaucracy on the same social structure of the Triple Alliance, it may seem superfluous to ask whether inequality existed in Mexico's Colonial Period. Some of the members of the then nobility became Don and Dona and, with their political connection, were able to grab the lion's share of the land. Through encomienda and repartimiento, their wealth grew substantially in the post-conquest decades at the expense of the less fortunate native Indians. Could upward mobility possible in such a structure? It is undeniable that some upward mobility existed through intermarriage, education and business acumen. The cases of merchants may be used to illustrate this assertion. As the New Spain economy was growing, fifty-six merchants were identified in the records (I. Altman 1991: pp. 425-427) some richer than others. Among them, Gregorio Yanez de Burgos and Juan Henche who got involved in the import business and also maintained a number of mining and commercial activities in the 1530s. Conceivably, in the mid1600s members of the liberal professions e-g lawyers, medical doctors had opportunities for upward mobility through their political contacts. However, these cases should not be interpreted to cover the racially heterogeneous society of New Spain.

In order to understand the behavior of the Crown and the New Spain colonists, their motivation must be revisited. Ferdinand II of Aragon and Isabella I of Castile were elated with the New World discovery by Christopher Columbus of a new route to the land of precious metals, silk and spices. They had sought and obtained ownership of the discovered lands and their contents from Pope Alexander VI. In Hispaniola, Cuba, and subsequently Mexico and Peru, the objective had not changed namely sending to Spain as much gold, silver and other resources that could be extracted as possible. Spain's interest was purely economic. It would be unwise and naïve to disregard the same motivation at the individual level as demonstrated by the crew members of Columbus and subsequently by Hernando Cortés. The system they both put in place driven by power, prestige and wealth ignored the uniqueness of the conquered inhabitants' culture. Economically, colonization was a success for the Crown. During the 16th century, Spain held the equivalent of US S1.5 trillion (1990 terms) in gold and silver from New Spain

Colonization of Peru

The Spanish colonization process continued its course in Latin America with Peru. In 1531 almost two decades after the fall of Tenochtitlan in Mexico, Francisco Pizarro with only 62 soldiers mounted on horses, 106 foot-soldiers and 1 cannon landed at Tumbes, a coastal city in Northwestern Peru. Its population at that time was in the range of 14 million, another demographic concentration in Latin America. Pizzaro led his army up to the Andes Mountains and on November 15, 1532, reached the Inca town of Cajamarca. After setting an ambush, Pizarro maneuvered to meet with Atahualpa, the Inca absolute ruler, seized him captive with the backing of the Spanish soldiers and claimed ownership of Peru to Spain. To be more accurate, the complete conquest of Peru occurred 36 years later with the defeat of Tupac Amaru at Vilcabamba, ending a three- hundred year Incan civilization.

A cold analysis of the swift capture of Atahualpa raises issues contemporary to his time and thousands of years preceding him. How the absolute ruler could have accepted the Spanish Conquistador request to meet? In my view, it is purely due to an underestimation of the Spanish military capability reinforced by the Atahualpa's overconfidence further to his recent victory over Huascar and becoming the incontestable emperor. The euphoria of success has a tendency of blurring any sign of danger. During the course of the war to establish his empire, the Atahualpa's army was estimated to be about 250,000 soldiers far larger than Pizarro's but this latter was magnified by the use of horses. Ironically, Atahualpa could have been on the same playing field as Pizarro's army if he had horses. After the formative period of the Norte Chico, the oldest Andean civilization in 3,500 BC, there were no large mammals in the Americas. They became extinct, more likely killed off by the first American natives.

Horses were among those extinct mammals. As the historian and geographer Jared Diamond put it: "Ironically, relatives of the horses that Cortez and Pizarro rode had formerly been natives of the New World. If Montezuma and Atahualpa had horses they would shattered the conquistadores with cavalry charges of their own". Humanity should learn that some of our current relentless actions against the ecosystem may carry a heavy price in the future.

Figure 4.5 Map of the Inca Empire

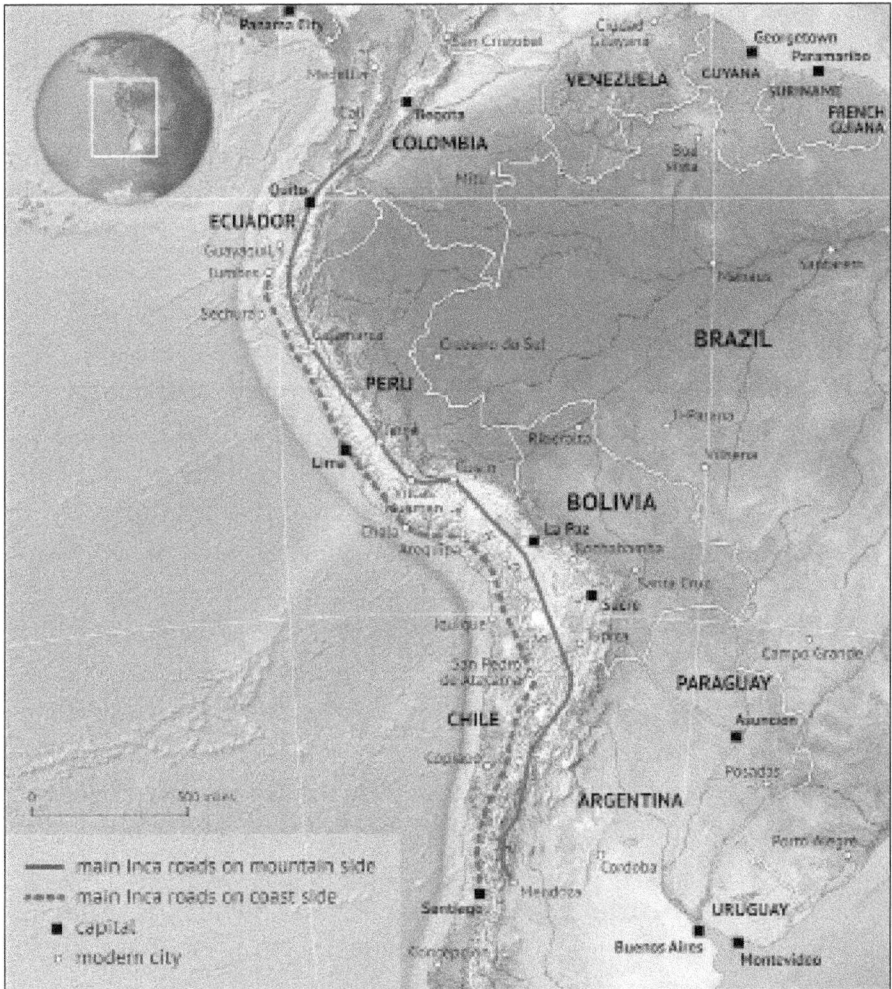

But more importantly, one may wonder how the absolute ruler could have been unaware of the Spanish presence and activities in New Spain (Mexico) and for that matter their whole warfare activities including the rebuilding of Tenochtitlan? It is in fact astonishing that up to 1533 there was no contact or trade between New Spain and Peru. Had contact been made with the Aztecs, Atahualpa would have known about the power and effectiveness of gunpowder. Lack of technology for shipbuilding cannot be invoked. The Incas had developed great balsa rafts which could have made the voyage possible by taking advantages of the favorable waters (W. W. Borah 1954: pp. 2-7, 8-11). As will be shown later in the Incas' ingeniosity and their way of living, natural limitations were no match for their creativity.

Two of the most important pillars of any civilization were absent in the Incas' namely handwriting and currency. Their commerce was internal. But bartering could still have taken place with the Aztecs. Moreover, in the context of South America's colonization, the Spanish established their first permanent settlement in the region of Darien currently a province of Panama. Darien was the point of departure of Francisco Pizarro to Peru in 1530. As can be seen in Figure 4.5 Columbia is basically in the backyard of the Northern Inca Empire. A distance of only 523 miles separates Panama from Columbia. Yet, no contact had taken place between the inhabitants of both countries. It seems reasonably certain that there was no communication* between the Inca Empire and the Aztecs of Anahuac, the south central part of the Valley of Mexico, at the time of the Conquest (W. W. Borah 1954: p. 131). This absence of communication between both civilizations will remain a mystery. History sometimes reveals some past events that carried enormous consequences. The Incas'case reminds me of a quote from Arthur Schopenhauer "every man takes the limit of his own field of vision for the limit of the world". In all likelihood for the Incas, no one besides themselves ever existed. It worked well for Spain, the serial conqueror of the Americas. Pizarro ordered the execution of Atahualpa on August 29/1533. This was a common military tactic used by both Cortés and Pizarro. However, the colonization of Mexico and Peru differs in mant ways socialy, economically and politically including special circumstances.

First, I will examine the emergence of the great Inca civilization. I will also look at the social stratification established by the supreme leader with particular attention to the relationship between the sociopolitical structure and inequality in the pre and post-conquest periods.

There are many mystical tales about the origin of the Incas people. However, based on archeological evidence, the Inca first settled in the Cuzco Valley in 4500 BC as hunter-gatherers in a band polity. The Incas spoke Quechua a language that originated in the central Andes Mountains. It was an Amerind language with about 10 million native speakers who lived primarily in the Andes Mountains (Bolivia, Peru, Ecuador, Colombia and Argentina). It eventually became the official language of the Inca Empire administration. They had a form of writing called Quipu, also used in other Andean cultures to record transactions, census data and events.

Quipu* is actually a device consisting of an arrangement of various colored and knotted cord attached to a base cord. Although this ingenious recording system was banned by the Spanish, some information has recently been deciphered by anthropologists on the life of the Incas.

Figure 4.6 Quipu

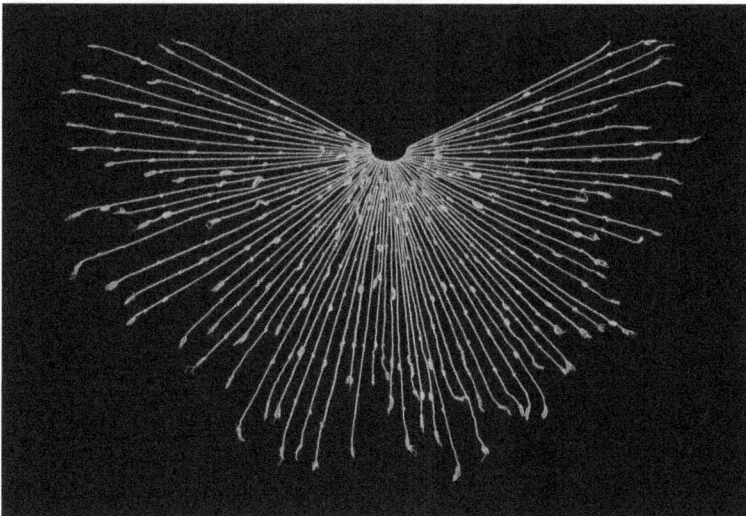

Again, there were no large mammals to carry heavy load. The llama was domesticated from the guanaco around 3000 B.C. in the Andes followed by the alpaca* and the vicuna*. This latter produces the finest wool in the world. It was reserved only for the Inca elite. Llamas were very docile which make a herd of 20 llamas easy to control by one person. A llama can carry a load between 50-70kg for twenty miles per day. A herd of 60 llamas can carry a substantial amount of goods. Since draft animals and wheel were not available and considering the geography of Peru, human muscles or other creative pulling system had to be used for the transportation of heavy loads. I mention this to give insight to the ingeniosity in the amount of work and manpower required to build the large Incas' stone structures and monuments.

The Incas' diet consisted of maize, beans, pepper, cashew, squash, avocado, sweet potatoes and other tubers. They drank llama milk and ate guinea pig, llama, alpaca, deer, fishes, domesticated ducks and birds for their protein. Llamas and alpacas furs were used for textile and their hide for rope. Vicuna produced exceptionally fine wool and was reserved for the elite.

Unlike the Aztecs, the Incas did not have public markets for the exchange or bartering of goods. This is understandable because the Incas did not use money or any other form of currency.

As was the case in most ancient civilizations, religion occupied a prime role in the life of the Incas. They were polytheistic. Their god and goddesses were revered in myriad ways by prayers, rituals including of human sacrifice. Like the Aztecs and through their Flower War strategy, their victims were mostly war prisoners from conquered territories. The Incas also had extensive knowledge of astronomy as can be seen in the structural design of their cities and agricultural development.

From the late AD 1400 and early 1500, the Incas embarked on ambitious campaigns to conquer neighboring territories, eventually building extending from Quito in the North to Santiago in the South. As shown in the following map, at its peak in 1527 the Incas Empire state covered the largest territory that the world had ever known, longitudinally stretching over 5,500 km. This expansion was carried out in three phases by King Pachacuti Inca Yupanki (AD1438-1471), his son Thupa Inca Yupanki (AD1473-93) who substantially extended the Inca kingdom up to the Maule River in northern Chile; and his grandson Huayna Capac (AD1493-1525) who continued the Northern extension up to the Angasmayo River and Colombia. The Inca kings ruled from Cuzco, the administrative and religious capital. At one point in time, there were ten million subjects speaking 30 different languages.

I thought it would be helpful to provide a brief summary of this patrilineal dynasty. Gordon. F. McEwan's book (2008: pp. 68-82). There were other kings in Peru before Pachacuti, notably Viracocha Inca (Gordon. F. McEwan's book (2008: pp. 68-82). But before Pachacuti, the succession did not follow the traditional laws or customs. Pachacuti set the foundation of the Inca Empire by conquering the neighboring states of Cuzco and undertaking the infrastructure projects including roads, aqueducts, bridges and temples. Upon his death which ended his twenty-year reign, his son Huayna Capac ascended the throne. Huayna Capac died of smallpox without designating which of his many sons and daughters from different mothers would succeed him. It all boiled down to the purest bloodline and the political intrigue with Huascar and Atahualpa emerging as the main contenders. The rivalry between the two brothers plunged the kingdom into a five-year civil war fueled by the political vacuum at the top and the panic caused by the smallpox epidemic. Huascar was eventually defeated and executed by Atahualpa.

This coincided with the arrival of the Spanish forces headed by Francisco Pizarro at Cajamarca in 1531. By the stratagem mentioned earlier, Pizarro defeated Atahualpa and kept him captive for eight months subject to an enormous ransom in gold and silver apparently equivalent to 50 million dollars by 2001 bullion standard*(M. E. Moseley 2001: p.8)

Despite the amount of gold paid by the Incas to free the emperor Francisco Pizarro retreated from his promise and ordered the execution of Atahualpa. The Spanish then installed a puppet ruler Tupac Huallpa (1532-1533). Huayna Capac's son also died shortly thereafter of smallpox. Tupac Huallpa was replaced by Manco Inca II (1533-1549) who escaped his captors and fled to the Amazonian rainforest in Vilcabamba, a neo-Inca state. He was joined there by Tupac Amaru (1571-1572), After a fierce battle with the Spanish military forces, the last Inca stronghold was defeated. Tupac Amaru was captured and executed. It took the Spaniards 36 years to completely conquer Peru.

The Inca Empire left an impressive infrastructure legacy that included many infrastructural projects. There was an efficient network of roads (40,000 km) that facilitated communication, transportation and trade in this vast kingdom. They built temples in the four corners of the kingdom one of which was the Coricancha (house of gold) complex erected in Cuzco. The floor, walls, ceiling and altar temple built to honor Inti, the sun god, were lined with 700 two-kilogram sheets of gold. Another temple was built with silver for the goddess Mama Kilya, Inti's wife, the Moon's mother and the regulator of women's menstrual cycles. Considering their insatiable appetite for gold, one can understand the amazement of the conquistadors in the face of such wealth. So much to plunder!

An advanced level of engineering was evident in the Inca construction of aqueducts and bridges. And the Inca had agricultural products unknown elsewhere in the world such as corn, beans, potatoes, squashes, tomatoes, peppers and peanuts.

The Inca did not enlarge their kingdom solely by war. Persuasion preceded confrontation. Pachacuti would send spies to regions he wanted to annex who would report back on the region's political organization, military might and wealth. He would then send messages to the leaders of these lands extolling the benefits of joining his empire, offering them luxury goods such as high-quality textiles, and promising that they would be materially richer as subject rulers. This strategy shows that the Incas were not warlike except by necessity. Most acquired territories accepted the rule of the Incas as a *fait accompli* and acquiesced peacefully. The subject ruler's children would be brought to Cuzco to be taught about Inca administration systems, then returned to rule their native lands. This was an effective means of indoctrinating new subjects in society and nobility. With luck, some would marry to Inca families thereby consolidating the empire's power.

In the span of a century, the population of the pre-conquest Incan empire grew to millions from thousands. The early few thousands were groups of people closely connected by family ties. Through expansion and military conquest the population grew. As such, the inhabitants of the territories conquered integrated into the kingdom were subjects and not Incas per se (M. E. Moseley 2001: p.9). Scholars can't agree on Tahuantisuyu's population for various reasons. Gordon F. McEwan attributed this to unavailability, unreadability and obscure meaning of source materials and lack of consensus on the methodological approach (G. McEwan 2008: pp, 93-96).

For these reasons, the pre-conquest Inca Empire population estimates range between 6 million and 14 million. A similar situation exists for the Incas themselves. However, estimates put the Incan population at about 40,000. But how could 40,000 Incas have governed a territory 5,500 km long with 10 million people speaking 30 different languages and without writing, money and the wheel? This was probably due to the Incas' sociopolitical and administrative structures. Maybe history was repeating itself with respect to the name of the Incas' territory - Land of the Four Quarters (Tahuantinsuyu in Quechua). Recall that Sargon of Akkad (2334-2279 BC) of Mesopotamia conquered what he called the "Four Corners of the Universe" and maintained order in his empire.

Sociopolitical structure and organization.

The Inca Empire maintained a strict hierarchy. It was headed by the Sapa Inca, the ultimate emperor in Quechua, and cascaded down to the smallest social unit. The emperor had an advisory council composed of the four governors of the four quarters who were usually close relatives of the emperor. At its peak in around 1527, the four quarters were divided in 80 provinces (M. E. Moseley 2001: p.8). Conceivably this partition reflected the ethnically heterogeneous Inca society. However, in order to govern this multitude of ethnically different people in such a large territory Quechua was imposed as the official language of the empire affirming thereby the cultural conquest all over the land.

The chain of command for the payment of taxes based on labor in kind was maintained by four levels of provincial hereditary (Curaca in

Quechua) administrators respectively responsible for 10,000 then 5,000 then 500 then 100 heads of households. This structure was followed by two-level nonhereditary officers (could be women), one for 50 heads of households and the other for 10 heads of households (G. F. McEwan 2006: pp 113-115). Basically, these administrators were tax collectors. This administrative structure required an accurate count of the work-force using the quipu. Unfortunately; this information was destroyed after the conquest.

In summary, four social classes were evident in this hierarchical orga-nization. The first class or level was the Sapa Inca and the high priest for his religious assistance. The second level was the royalty which included the royal advisory council. The third class was made up of the provincial governors and nobles who attained distinction because of their excep-tional performance in the field. The fourth and by far the largest class consisted of the commoners or ayllus*(40).

Commoners included metal workers, artisans, textile weavers and what is known today as specialists in any particular trade involved in the design and construction of bridges and aqueducts, terraces and the decoration of the temples.

A married couple was viewed as a basic economic unit which by itself could not meet the basic necessities of life. Endogamy was compulsory in Incan society. Remember that this society did not use money. Payment in kind for labor was the currency. It was a reciprocal beneficiary obli-gation. Labor was provided by family members of both partners so the marriage of members of large families was advantageous. This was the concept of Ayllu in which a social unit is the basis of economic activity. Ayllu members worked the land and cared for the cattle for food and clothing. They also worked as miners and weavers. Everyone was obliged to work and contribute to the *mita* or tax. In exchange, the Inca would supply food throughout the year and provide agricultural products not produced in the area, education and healthcare. If family A needed help with a harvest and family B needed help with seeding, an exchange of labor for the same amount of time would meet the need of parties.

At the macro level, this obligatory labor system included working on infrastructure projects, government buildings, temples or any initiative of the Sapa Inca. In this agrarian state economy, one-third of the production went to the nobility, one third to the clergy and one third to the ayllu members for their own needs. This forced labor system, called Mita* in Quechua, sustained the lavish lifestyle of the nobility and allowed the empire to build and fill food storage warehouses in each province for redistribution in times of poor harvest. Nevertheless, to maintain peace, festivities were organized by the emperor or the governors with gifts to the curacas for their work

As can be seen, many actions were taken by the Incas to maintain and stabilize this heterogeneous society. This can be seen in the partitioning of the territory into four quarters, the strict hierarchy of command and the various religious ceremonies and festivities. The pillar of this political structure was the myth that harmony between humans, nature, and the gods was essential. However, Inca subjects (the non-Incas) were allowed to continue to practice their own religions provided that Inti, the sun god was predominant. The conquest of Peru by Pizarro makes it difficult to assess the viability of the Inca hierarchy in such a culturally diverse society.

By all accounts, the Inca ruler reinforced the class differential between the nobility and the commoners. Prior to the Spanish conquest, nobles displayed their status by their attire which included the finest textile clothing. Only the Sapa Inca wore clothing made from vicuna rule decorated with gold and other ornaments. Nobles were identifiable by their earing. They were called big ears, *orejones* in Spanish; the larger the earing the higher the social status.

But this visible social class differentiation was the tip of an iceberg of profound systemic discrimination. The authoritarian Inca regime confined the non-Incas to a rigidly controlled life. Even marriage had to be approved by the chief. This is not to say that exogamous marriage never occurred in the nobility but depending of the circumstances, this marriage could lower the status of either party.

The Inca education system was gender discriminatory. Young men of royal blood and selected young members of conquered territories chosen to administer the region were orally educated between the age of 13 and 19. Teachers, called mawtakuna in Quechua, taught Inca religion, government, quipu, physical education and military techniques. Young women were taught the art of womanhood, governance skills (limited levels) spinning, weaving and chicha (brewing alcoholic and non-alcoholic beverages from corn and fruits). At the completion of their schooling, a few of these young women would stay to pass on their knowledge to new students or become secondary wives of the Sapa Inca. They could also be sent as a reward to exceptional men because of their service to the Sapa Inca.

Commoners could not attend formal school except perhaps in Quechua, the official language. They learned their trade from their parents and co-workers. They wore basic clothing and were prohibited from owning gold or silver. The black market was non-existent. In the same vein and contrary to the Aztec Empire, the market as a transaction place did not exist in the Incan Empire thereby eliminating private exchange for food and personal items.

Another form of discrimination was apparent in the Inca taxation system. The upper classes including the Sapa Inca, the nobility and a subgroup of the curacas, the special servants of the empire (yanacona in Quechua), specialists of a particular trade (camayos in Quechua) were tax-exempt. The tax burden rested on male commoners monitored by the royal inspectors. It becomes obvious that the possibility of upward mobility was very limited except perhaps for the special servants of the empire. Since they performed a variety of special services to the nobility, this could be a path to the upper class (G. McEwan p.100).

Women made a substantial contribution to the Incan economy. Although rare, some women occupied the position of curaca. They complement the role of their husband on the field and under the marital roof with the children. Each new couple was granted a house by their village. It appears that the trial of marriage in the common class was practiced and the relationship could be dissolved if it did not work. Among the educated young women, the chosen ones, Quechua Aclla Cuna ("Virgins of the Sun"), lived in temple convents under a vow of chastity. Their duties included the preparation of ritual food, the maintenance of a sacred fire, and the weaving of garments for the emperor and for ritual use.

Figure 4.6 Machu Picchu

Clearly educational and economic inequality was rampant in the pre-conquest Incan civilization. The words of Garcilaso de la Vega reveals the attitude of Tupac Inca Yupanqui on education. In his chronicle, he stated, "Science was not intended for the people; but for those of generous blood. Persons of low degree are only puffed up by it, and rendered vain and arrogant. Neither should such meddle with the affairs of government; for this would bring high offices into disrepute, and cause detriment to the state". However, had Atahualpa soldiers more educated perhaps they would have been able to detect Francisco Pizarro's ruse. Better weapons do not always determine the outcome of a war, only the way it is fought. The courage, wit, self-determination of a well-trained army could have changed Atahualpa's fate.

The Inca civilization was at its peak from 1438 to 1532 and remains one of the world's marvels until today. Visitors are still impressed with the Machu Picchu citadel in the Jo Mountains.

The Inca's magnificent engineering feats including their road and agricultural terraces in mountainous terrain across the roughest terrains in the Andes were one key to the expansion and success of the empire. Through a system of collective property, labor and advanced centralized economy, the Incas were able to secure unlimited manual labor to support the empire. Most importantly, the Inca did not use what is known today as the three pillars of social development: the wheel, money and formal writing. Archeological studies and witness accounts shed light on the motivations of the absolute ruler for territorial expansion. Besides power and prestige in the deep-rooted tradition, each emperor had to build his own wealth. In an early account of Inca culture written 300 years ago by Jesuit priest Father Bernabe Cobo, "for therein were many palaces of dead kings with all the treasure that each amassed in life; and he who began to reign did not touch the estate and wealth of his predecessor but built a new palace and acquired for himself silver and gold and all the rest". In other words, the dead ruler remained the owner of the property he had accumulated in life. Ironically, this kind of thinking had well served the conquistador's wealth appetite.

There is a belief that ethnic changes in the composition of a native colonized population and the administrative requirements to support this change tend to have long term consequences on the mixed population by reinforcing social stratification. In fact, scholars' opinion about the long term effect of colonialism varies widely from non-consequential to detrimental politically, culturally and economically for the colonized countries.

Summary of Political Processes and Events preceding modern Mexico and Peru.

MEXICO

Mexico history can be divided in four periods: pre-colonial up to 1519; Colonial (1519-1821); national (1821- 1910); Modern (1910 to present).

Mexico was plagued by internal dissensions fueled by the thirst for power and wealth inherited from the pre-independence rulers. The past social problems found their way into the Mexican culture which created a fertile ground for political instability. You will recall that it took Hernando Cortés two years to conquer Mexico. In 1521 it became a colony of Spain. Cortés totally razed Tenochtitlan and built Mexico City on its ruins, the premier European center of the New World. It did not take long for Cortés to socio-economically reorganize the country by putting in place the institutions for securing prosperity. Who could then be the beneficiaries? Surely Spain but also the nobility members by their close contact with those in power. As mentioned earlier, encomienda, the right of a colonist to demand tribute and forced labor from the Aztecs was introduced. A chart in the Note section of Appendix I shows the population decrease by smallpox and cocoliztli. Later on, slavery became common as the rich encomienda holders diversified their investments in labor-intensive economic sectors such as textile and sugar cane, rice and grapes. These instruments of extractive institutions left their marks decades later.

Mining and agriculture were the main extractive resources for Spain. The Crown's prosperity was enhanced by New Spain's regular supply of silver, foodstuffs and domestic textile. The landowners in New Spain got their share of wealth while the largest sector of the population while the indigenous lived on a minimum level of existence.

The invasion of the Iberian Peninsula and the abdication of Spanish king Ferdinand VII in 1808 and his return to the throne in 1815 created political turmoil in Latin America. The promulgation of the revised Cadiz Constitution abolishing all forms of forced labor convinced the colonial Spanish elite of both Mexico and Peru that independence was the best political solution. Jose de San Martin is known as the libera of Argentine, Chili and Peru in 1821; Simon Bolivar for Venezuela in the same year and Augustin de Iturbide for Mexico in 1824.

In Mexico, the political maneuver of Agustín de Iturbide in 1821 promising equal rights and upper-class status for the Spanish and mestizo population. But as a creole aristocrat, he served only the interest of his social class. He was seen as the promoter of the Spanish rules. He was accused of treason and executed in 1823.

The case of the political maneuver of army general Agustín de Iturbide deserves to be underlined. True, he led towards the independence of Mexico but the end of his tenure as an authoritarian ruler signaled the beginning of an era of political instability. Soon after the independence of Mexico, he declared himself emperor, dismissed the congress and replaced it with a junta conceivably composed of his acolytes. He stayed less than two years as emperor leaving Mexico in total political instability. Between 1824 and 1867 there were fifty-two presidents in Mexico, few of whom assumed power according to any constitutional sanctioned procedure (Acemoglu & Robinson 2012: p. 31).

Internal dissensions continued between the inhabitants of Texas, then part of Mexico, and Santa Anna the leader of the resistance against Spain's unsuccessful attempt to repossess its colony. Santa Anna resigned in 1844; friction between the US and the Mexican residents cause the US-Mexico War. As a result of an agreement reached between the two countries the US, Rio Grande became the boundary of Texas, California and Nuevo México were ceded to the US. In addition, the US agreed to pay $15 million as compensation for the seized land.

The list of political disturbances can go on and on reflecting a period of riots and instability until World War II. In fact, close to 1 million Mexicans have emigrated to the United States for better living conditions.

In 1946 Miguel Aleman of the PRI (Partido Revolucionario Institucional) became president followed by Gustavo Diaz Ordaz in 1968. Mexico benefited from a period of industrial development and economic growth. As a result, this country was selected to host the Olympics regardless of a bloody demonstration against the economic inequality between the haves and the have nots two days before the game. Among other upheavals, the Chiapas rebellion* of 1994 and the War on drugs had created an atmosphere of insecurity.

But, today Mexico is a different country. It is led by Andrés Manuel López Obrador of the Morena party, a coalition of three left-wing political organizations. He was elected on a political platform to battle corruption, to reduce violence and to deal with the longstanding challenge of inequality.

There are many multinational companies operating in Mexico including América Móvil, CEMEX, FEMS and the companies of the Mexican business magnate Carlos Slim. Mexico is ranked as the 13th richest economy in the world. But it also listed among the countries of poor people in the world. However, based on the most recent information, Mexico's poverty rate for 2016 was 34.80%, a 5.7% decline from 2014. According to the Economic Research of the Federal Bank of St Louis, the Gini Index of Mexico was 45.4 in 2018 compared to 48.7 in 2014.

PERU

Similarly with Mexico, the political dynamic of Peru can be divided into four periods: pre-colonial-1532; colonial (1532-1572); pre-modern (1572-1821); modern Peru (1821 to present).

Atahualpa, the last Inca emperor, was executed eight months after his capture despite the amount of gold, silver and precious stones naively submitted for his liberation. This execution practically ended the Incan civilization but not officially until the destruction of the Incan neo-state of Vilcabamba with the death of Amaru Thupa in 1572. Again, this was not the end of the colonial period. The Viceroyalty, a Spanish imperial administrative structure, governed the country from Lima until independence in 1821.

The Viceroy continued to enforce encomienda for the benefit of his army. Economic development was sought through commercial monopoly and mineral extraction, mainly from the silver mines of Potosi. Wars, Mita* and infectious diseases have taken a heavy toll on the population. Over 200 indigenous communities had to send one-seventh of their adult male population to work in the Potosi silver and Huancavelica mercury mines. The Mita* ran selectively between 1573 and 1812 in that a dividing line exempted some communities while fully enforced in the adjacent communities. According to Melissa Dell, the Mita effect lowers household consumption by around 25% and increases the prevalence of stunted growth in children by around 6 percentage points in subjected districts today. The products in the form of tax collected were sent to Spain in return for converting the natives to Christianity.

José de la Serna e Hinojosa was the last of 52 viceroys of Peru from 1532 to 1821. The movement for an independent Peru forced him to abandon Lima in June 1821.

A series of events that have led to the republic of Peru occurred between the last Incan rebellion in 1780 around the highlands near Cuzco and attempts for restoring democracy in the country since 1979. The Incan rebellion was an uprising of native and mestizo peasants against the tax increase in the Spanish Viceroyalty of Peru.

External political events precipitated radical changes also in Peru. The effects of the European Enlightenment period disseminated in Peru by the intellectuals convinced of the philosophy of Voltaire, Montesquieu, Rousseau and others promoting the value of knowledge, freedom and happiness. These ideas found fertile ground in Peru. The Napoleon invasion of Spain in 1808, instilled the idea of independence particularly between the Creoles (those born of European descent in America).

Pre-modern Peru had to deal with the thirst for power of the military leaders who had become more visible in the battle for independence. In addition, the leaders had to build a new political structure for governing a pluralist society composed of Indians, Creoles and Landowners.

Despite the liberal constitution adopted in 1828, General Augustin Gamarra took power illegally and so did his successor General Felipe Salaverry in 1835. A succession of political parties, liberal and conservative with inconsistent worsened the situation. General Ramon Castilla was president from and 1845 to 1851 and 1855 to 1862. He was popular for promoting national prosperity from the taxation of companies exploiting Guano deposits, for his social reform by the abolition of payment of tribute by the Indians, the emancipation of the black slaves, for his primary, secondary state education system and the adoption of a Constitution.

But this honeymoon with the population did not last long. The second half of the 19th century witnessed the formation of a Civilian Party representing the landowners and the merchants. The major public works undertaken by this political party in the presidency plunged the country into debt. The war of the Pacific (1878-1883) between Peru and Chile which the latter won was economically detrimental for the country for at least the following four decades. Peru became predisposed again for political change. Hence the Democratic Party accession to power by its leader in 1895 rivaling with the Civilian Party; a leftist party, the American Popular Revolutionary Alliance 1924-1930 and the return of the generals by a military Junta. A bloody period ensued until World War II in which Peru cooperated with the United States by authorizing Allied use of airfield and the sale of petroleum, cotton and minerals. Two periods of military rules by junta promoting economic development followed by the return of civilian leadership bring the political history of Peru to the current decade. Pablo Kuczynski whose presidency was tainted by corruption resigned in March 2018. He was replaced by the recent Peruvians Party for Change with Martin Vizcarra in 2018. This is a politically eventful history in this country's trajectory to democracy and economic stability.

Modern Peru substantially contrasts with its premodern economic period. In 2012 Peru was one of the world's fastest economy with a GDP growth rate of 6.3% slowed to 3.9% in 2018. According to the World Bank, the poverty headcount ratio at the national poverty line (% of the population) in Peru was 20.5 in 2018, a poverty reduction of more than half compared with 2004 which was 58.7. The national poverty rate is the percentage of the population living below the national poverty line. The Gini* income coefficient of Peru for 2010-2017 was 43.8 a five-point reduction compared with the preceding 2000-2010 period of 48.1

Culturally, approximately 4 million Peruvians today still speaks Quechua. On an overall population of 31.2 million in 2018, 45% is indigenous people, descents from those who had inhabited Peru prior to the conquest period; 37% is mestizos; 15% is white European from various ethnic backgrounds (Spanish, Italian, German, French, British, Croatian, Jewish and Irish) ; 3% is Asian, Afro-Peruvian, Mullato and Zambo. The Mullatos are citizens of Peru of African and European descent while the Zambos are of African and Amerindian ancestry.

Legacy of Colonialism

I s it fair to say that some of the political instability experienced by both Mexico and Peru in the pre-modern period has its roots in colonialism? There is a belief that political, economic and ethnic changes in the composition of a native colonized population and the administrative requirements to support this change tend to have long term consequences on the mixed population by reinforcing social stratification. Recall the case of the Mexican aristocrat creole Agustin de Iturbide and his authoritarian regime. His administration was a copycat of the Spanish regime. He did not know any other way. The same situation prevailed in pre-modern Peru. Although an independent country in 1524, the last viceroy left only in 1821. The Civilian Party of the landowners and the merchants knew how to satisfy their economic appetite at the expense of the larger population. The perpetuation of extractive institutions created infighting and political instability, building a strong motivation to play musical chair in the replacement process of the existing elite.

Could the sequel of colonialism accreted over centuries still be felt today in modern Mexico and Peru?

Opinions about the long term economic effect of colonialism vary widely from detrimental (S.L. Engerman and K.L. Sokoloff 2005) to non-consequential J. G. Williamson 2015) for the colonized countries. The former suggests that "it was those colonies that began with extreme inequality and population heterogeneity that came to exhibit persistence over time in evolving institution that restricted access to economic opportunities and generated lower rates of public investment in school and other infrastructures consider conducive to growth. These patterns may help to explain why a great many societies with legacies as colonies with extreme inequality have suffered from poor development experiences".

The latter posits that "compared with the rest of the world, inequality was not high in the century following 1492, and it was not even high in the post-independence decades just prior to Latin America *belle* époque* and started with industrialization. It only became high during the commodity boom 1870-1913, by the end of which it had joined the rich country unequal club including the US and the UK. Latin America only became relatively high between 1913 and the 1970s when it missed the Great Egalitarian Leveling which took place almost everywhere else. That Latin America has its roots in its colonial past is a myth".

Generalization is always risky. In fact, exception dampens generalization. In the assessment of the impact of colonialism on modern Mexico and Peru, many factors must be taken into account including the demography, the climatic conditions of these countries and also the overall European political environment. In this context, demography is used in its usual meaning that is the size and movement of populations and their relationship with the natural environment.

The discovery of the New World brought enormous wealth to the Spanish Empire. Gold has always been a precious sought-after commodity. The presence of gold and a large workforce were the first observations of Columbus as well as Cortés and Pizarro. The large and dense population of both Mexico and Peru make them the perfect source of wealth for their empire. Hence, the development of the necessary extractive institutions. It is politics and political institutions that determine what economic institutions a country has (D. Acemoglu and J. Robinson 2012: p. 43). They produced regularities that shape and are in turn shaped by individual behaviors. (T. Kuran 2011: p.6). The invisible entrenched power of institutions also determines a country's success or failure to capitalize on opportunities for economic growth and social stability. These institutions, with the assistance of the elite, continued in the premodern or modern period of both countries with the political instability described earlier.

That said, a departure from this extractive system has always been possible by making the right choice. Acemoglu and Robinson (2017: Volume I) illustrate this point with the case of the Potosi silver mine. The huge system of forced labor set up by Viceroy Francisco de Toledo was abolished when Peru became independent in 1821. However, forced labor continued until 1952. This is just one example to prove that the current economic inequality of these nations should not be attributed to their colonial past.

Recall that I have mentioned demographic environment as one of the factors taken into consideration in the colonization process. From a broader perspective, an extractive institution is not the only hallmark of colonialism. After many unsuccessful attempts, the first permanent British colony was established in Jamestown, Virginia in 1607. This was a sparsely populated area also meaning no available labor force to coerce. In fact, incentives had to be given to the first British settlers to encourage them to stay and work. The institutions created for this purpose include political rights and access to land and are called inclusive because they sustain individual growth and well-being. A large tax base was created to the benefit of England in addition to the trading relationship.

Extractive institutions were designed for countries' proneness to disease. Yellow fever, malaria also killed a large proportion of the French army in Saint Domingue (currently Haiti). Acemoglu and Robinson called West Africa the 'white man grave'. These countries had extractive institutions with limited migration of settlers.

In summary, the colonization of Mexico and Peru was driven by the demographic and environmental characteristics of these countries. That said, even after their independence, the income inequality continued to grow. The Gini coefficient increased from 0.57 to 0.65 from 1870 to 1914 during *la belle époque*. This trend cannot be attributed to colonialism but to the greed of the elite.

Background

HISPANIOLA

The written work for which Bartolomé de las Casas is most famous is the Brevísima relación de la destrucción de las Indias. This short track damned the Spanish treatment of the Indians of the New World, reporting atrocities committed by the conquistadores and documenting the scope of the genocide that had taken place. Source: Samuel M. Wilson – Hispaniola. *Caribbean Chiefdoms in the Age of Columbus*

Endnotes

MEXICO

4a. From a chronological perspective the term "Kingdom of England" encompassing Wales, Scotland and Ireland can be used for the period up to May 1st, 1707. The appellation Great Britain came into practice on January 1st, 1801 when Ireland entered the Kingdom as per the Act of Union. The name United Kingdoms of Great Britain and Northern Ireland was established by the Royal and Parliamentary Titles Act 1927. Until today the abbreviation UK is meant to identify a country that includes England, Scotland, Wales and Northern Ireland. This convention may not always be followed depending on the source document.

4b. This term is usually applied to attacks on Jews in the Russian Empire in the late 19th and early 20th centuries. On June 6, 1391, mobs fueled by anti-Semitic preachers carry out pogroms in Sevilla, a city incorporated into the Christian kingdom of Castile, devastating one of Europe's most vibrant Jewish communities. Source: Timeline of Spanish Inquisition – britannica.com

4c. The Batey is a space bordered by stones that sometimes had drawings of the deities and wood or stone figures used to represent them.

4d. Conuco: A small plot of land or orchard usually cultivated by a farmer for his own subsistence. It is then a mode of agriculture in which part of the land produces only enough to feed the family that works there. Commonly, the extensions of land for this purpose are called Conuco.

4e. *Encomienda* is a grant by the Spanish Crown to a colonist in America, conferring the right to demand tribute and forced labor from the Indian inhabitants of an area.

4f. *Repartimiento* was a colonial forced labor system imposed on the indigenous population.

4g. Nahuatl the original written language of the Aztecs can be characterized as a pictographic script that is a form of writing which uses representational, pictorial drawings, similarly to cuneiform and, to some extent, hieroglyphic writing which also uses drawings as 1130 – 1350 AD. By 1500 their population grew to over 3,000,000.

4h. A city-state is a sovereign state that consists of a city and its dependent territories. I must point out that non-sovereign cities may enjoy a high degree of autonomy and could be considered a city-state.

4i. La Noche Triste ("The Night of Sorrows", literally "The Sad Night") of June 30, 1520, characterizes the heavy loss incurred by the Spanish army and their indigenous allies retreating from Tenochtitlan following the death of the Aztec emperor Montezuma II who had been held hostage by the Spaniards.

4j. Crypto-Jews are of Portuguese descent. Many converted Portuguese Jews came to New Spain looking for commercial opportunities. In 1642, 150 of these individuals were arrested within three or four days, and the Inquisition began a series of trials on suspicion of still practicing Judaism. Many of these were merchants involved in New Spain's principal economic activities. Hamnet 2006: p.92) The Africans also experienced difficulty with the Inquisition. They were accused, more likely by their owners, of witchcraft and sorcery. Although they had proven to the Holy Office that they were Christians by their knowledge of catechism and liturgy, the punishments exacted could be more seen as a form of social control than religious. In the beginning, free slaves of African descent had to pay a special tax and were subject to the law to keep them in a state of servitude. Nonetheless, as time went by, African bozal (a black slave without exposure to Spanish culture) or ladino (already acculturated) or at any stage in between, made a substantial contribution to New Spain's economy. (I. Altman et al 2003: pp 204-222).

* *La belle époque*

The beginning date of *la belle époque* varies among authors either 1871 or 1890 like in this definition. In this quote it was a period from 1890 to 1914 characterized by the very rich's inability to deal with the grim reality of modern life, and, as a consequence, their retreat into a frivolous, fairy-tale kind of existence of their own making. Choosing to live out of time and place, this aristocracy rejected reality and thus dissociated itself from the real world.

Instead, this elite constructed a rigidly structured society based on the domination of the weak—whether the poor, the opposite sex, or children.

Thus, the rich judged people according to social standards in no way connected to merit.

Source:https://www.mdc.edu/wolfson/academic/artsletters/art_philosophy/humanities/belleepoque.htm

PERU

4k.Notwithstanding the absence of trade communication during Atahualpa's reign, the presence of smelting copper and bronze smelting in Peru indicates that there had been some sea communication between both countries in the past. Considering that this technology was common in Mexico in the 10th and 11th centuries, according to Rivet & Arsando (1946: pp. 178-187) this communication had taken place prior to the social evolution of the Aztec and Inca Empires. Evidence of trade between Mexico and Peru started in 1536, three years after the execution of Atahualpa. (W. Borah 1954: p.131)

4LThe Mita was a system established by the Spanish to construct buildings or create roads throughout the empire. It was later transformed into a coercive labor system when the Spanish conquered the Inca Empire. Mita was used for the extraction of silver at the Potosi mine and the cinnabar was hauled out at Huancavelica for extracting mercury. The Mita system allowed the natives to pay off their debts, the Encomienda did not. Encomienda was like slavery.

4m. Alcapa is a wool-bearing camelid in the species of the llama.

4n. Vicuna is a smaller species of llama and Alcapa found in the Andes.

4o. The Chiapas rebellion refers to the 1994 Zapatista uprising, the 1995 Zapatista crisis and their aftermath, and tensions between the indigenous peoples and subsistence farmers in the Mexican state of Chiapas.

4p. To have a preliminary understanding of how a quipu could be used to calculate please follow this link: https://www.youtube.com/watch?v=EYq-VtyAd2s

PART V
Evolution of Political Governance

America's abundance was created not by public sacrifices to the common good, but by the productive genius of free men who pursue their own interests and the making of their own private fortunes. They did not starve the people to pay for America's industrialization. They gave the people better jobs, higher wages, and cheaper goods with every scientific discovery or technological advance – and thus the whole country was moving forward and profiting, not suffering every step of the way.

Ayn Rand

Introduction

PART V focuses on the development of capitalism, the free world economic system, with the objective to address income and wealth inequality. The association of capitalism with democracy will drive the continuation of the analysis in the next PART. Capitalism and democracy have proven to be beneficial to the free world when the nature and limit of their respective field of jurisdiction are understood and established. They have been interacting with each other for millennia considering that the long trading practice of goods and services

From PART II to PART IV, I have reviewed the emergence of inequality in society embedded in the evolution of social complexity from band to state and empire. I looked at unified empires in Mesopotamia, Egypt, the Indus Valley, and China in the Old World and Mexico and Peru in the New World. The assumption was that the stratification resulting from extended territorial dominance would make more visible the political culture implemented by their rulers, and facilitate the analysis of inequality. It worked. In each of these empires, inequality did exist. Centralized, monarchial and theocratic governments could have ruled a stratified society in accordance with social justice norms, but this was not the case. Same for the empires of the New World before the colonization. Sadly, the political culture of the past was carried over to the present.

There are five stages in social organization at specific period of time around the globe; (1) primitive communal; (2) feudalism (particularly experienced in Mesopotamia, France, China and the overseas possessions of England, Spain and Portugal) (3) slave plantation; (4) capitalism (5) socialism. It is worth noting that Cuba remains the only country who has made the transition from capitalism to socialism. The first and third stages have been covered indirectly in the band, tribe politics and colonialism, keeping in mind that slave plantations were an extension of mercantilism, a politico-economic system to be reviewed in the following pages.

Feudalism

The emergence of feudalism in so many civilizations from Asia to Europe supports the theory that it is a necessary and inevitable stage of political development. As mentioned earlier, feudalism is a decentralized form of government in which a monarch or lord divides and allocates lands called fiefs in exchange for military services.

In Europe, feudalism was abandoned in the 13th century. Causal factors include the shortage of labor resulting from the Black Death which killed more than a third of Europe's population. The introduction of coinage in the 13th century also weakened the feudal system because money could be used to buy military service instead of vassal service.

As feudalism disappeared, a rich class of merchants emerged whose loyalty was only to the payer. This class played an important role in the commercial supremacy of Europe, particularly England. The end of feudalism was also marked by an increase in the urban population. Towns that had an average population of 125 in the 14th century and 154 in the 16th century grew to 10,000 or more in the 17th century. According to the historian Jan de Vries, Europe's population (excluding Russia and the Ottoman Empire) grew to 61.6 million in 1500, 70.2 million in 1550 and 78 million in 1600. This increase could be explained by increased medical knowledge and care and faster dissemination of medical information – thanks to Gutenberg's movable type printing press. There were also cleaner living conditions and increased food production due to labor-saving agricultural implements.

The three centuries of the medieval period and the Renaissance saw significant technological advances in Europe with a substantial acceleration at the turn of the 20th century (Toussaint 2017: pp. 7, 40). Inventions such as gun powder ~1249, the spinning wheel, mechanical clock ~1300 and the Gutenberg printing press ~1436 are worth mentioning from a military, commercial and cultural and perspective (ibid)).

With the number of major inventions in the 1500s, Europe achieved a technological edge over all other civilizations. What emerged was a commercial economy but not a capitalist one yet. Parallels can be drawn with the Aztec civilization where wage labor was rare, as were sales of land. Commercial practices such as books of account, partnerships, and loans existed but only in rudimentary fashion (M. E. Smith 2017: pp.45-46). Another view is expressed by Karl Polanyi about this pre-capitalist market system. Polanyi's distinction between the market place and market system was an attempt to deal with the pre-capitalist commercial exchange. Money and commerce certainly existed in the pre-capitalist market places but the mechanism to determine prices in these markets differed from the supply-and-demand mechanism in capitalist market (Scarborough and Clark 2007: pp.177-178). Nonetheless, Europeans felt equipped for worldwide expansion.

Sixteen century Spain with its colonies in the New World raised the competition bar and other countries felt the pressure to improve their economy. Britain, France and Netherland took up that challenge and followed Spain's suit in the Americas and Africa. The Dutch East India Company became a dominant player in the spice and silk trade after founding a colony in the Cape of Good Hope on the southern coast of Africa thereby curtailing the Portuguese trading posts on the western coast. Large plantations in the Third World worked by the slaves, capital investment and technological innovation in commercial shipbuilding and maritime transportation all contributed to an explosion of international trade. The mercantile system was born.

Mercantilism

In this commercial and social evolution continuum, mercantilism met the requirements of a centralized state. Mercantilism posits that a nation must obtain as much wealth as possible from its colonies and maintains a positive trade balance meaning exports must exceed imports. This, naturally, led to the Navigation Acts and Sugar Acts (See the Note section of Appendix I). A nation's goal was to become self-sufficient and independent from other countries for goods; so was the thinking!

Mercantilism which emerged in the 16th century coincided with the publication of The Prince by Machiavelli in 1532, five years after his death. In the Machiavellian spirit, the goal of any government is to stay in power; practically speaking, the end justifies the means. The colonies were 'captive' markets and their purpose was to enrich the mother country. Raw materials were sent to the mother country and finished goods were sold back to the colonies. Competition for the colonial markets characterized European imperialism and found justification in mercantilism. The application of the mercantilist theory led to the development of a skilled labor force in the colonizing country in the clothing, footwear and jewelry industry to meet the growing need of the upper class. Needless to say that the imposition of heavy taxes and restrictions frustrated the colonized particularly in North America eventually leading to the American Revolution.

The dimension and solution to problems such as shortage of labor and the introduction of coinage which had led to the demise of feudalism pointed to the direction of the state. No economic policy other than mercantilism could have had the power to effect such a substantial change at the politico-economic. The macroeconomic policy of mercantilism became the dominant ideology for two and a half centuries because it was carried out by the governing body with the merchants' participation. This begs the question as to what advantages merchants could gain from their participation. The answer resides in the definition of rent. Rent is any payment or financial advantage legally given to an individual or a corporate entity in excess of the cost needed to design and carry a production. Rent-seeking, a common practice in the current century, refers to all largely unproductive, and expropriative (or extractive) activities which bring a positive return to the individual but not to society (A. Krueger 1974: pp.291-303). As will be substantiated later in the examination of capitalism, to the extent that resources are spent to capture monopoly rents in such ways as lobbying, bribery, and related activities, these resources are basically wasted from an economic and social point of view (Ekelund and Tollison 1981: p. 19).

Rent seekers are known to get a bigger slice of the financial pie without increasing the pie itself. Put differently rent-seekers increase their companies' share of wealth without creating a new one. From this perspective, they not only bring inefficiency to the economy but also increase the gap between the haves and the have-nots. Rent-seeking merchants and governments developed and enforced mercantilist policies. Merchants benefited greatly from the enforced monopolies, bans on foreign competition, and poverty of the workers. Governments benefited from the high tariffs and payments from the merchants (J. Niehans 1990: p.19). At first glance, these practices look like a conspiracy against the workers.

One of the mercantile system's policies was to maximize production for export purposes without consideration of the workforce's wellbeing. By depriving the lower class of free time, education and extra money, this institutionalized injustice was seen as a remedy to prevent vice and laziness and protecting the economy. The elite embraced Voltaire's words that "work spares us from three evils: boredom, vice and need". However, Voltaire's quote needs to be put in the proper context. Opposing the mercantilism economic theory was physiocracy, an economic theory of the 18th century Age of Enlightenment which posits that the wealth of nations is derived solely from the value of land or its development and that agricultural products should be highly-priced.

At the time the physiocrats were formulating their ideas, economies were overwhelmingly agrarian. That is presumably why the theory considered only agricultural labor to be valuable. Physiocrats viewed the production of goods and services as equivalent to the consumption of agricultural surplus, since human or animal muscle power provided the main source of power and all energy derived from the surplus from agricultural production. Profit in capitalist production was really only the "rent" obtained by the owner of the land on which the agricultural production took place. No wonder Voltaire encouraged hard work for the lower class, being himself a landowner.

Adam Smith rejected the mercantilist focus on production, arguing that consumption was paramount to production. In his words "consumption is the sole end and purpose of all production; and the interest of the producer ought to be attended to, only so far as it may be necessary for promoting that of the consumer" (A. Smith 1993:pp. 376-377). But in the mercantile system, the interest of the consumer is subsumed by the interest and needs of the producer. Mercantilism considers production, not consumption, as the ultimate end and object of all industry and commerce.

Arguments against mercantilism increased as the negative consequences of some of its policies and the evolution became evident and the European political environment evolved. Still, scholars remain divided over the cause of the end of mercantilism. Those who believe the theory was simply an error hold that its replacement was inevitable as soon as Adam Smith's philosophy was unveiled. Those who feel that mercantilism amounted to rent-seeking hold that it ended only when major power shifts occurred. But there is a third argument which perhaps escaped the thinkers of the mercantile system. This argument and its corollary go to the core of global exchange and remain valid today. At the heart of Smith's argument about the free-flowing of goods and services by eliminating tariffs is the implicit concept of freedom between trading partners. Montesquieu, a French philosopher of the enlightenment period, posited that "if all necessities could be produced within one political boundary, this would lead to despotism whereas if necessities had to be exchanged between political entities, this would encourage freedom"*(A. MacFarlane 2000: 40).

Commerce encourages freedom. But if commerce encourages freedom it is also a consequence of it. Commerce can only flourish where there is a certain amount of freedom. Increased consumption follows commerce which creates healthy business relationships between trading partners. This is contrary to the atmosphere of distrust and animosity which existed between England and its American colonies. Moreover, in Smith's line of thought, the positive social impact of this freedom is contagious. The reciprocal relationship that people voluntarily establish, channels self-interest to mutual advantage and promotes a prosperous social order.

With the wisdom of time, it is easy to identify the many pitfalls of an economic system championed by the ruling state. Perhaps sheer urgency of rapid gain prevented the political thinkers to foresee these pitfalls and their consequences or they were inept to address them. Mercantilism was supposed to enhance and protect the state by extracting and accumulating as much wealth as possible and maintaining a positive trade balance in a ruthless zero-sum process. In the finite number of markets in the conquered territories, this zero-sum game pitted nations against each other. Indeed, the 17th and 18th centuries were among the most violent periods in Europe. Since it was related to the Navigation Acts, mercantilism was clearly a factor in the twenty-year Anglo-Dutch*war. And, the bloody Franco-Dutch war (1672-1678) can be attributed to French imperialism in the acquisition of the Spanish Netherlands*.

Given the unique characteristics of each European country, the abandonment of mercantilism did not occur simultaneously on the continent. In England, over the course of the 18th-century, mercantilism law and regulations were repealed and replaced with the *laissez-faire* economics of Adam Smith. France made this change only as part of the socio-economic and political revolution of 1789. In Germany, mercantilist ideology prevailed throughout the 19th and 20th centuries when the German Historical School of economics was paramount (Wilson 1966: p.6). This school of thought supported protectionist economic policies as an instrument of nation-building.

However, the measure of a nation cannot be limited to such a simplistic and adversarial approach. The main beneficiaries are the state and the wealthy merchants at the expense of the lower class that make up the majority of the population. In capitalism, capital accumulation as a result of freedom of action, the capital and labor nexus, and the laissez-faire approach provide a more sustainable system for economic development. The hope invested in this economic system and its prevalence today require not only a review of its beginning but also of the events preceding its development.

Let's go back to the pre-industrial stage, a phase known as Pro-industrialization. Coined by the historian Franklin Mendels in 1969 and popularized in his 1972 article on the Flemish linen industry in the 18th century, proto-industrialization is defined as the rapid growth of traditionally organized but market-oriented, rural industry accompanied by changes in the spatial organisation of the rural economy(F. Mendels 1972: pp. 241-261). Later this term was used to mean the initial steps towards European industrialization between the 16th and the 19th century - the intermediate developmental stage of capitalism.

There is no consensus that pro-industrialization led to capitalism. I believe the socioeconomic uniqueness of each European country has to be taken into consideration. Proto-industrialization has been criticized because the cause and effect dynamics for industrialization could not be established in any European country even in a particular pro-industrial region.

Deeper empirical studies are needed to ascertain whether the economic growth and demographic changes experienced in those locations were a stepping stone for industrialization. But, certain limiting factors need to be built into the definition of proto-industrialization. D.C. Coleman states: "Proto-industrialization is thus defined by the simultaneous occurrence of three ingredients within the framework of a region – rural industries, external destinations and symbiosis of the rural industry within the regional development of a commercial agriculture". Implicit in Coleman's definition is the assumption that an expansion of the population will occur as a result of income accumulation of merchants and be a precursor to industrial revolution. Regional workshops experiencing proto-industrialization will favor labor-saving mechanical devices because of a shortage of human resources. In an article titled The Theories of Proto- industrialization Sheilagh C. Ogilvie reviewed Mendels' theory and the positions of Kriedte et al and others on this matter. She concluded that no specific theoretical framework fits the evolving conditions of continental Europe from the medieval period to the 19th century. There is a recognition that proto-industrialization does not explain the European economic and demographic growth preceding the industrial revolution. A series of important financial, political and technological changes set the conditions for the Industrial Revolution

Pre-capitalism

As part of this economic development process, a key agent emerged namely the merchant/entrepreneur hereafter shortened to entrepreneur. They played a fundamental role in everything from the delivery of the raw material to the finished product. They were the liaison between the workers, the artisans (the producers) and the consumer (the market). Market forces drive innovations for profit-making in the free market system, the objective of all entrepreneurs. A crucial stage in the development of capitalism occurred when the entrepreneur started paying a wage to the producers for the finished goods and paying in advance for the raw material. Presumably, producers accepted the terms of this arrangement with the entrepreneur because it was advantageous to both parties. On the one hand, the producer did not have the required borrowing capacity or credit. On the other hand, the entrepreneur had an opportunity to increase production. The entrepreneur is this steel-nerved human creature with the flair and competence to comb the socioeconomic environment to find and capitalize on profitable business opportunities. Entrepreneurs are profit-driven and ready to jump on the most promising technological innovations for this purpose in the free market system. They must be able to plan, organize and manage a business and its inherent financial risks. The entrepreneur is not villain as often described in the capitalist economic system. The 18th-century Irish French economist Richard Cantillon defined an entrepreneur as a person who pays for a product at a certain price and resells it at an uncertain price. From this perspective, profit is then a fair reward for risk-taking.

Although I could not find detailed information about business loans and investments in the proto-industrialization (pre-capitalist)* phase, there is evidence of banking institutions and their financial intermediaries from the 15th century in Italy, Germany and Belgium. Moreover, the corporate financial structure was already in place. Fund holders were able to finance business ventures through a joint-stock chartered company. A charter is a legal document granted by the Crown giving the business owner of a company the monopoly on trade within a specific region for a given number of years. This prerogative also confers strong legal powers to the owner to enforce orders in distant shares of the company.

In England, the Muscovy Company was the first joint-stock company that received its charter in 1555. They were followed by the Dutch East India Company, a chartered company established in 1602 when the States-General of the Netherlands granted it a 21-year monopoly to carry out colonial activities in Asia. The Dutch East India Company is considered the first multinational corporation in the world and also the first to issue stocks.

The large sum of money necessary for these ventures required many investors each of them holding the first permanent English settlement. In North America, this settlement was near present-day Williamsburg in East Virginia. This colony was a private venture organized by the Virginia Company of London. King James I, granted a charter to a group of investors for the establishment of the company on April 10, 1606. The charter gave the company the right to settle anywhere from roughly present-day North Carolina to New York State.

During the 17th century, production from the home, known as the cottage industry, boomed. This changed with technological/manufacturing innovations and the development of factories throughout England setting the pace for the First Industrial Revolution. By the beginning of the 18th century, England had a robust reputation in the woolens industry. However, the early manufacturing industry also included silk production, clock and instrument making, firearms manufacturing, steam pump manufacturing and glassmaking.

On this latter product, coal was more likely used since England had rich coal mines that could be supplied for this purpose and residential heating. But, the appropriate technology for smelting iron, was not yet available. The Bessemer iron smelting was implemented in 1855 and with a whole range of technology that facilitated mass production processes. It is fair to say that the socioeconomic environment of the First Industrial Revolution was favorable for the emergence of capitalism.

Capitalism

As can be seen in the above graph, Great Britain was in a good position to signal this era of technological development with the Great Exhibition of 1851 less than two decades before the Second Industrial Revolution. Prince Albert, the husband of Queen Victoria stated that "the aim of the exhibition was to develop a fertile promotion of all branches of human diligence and the strengthening of the bonds of peace among all the nations of the Earth". England was indeed in a good position technologically, economically and politically to show its power to the rest of the world.

Figure 5.0

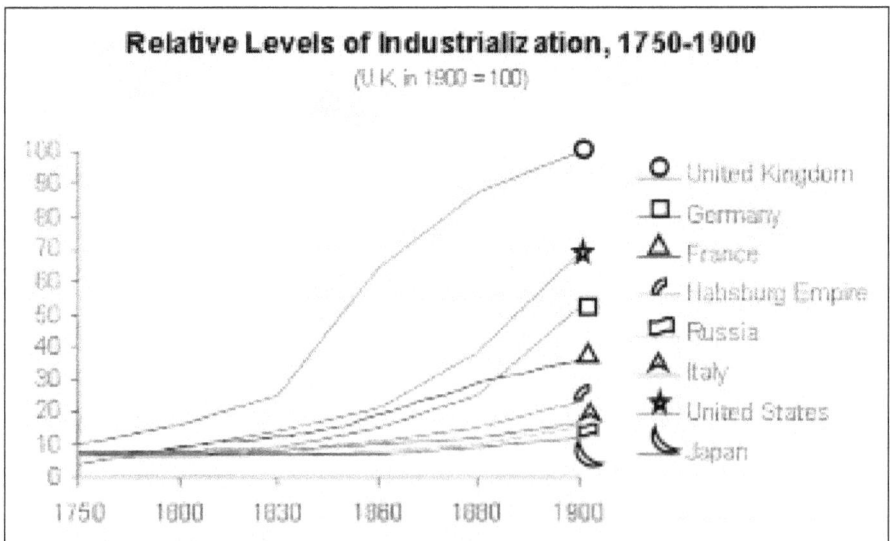

Relative Levels of Industrialization, 1750-1900
(U.K. in 1900 = 100)

Canada, then a colony of Great Britain but on the verge of becoming a self-governing dominion of the British Empire, took this opportunity to showcase its minerals, timber and agricultural products. Canada's goal was to attract investments and stimulate immigration.

At the same time, America was undergoing a great transformation. The South, an agrarian society still under a semi-feudal system, was very different than the industrialized North. The latter was more densely populated, mostly due to the influx of European immigrants. It was also more urbanized and economically more diversified. In the South, the combined effects of slavery and fewer and smaller cities were not conducive to technological innovation.

This not to say that the South was not wealthy but the skyrocketing price of cotton* made investments in diversification less attractive to the landowners. The American exhibits at the Great Exhibition that attracted the most attention were the grain reaper (McCormick), the specimens of firearms (Colt, Harford) and the rubber goods (Goodyear, Heaven), some familiar names until today.

In the wake of the highly successful 1851 Great Exhibition, the United States had the Exhibition of the Industry of All Nations, a World's Fair held in 1853 in what is now Bryant Park in New York City. It was the first US World Fair. A total of 22 countries participated in the exhibition including Canada, West Indies, Mexico, Austria and Russia. The exhibition showcased new industrial achievements and the nationalism of a relatively young nation and its values. Open from July to November 1854 the fair was visited by over 1.1 million visitors.

The fair featured its own glass and iron exhibition building – the New York Crystal Palace. Exhibits included Eli Otis's elevator, the sewing machine, exhibits from various foreign nations, and a bearded lady. There were 31 classes of exhibits with the Mineral Department deemed most interesting by the New York Times. American exhibits took more than half (54,530 of 98,749 square feet) of the display space.

To recap, a combination of events facilitated the development of capitalism: the First Industrial Revolution (1760-1840), the needs created by the American Civil War, the additional markets created by the tree trade imposed on Egypt based on the Anglo-Ottoman Agreement and the Second Industrial Revolution (1870-1940). All gave momentum to the capitalist system. The Second Industrial Revolution led to a technological and economic explosion throughout America and Europe. Germany's pig iron production soared from 40,000 tons in 1825 to 250,000 in the early 1850s.

Private and public financial investments transformed the economic market environment into a state that could be called capitalism. It was an economic system characterized by private or corporate ownership of capital goods, by investments that are determined by private decision, and by prices, production, and the distribution of goods that are determined mainly by competition in a free market. In essence, this is the role of Adam Smith's invisible hand which he described in "*An Inquiry into the Nature and Causes of the Wealth of Nations*" (1776). The government* role (the visible hand) is confined to protecting individual rights and not intervening in the economy.

The profitability of a business increases when its goods and services reflect needs. This was Richard Cantillon's position in his book "*An Essay on Economic Theory*" (1755). Indeed, he may have inspired Adam Smith.

It was also during the Second Industrial Revolution period that the United States surpassed Great Britain in industrialization to become the workshop of the world - the world's industrial powerhouse. Transportation technology played an interesting role in the race for this supremacy. Steam locomotives were first developed in Great Britain during the early 19th century and used for railway transport. The first steam locomotive to haul passengers on a public railway was built in 1812–13 by George Stephenson and his son Robert's company Robert Stephenson & Co in Great Britain. However, by 1850 the United States had built a network of 14,518 kilometers of rail compared to only 9,797 kilometers in Great Britain and 5,856 kilometers in Germany.

A contagious feeling of optimism buoyed the American nation invigorated by new technologies. The American optimism crossed the Atlantic and created a much-needed migration windfall for the United States.

As American wages exceeded those in Europe, especially for skilled workers, millions of European came to America. They were anxious to start a new life full of hope, a forerunner of the 1931 James Truslow Adams' American Dream. The total population of American cities grew from 38.5 million in 1870 to 76.2 million in 1900.

With the passage of time and economic development, the supporting institutions, policies evolved. In addition, the Bank of England created in 1694 to supply currency was followed by many second-tier banks to handle merchants' and business owners' commercial instruments. Many other financial institutions were already operating in France Belgium and Italy for trading government securities. A similar situation occurred across the Atlantic, the Bank of New York was founded with a nominal capital base of $500,000 on June 23rd, 1784. Thirty-three years later on June 23rd, 1817 Canada's first banking institution, the Bank of Montreal was established. With a capital base of £250,000 ($21,178.40)* they offered public and private monetary and financial services to the public. The banks played an active role in building up the economy of their respective nations by providing loans to businesses and their government.

The advent of banks, the incorporation of businesses, the risk-taking, and the lending and investing signaled the institutionalization of the sought- after wealth in North America. As mentioned earlier, Western Europe preceded the New World in this undertaking. From this point onward, household revenues came from a business source, wages and later on government assistance.

Technically no stock market existed until1817 when the New York Stock Exchange opened. This marked a turning point in corporate finances and responsibilities. Until 1825 the British Government banned the issuing of shares to prevent abuse by dishonest companies. With the establishment of the stock market, the risk concept took on a different meaning. People could reduce their risk by investing in different companies. However, as it still happens today, in times of economic boom, the anticipation of gain drove many investors to ignore the possibility of loss. An event such as the collapse of the price of cotton in the first half of the 19th century and faulty investments in the railroad industry brought this truth home to investors. In modern words, they became victims of their irrational exuberance*.

Two important observations in these successive economic booms and crises need to be made. First, the last decades of the 19th century were satirically dubbed the Gilded Age by the American author and humorist Mark Twain. This was because of the extravagant opulence and wealth resulting from unparalleled technological development and the increased efficiency of the labor force. But the Gilded Age was also a period of horrific labor conditions for men, women and children. The growth of capitalism parallels the increase of inequality. The labor movement initiated in 1840 had stopped as the price of labor had plummeted. Second, the devastating effect of the Long Depression* raised the American population's opinion of expecting more from their government; an example of the need for the visible hand. Again, it refers to the government's role in the economy and the invisible hand to the market; more on these concepts in Part VI.

When Franklin D. Roosevelt became president in 1933, he reversed the previous administration's policy of non-intervention in the economy. Early in his term, Roosevelt passed legislation to reform the banking system to institutionalize depositors' account protection and to regulate the stock market to prevent the abuses which led to the 1929 crash. He also introduced the Fair Labor Standard Act to minimize the use of children in the labor force and the Interstate Commerce Act to redress the inequality in the railroad industry caused by the preferential treatment of large shippers over small businesses. In addition, Roosevelt reformed the Social Security system and instituted Unemployment Insurance and subsidies for farmers. This demonstrates a role that political authority (the visible hand) can play as part of the capitalist governance system.

If capitalism is an economic and political system of governance, why is there inequality in democratic capitalist states? With a few exceptions, this is the dilemma of the free market economy. It is conceivable that inequality is embedded and inevitable in the process of keeping profit leadership in the private corporate world. The success of the most productive business can be seen as the outcome of a "natural selection" in the competitive market place. The firm with the wisest combination of labor and capital (skills, technology and business strategies) gets the financial rewards and distributes them as they wish. The firm's shareholders get the lion's share of the reward followed by some to the management board and the rest perhaps nothing. Employees who get their salaries or wages should be happy to have a job.

The preceding argument is not intended to portray the corporate world as the villain. After all, corporate businesses are vital to the economy. At the macro level, capitalism is designed to promote productivity and profit. But, it can also be expected to sustain inequalities of income and wealth since first movers may keep their advantages for decades (B. R. Scott 2011: p. 59).

In other words, inequality is the natural state of capitalism, a position disputed by Joseph E. Stiglitz who suggests that inequality is a product of political and not merely macro-economic forces. In another level, he also suggests that inequality is not an an inevitable byproduct of globalization - the free movement of labor, capital, goods and services, and technological change - that favors better skilled and better educated employees (J. Stiglitz 2015: p.120). I will come back to this point in a moment.

Earlier, capitalism was defined as one of the two systems of governance for economic relationships, the second being democracy sustaining freedom of action. But a core element of democracy is the freedom of action, provided that some cardinal rules are respected. Corporations of different sizes enter the market every day, some open to the concept of social justice than others. Besides some tax advantages, bending the rules for one is rightly seen as unjust to others. Multinational corporations have more effective conduits to maintain their supremacy. The financial rewards mentioned in the preceding paragraph may come from modifying market rules through legitimate accommodation. The resulting impact is enhanced economic inequality in the corporate milieu with a rippled effect on society at large. If the problem becomes a concern at the national level, it can be addressed by means of the electoral process through the democratic engine, the other system of governance.

Generally, when inequality is high, citizens attribute it to the malfunctioning of the political system. In representative democracy, citizens elect their government. The political scientist R. A. Dahl has defined (liberal) democracy as a regime in which there is meaningful and extensive competition, sufficiently inclusive suffrage in national elections and a high level of civil and political liberties. He acknowledged the fact that democracy's inability to address persistent economic inequalities leads to "resentments and frustrations which weaken allegiance to the regime" Dahl 1971: p. 103). However, it has never been the role of democracy to correct inequality. The responsibility falls on the government, the visible hand of capitalism, to provide freedom of action to the many players within a legal and regulatory framework that are essential to capitalism. Political authority ensures fair play among competitors (B. R. Scott 2011: p 47). Without this safeguard the confluence of corporations' laudable objectives to respond to the market needs and the sheer urgency of profit-making in a competitive environment may lead to non-beneficial outcomes to all. However, despite this safeguard, some actions or pricing strategies still fall through the crack.

The following are some practices supporting economic inequality - some better known than others.

Market Imperfections

Economic rent

Much has been written by prominent economists and political scientists about financial practices leading to what is known as economic rent. It is the extra money or payment made by a buyer over and above the amount expected by the other party. As an example, paying an extravagant amount of money to a public figure for just showing up at an event. The economic rent is the difference bewween the real price the guest should charge and the amount paid. Economic rents result from market imperfections because the amount of money offered by the buyer is outside of the market competition mechanism.

If this concept is extended to a corporation, it means because of the particularity of the product or service offered, the corporation is allowed to sell for a certain price regardless of what the market can bear. It is not difficult to identify the beneficiaries of this extra profit. In normal business practice, the selling price includes the production costs and profit taking into account what the target market can bear and the competition. Such a formula leads to what is called an economic profit resulting from the business operations. This is quite different from the additional monopoly rent received like in the case of market dominance of a product by a particular corporation. Nobel Laureate Paul Krugman quite aptly calls monopoly rent "Profit without Production".

The disjunction between both types of income is quite evident. Shareholders' income does not necessarily filter down to the employees in the form of higher wages and salary. More likely the product and services will not change substantially over the duration of the rent lifespan. It then begs the question who wins in monopoly rents? The beneficiaries are the corporation's shareholders, the CEO and his team followed sometimes by the lobbyists and the government in the form of permits or other fees. Employees are neither part of this list nor the general public both victims of the corporation's market dominance. It follows that monopoly rents sustain economic inequality in society.

Nonetheless, not all market dominances are necessarily bad. Sometimes they are the outcomes of decades of research and financial resources. For example, consider the exclusive rights of pharmaceutical companies for patent drugs. Companies must recuperate their costs. Protection of intellectual property, in this case, will remain a debatable issue. Should the right to live be contingent to the ability to pay (J. E Stiglitz 2015: p. 77)? Perhaps the government should subsidize more certain drugs to make them more affordable.

Globalization

It may be helpful to remember J. Stiglitz's earlier quote that inequality is not an inevitable byproduct of globalization but macroeconomic policies. These words infer that globalization has been mismanaged. I will illustrate this case with an example.

A common starting point for tracing the evolutionary process of the diffusion and economic integration of major economic powers is the Age of Discovery between the 15th and 18th centuries. However, trade with the West officially began much earlier with the Han Dynasty in China in 130 BC and the Silk Road. It was an early form of globalization that facilitated the long-distance exchange of culture and goods.

The Silk Road remained in use until AD 1453 when the Ottoman Empire blocked the trade between China and Western Europe. tAs mentioned earlier, this blockade played an important role in the discovery of the New World. A mercantilist economy followed' and goods and services were channeled towards the Spanish and Portuguese empires.

Globalization is a complex phenomenon and the role it plays in the development of inequality has been highly debated among scholars. In public discourse, it is associated with the rise of inequality in the middle class. Is this claim justified?

It may be useful to start this evaluation with a definition of globalization. In the 2019 World Economic Forum (WEF) globalization was described as an outcome of socio-economic evolution - a phenomenon driven by technology and the movement of ideas, people and goods differentiating it from globalism which is the priority of neoliberal order over national interests.

There is no consensus on a definition of globalization. The WEF' definition of globalization is useful because it completes the IMF's in the World Economic Outlook of May 1997. This organization describes globalization as the growing economic interdependence of countries worldwide through the increasing volume and variety of cross-border transactions in goods and services and of international capital flows, and also through the more rapid and widespread diffusion of technology.

At the core of this concept lies the principle that products and services are produced where there is a comparative advantage to do so based on myriad factors such as material availability, labor force cost, capital requirement, technology, legal and political environment. This international strategy implies a mutual gain on both sides, the receiving producing organization called B, the host and the foreign ordering corporation A, the home. However, this win-win outcome is not as obvious as it may look. On the one hand, assuming that 'B' is part of Global South*, it may benefit from lower unemployment, higher living conditions and technology transfer. On the other hand, 'A' might cash in on the competitiveness of its product or service, probably get some tax advantages and a wider range of investors.

However, if this micro situation is extended to a macro or even global level, the impact is more complex. The elite and perhaps the top middle class of 'A' benefit much from globalization respectively from higher profit and lower price of goods and services. But the workers are the big losers as a result of the obvious economic policy designed to outsource their jobs. The profit made by 'B' does not necessarily improve the financial conditions of its middle class since the product is for an overseas market. Undeniably, the factory workers got a job; lower-income people have minimally benefited from globalization. While society as a whole benefits from this process of economic development, the gains are unevenly distributed. As reported in one of the American Economic Association articles, globalization has contributed much to changing the world but potentially too much to blame. Indeed, over the last 25 years, inequality between countries have decreased (A. Revenka & M. Dooley – Brookings May 2019). However, inequality within countries have increased. This is why the net benefit of globalization is often challenged. It is difficult to be totally positive about the net benefit of globalization.

Maleficent Business Practices

In another area, conventional wisdom suggests that a business cannot prosper in the long run with maleficent practices. Without expanding too much on this, these practices generally refer to purposely designed malicious activities for financial gains. They are maleficent because they operate contrary to operating procedures established for corporate entities and drive inequality by their financial ramifications. Among these practices are the various forms of distorted transfer pricing and tax havens.

Transfer Pricing

A tremendous amount of research has been done on transfer pricing including the work of Raymond Baker former President of Global Financial Integrity and Alex Cobham CEO of the Tax Justice Network. Transfer pricing is the pricing of transactions between different related units of an MNCs (multi-national corporations) operating in different countries. The price of goods and services is based on their stage of production. Transfer pricing goes back to 1995 when the Organization of Economic Cooperation and Development (OECD), following the initiative of the United States, published the transfer pricing guidelines which have been amended in the last decade. It was originally created to streamline business operations such as the reduction or exemption of customs duties. In addition transfer pricing facilitates the flow of goods, services and intangibles particularly between related corporate entities for the purpose of financial reporting, and avoidance of double taxation of profit between related corporations. However, over time and with the evolution and expansion of globalization, it has become a convenient tool for channeling wealth to some MNCs.

Transfer pricing occurring between non-related corporations trading internationally is generally fair because it is deemed to reflect the market price. In this case related companies, inflated or deflated price discrepancies with the market can be established from the paper trail of customs documents and the market price of the item.

It has been estimated that one-third of international trade takes place between related corporations. But this process to facilitate inter-related company trade is sometimes distorted in a malicious way; falsification of invoices being part of the process to escape taxation.

Mis-invoicing

Trade mis-invoicing occurs when importers and exporters deliberately falsify the stated prices on the invoices for goods they are importing or exporting as a way to illegally transfer value across international borders. Mis-invoicing as a fraudulent activity is dealt with outside of transfer pricing. In the same vein, re-invoicing is the falsification of an exporter invoice by a tax haven firm. The following diagram illustrates how this system works. A corporation in a developing country, hereafter called the importer has decided to buy 50 used cars from a firm in a developed country, the exporter. The importer requests that the exporter send the invoice for $1 million to a tax haven somewhere in the Caribbean. The tax haven re-invoices the importer at more than the market value of the cars at $1.5 million. The importer pays $1.5 million to the tax haven. This latter pays $1 million to the exporter and diverts the rest in an offshore account.

Bottom line, the importer has successfully pocketed $500,000 of which he will never be taxed. Mis-invoicing and re-invoicing are big business with many shell companies willing to help this kind of importer. In 2013, the profit from this practice on international trade is estimated to be about $700 billion per year.

According to Global Financial Integrity, there was a total value gap in reported trade between 135 developing and 36 advanced economies of $8.7 trillion. The value gap is the difference between the exporter and the imported dollar amount for the same commodity for the same date.

Graph 5.1 Mis-Invoicing and Re-Invoicing Process

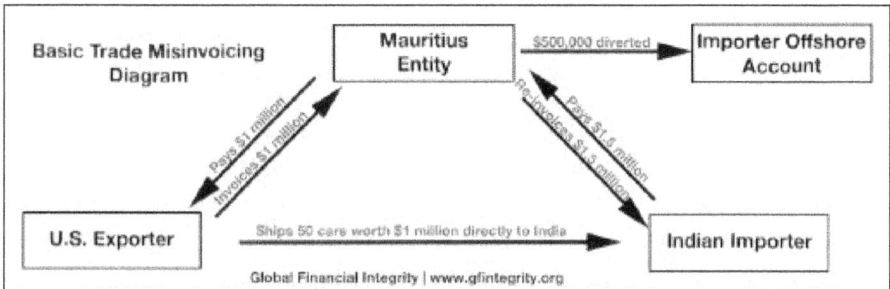

Trade mis-invoicing amounted to approximately 80% of illegal outflows from developing countries. Surely, ending this practice could provide part of the funding to address economic inequality in these societies. In terms of financial magnitude, in 2012 the Global South*, received a total of $1.3 trillion in foreign aid, investments and income from abroad. In the same year, $3.3 trillion flowed out of it. Net resource transfer for all developing countries has been mostly large and negative since the early 1980s, indicating sustained and negative outflows from the developing world (infomineo.com). Raymond Baker defined the combination of illegal financial flows and offshore tax havens as the greatest driver of inequality in developing countries.

Tax haven

An inherent characteristic of capitalism as an economic doctrine is its tendency to expand because of its simplicity and psychological attractiveness. Regardless of ethnicity, gender or geographical location, capitalism is a concept easy to understand and ethically acceptable unless prohibited by someone's religious belief. Working to earn wages or salary as part of an active workforce or running a business is a straightforward, laudable and respectable objective. Problems emerge when the financial evolution results in the establishment of certain rules that cause socioeconomic dislocation in their application.

Many eminent writers have underscored this deplorable situation. The former Secretary of Labor in the Clinton administration Robert B. Reich in *Saving Capitalism for the Many not the Few* quoted Karl Polanyi that those who argue for "*less* government" are really arguing for a *different* government – one that favors them or their patrons. But a deeper analysis of what people want has revealed that it is not only a different government but also one with equitable rules.

The 17th-century, French fabulist Jean de Lafontaine *In the Wolf and the Lamb,* rebuked that might makes right by inferring the abuse of the aristocracy. Inevitably wealth leads to power which leads to influence. But accepting this outcome would be contrary to the spirit of most constitutions of the free world which guarantee the civil liberties and equality of all citizens before the law. Institutions are created and run by people. Having a standard marketing mission statement to meet the needs of customers is a necessary and acceptable long term goal but insufficient if it is inconsistent with (inter)national laws.

Tax havens are the next vehicle of financial abuse. A lot needs to be said about the ramifications of this maleficent business practice. In the foreword to *The Hidden Wealth of Nations – The Scourge of Tax Havens* by Gabriel Zucman, Thomas Piketty states that tax havens with their financial opacity are one of the keys drivers of rising global inequality. It allows a large portion of the wealthiest groups to pay negligible taxes while the rest of us pay large taxes in order to finance the public goods and services that are indispensable for the development process. According to Zucman's conservative estimates, "eliminating the US tax revenue losses would be equivalent to an average tax increase of about 20% for all taxpayers within the top 0.1% income group". Under the cover of anonymity, billions of dollars in taxable revenue are stashed out of taxpayer home country.

The following table provides an overview of a conservative tax loss estimate calculated by continent or country.

Figure 5.2 Financial Wealth in Tax Havens in 2014

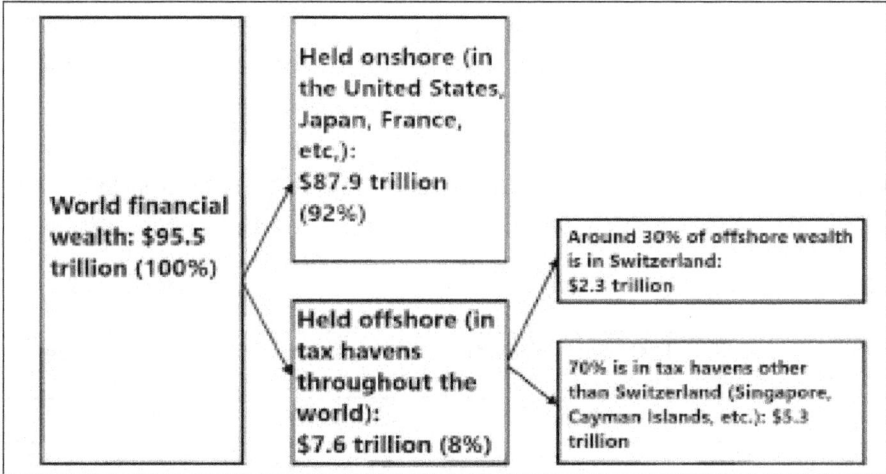

Reproduced with Permission. Source: Gabriel Zucman - The hidden Wealth of Nations

Globally, it is estimated that $200 billion in tax was lost in 2014. Where does this amount come from?

G. Zucman calculated that 8% of household wealth worldwide is held in tax havens. Household wealth is defined as the sum of all the bank deposits, portfolios of stocks and bonds, shares in mutual funds, and insurance contracts held by individuals throughout the world, net of any debt. Based on information published by the Federal Reserve in the United States and the Office for National Statistics in the United Kingdom, the global household wealth amounted to $95.5 trillion in 2014, surely more at the time of writing this book; hence the total amount of $7.6 trillion in the second column of Figure 5.2. This amount of money held in offshore account may look conservative base on different approach and method of calculation. Based on a study carried out by the economist James Henry for the Tax Justice Network, he estimates that the global private financial wealth held in offshore accounts - excluding non-financial assets such as real estate, gold, yachts and racehorses – to be between $21 and $32 trillion.

As per Figure 5.3 continental Europe and Asia seem to have had a big hit followed by the United States. However, Russia and the Gulf Countries have held the biggest share of their household income in tax havens. Considering the stiff sanctions on tax evasion by the Russian Federation, the relevant amount may have been collected by now. With respect to the Gulf Countries, they do not tax income or inheritances. The third column amounts excluding Russia and the Gulf countries are not small amounts. Putting this number in perspective, for example in Canada, the revenue loss of $6 Billion is close to the 2014 Gross Domestic Product of one of its provinces - Prince Edward Island (~ $5.2 Billion).

Table 5.3 Offshore Wealth and Tax Evasion

	Offshore Wealth	Share of Fin.	Tax Revenue Loss
	($ Billion)	Wealth held	($Billion)
Europe	2,600	10%	78
United States	1,200	4%	35
Asia	1,300	4%	34
Latin America	700	22%	21
Africa	500	30%	14
Canada	300	9%	6
Russia	200	52%	1

Gulf Countries	800	57%	0
Total	7,600	8%	190

Reproduced with permission. Source: The Hidden Wealth of Nations.

It may be of interest to briefly review the engineering of this system that facilitates the wealthy of many nations not paying their fair share of tax.

Participants open accounts in Switzerland, Singapore, Cayman Islands, Panama, Luxembourg and the like to access the customized services that these countries provide for {tax evasion}. Despite this apparent multitude of tax heavens, it would be destructive for them to compete with each other. They each specialized in a component of the wide range of the wealth management processes. Switzerland is the custodian of securities; Luxembourg specializes in mutual funds; Hedge funds are kept in the Cayman Islands. All funds are taxed where they are located, hence the benefit of certain countries with low tax rates.

How could this situation have gone for so long? Zucman has stressed a troubling fact. The foreign wealth held by Switzerland increased by 15% after the 2009 G20 meeting ending banking secrecy. It stood at $2.3 trillion in 2015. Never underestimate the creativity of the Swiss bankers for ignoring regulations. They have transformed a difficulty to an opportunity.

It is not in the scope of my review to go through the various corrective measures taken. Nonetheless, substantial progress has been made in the long path towards eliminating tax-havens. A case in point is the Foreign Account Tax Compliance Act {FATCA} which requires an automatic exchange of data between foreign banks and the Internal Revenue Service. This law stipulates a 30% tax penalty for the refusal of foreign banks to disclose US citizen accounts. As can be seen, trillions of dollars that could be used to redress inequality are diverted from governments only to evaporate in tax havens and be absorbed in illegal business practices.

Rent-seeking, patent protection, occupational licensing, transfer pricing manipulation, mis-invoicing, tax haven and various forms of accommodation to reduce competition take a slice of the tax base. I was not able to find a realistic estimate of the cost of all these activities but in the case of occupational licensing it results in 2.85 million fewer jobs in the United States with an annual cost to consumers of $203 billion (Kleiner, Kruger and Mas 2011). Nobel laureate economist Angus Deaton warned that rent-seeking could kill capitalism. Rent seekers do not produce anything, in fact, they reduce economic growth. In *Capitalism Alone* Branco Milanovic argues in a similar way by saying "it is the reneging on some crucial aspects of this implicit value system, namely a movement towards the creation of a self-perpetuating upper class and polarization between the elites and the rest that represents the most important threat to the longer-term viability of liberal capitalism. This threat is a danger both to the system own survival and to the general attractiveness of the model to the rest of the world".

In the preceding paragraphs, the focus was on the wealthy not behaving as good (corporate) citizens. Let's now shift the focus on the middle class.

Several reasons justify this shift. First, people of this stratum are the biggest victims of inequality, one of my main considerations. Second, they represent slightly more than 50% percent of the world's population and globally will reach 4 billion by the end of 2020 and 5.3 billion by 2030 and with enough discretionary expenditures to meet the criteria of the middle class. On the trajectory of socio-economic development, they are unlikely to fall into extreme poverty barring a major economic catastrophe. The middle class is preceded by the wealthy elite and followed by the poor and the extremely poor stratum whose household spending was less than $1.90 per person per day. The middle-class household spending was in the range of $11 - $110 per day in 2011 purchasing power parity.

Table 5.4 Partial Middle Class Potential Market

China	India	India	USA
2030 Potential Market ($trillion)	14.1	12.3	15.9

This profile of the middle class made by Brookings scholars also has a few interesting characteristics. They have enough discretionary income to buy durable goods, entertainment and vacations. Globally, this stratum is rapidly growing. While every second one person escapes extreme poverty, five persons join the middle class.

The ramifications of this middle-class growth are enormous from an economic and political standpoint. This class is the engine of the economy not only because the magnitude of their spending is greater than the one of the elite class but also by the nature of these expenses as described earlier. Moreover, the sheer magnitude of this social stratum requires politicians to listen to their voices. In this context, the middle class can make a difference in the political future of a country.

Considering the economic gap between the upper and the middle class, recent political events suggest that this latter stratum felt abandoned by their leader. They reflect a clear picture of economic inequality. Access to education, employment affordable housing and healthcare are on the top of their preoccupation. Current findings of OECD* reveal that the top 10% in the income distribution holds almost half of the total wealth, while the bottom 40% accounts for only 3%.

Reducing the gap between the upper and middle classes is the right thing to do morally and economically speaking. Everyone benefits from the economic development of this stratum.

Endnotes – Part V

5a. Spanish Netherlands was the name for the Habsburg Netherlands ruled by the Spanish branch of the Habsburgs. For a long time, the Netherlands were part of the Spanish empire. In 1588, the Netherlands became a republic independent of Spain.

5b. Werner Sombart divided capitalism into different stages: (1) proto-capitalist society from the early middle ages up to 1500 AD, (2) early capitalism in 1500–1800, (3) the heyday of capitalism from 1800 to the First World War, and (4) late capitalism since then. Werner Sombart. Modern Capitalism. Publisher K A Nitz. November 29/2019

5c. Events of the 20th century have shown that the government must sometimes intervene in the market to establish an equitable playing field for the actors. Hence, the case can be made that certain elements of socialism can be found in modern capitalism, notably in Canada and Northern Europe.

5d. Computing 'Real Value' Over Time with a Conversion between U.K. Pounds and U.S. Dollars, 1791 to Present.

Source: measuringworth.com

5e. Coined by Alan Greenspan, the former Chair of the Federal Reserve of the United States, irrational exuberance refers to investor enthusiasm that drives asset prices up to levels that are not supported by reliable data supporting the stability and health of the asset.

5f. The Long Depression was a worldwide price and economic recession beginning in 1873 and running according to some economists either until 1879 or according to others until 1896.

5g. Global South is the name used by the World Bank and other governmental organizations to designate newly industrialized or in the process of industrializing countries. They are largely considered by freedom indices to have a lower level of democracy and have a history of colonialism by Northern, often European states. (See Map in Appendix I)

5h. OECD (2019). Under Pressure: The Squeezed Middle Class, OECD Publishing. Paris. https://doi.org/10.1787/689afed1-en

PART VI
Economic and Political Dimensions of Inequality

Almost all of the revolutions which have changed the aspects of nations have been made to consolidate or to destroy inequality. Remove the secondary causes which have produced the great convulsion of the world, and you will almost always find the principle of inequality at the bottom. Either the poor have attempted to plunder the rich, or the rich to slave the poor. If then a state of society can ever be found in which every man should have something to keep, and little to take from others, much will have been done for the peace of the world.

Alexis de Tocqueville –
Democracy in America, Volume II

Introduction

Why do people behave differently when they attain power, prestige and wealth? More to the point, why self-interest often overrides human values?

I was inclined to seek the expertise of psychologists specialized in the lore of human instinct. However, the craving for prestige and wealth which characterize the upper class of most nations is unfriendly to any constraint or limitation. I would then had to add a plethora of other experts including political scientists, sociologists and economists. This is to say that greed, the outcome of power, prestige and wealth, and one of the drivers of inequality is a multifaceted issue. It is pertinent to raise this question now when many fundamental issues have been addressed. The complex ramification of inequality can better be articulated and understood.

Let's proceed with some illustrations of inequality and the solutions considered. Originally this book was entitled *Greed - the Trilogy of Power, Prestige and Property.* As mentioned above, inequality would be an outcome of greed which is not always the case. Although I have taken this position particularly in the analysis of the chiefdom polity and the role of the Big Man, I now think that this approach could be expanded based on the evolutionary phases of political structures from egalitarian, ranked to stratified societies. Recall a ranked society is a social structure in which positions of valued status are limited so that not everyone with the requisite talent and qualifications can reach them (M. F. Fried 1967: p.109). This definition means that there is a systemic and structured inequality across groups in their access to resources and opportunities.

I have profiled the socioeconomic ramifications of inequality at each stage of the cultural evolution. However, beside differentiating economic, social and political inequality little has been said at the scope and definitional level. For example, is inequality a particular trait of human or common in the biosphere? If it is found elsewhere, what is its intrinsic nature and how did it emerge? The reality is that inequality, as a multi-dimensional concept, covers many bases. This explains why there has been so much analysis of this subject and why it is so difficult to managing it.

The study of inequality is sometimes embedded in the study of poverty although the latter is broader than the former. Various forms of inequality exist in society. Economic inequality which involves the differential position based on income and wealth. This latter infers wealth accumulation. Social inequality (gender, class, age, race, sexual orientation, immigrants) refers to the status or perception of members of these groups by society. Political inequality is the unequal influence over decisions made by political bodies and the unequal outcomes of those decisions

Wealth accumulation or the dominance of the elite has attracted a lot of attention in the last decades perhaps due to the 2008 financial meltdown, despite the housing market recovery. Understandably, the narrative about economic inequality encompasses more than wealth because wealth is derived from (passive) income. However, wealth inequality gives a more accurate picture of the economic class differentiation of society (T. Piketty 2014: 274-8) based not only on income distribution but also on the cultural acceptance of the concept of saving. There is a need for a clear understanding of the wealth-building mechanism and the roles of policymakers and society.

Wealth can be defined as the total accumulated tangible and non-tangible assets on a net basis. This includes liquid cash, real estate holdings, intellectual properties, savings and investments minus any short and long-term debts, personal and commercial. Income can mean different things depending on the end-use. But for the sake of simplicity, income is a regular flow of cash from salary or wages, investments or private or social benefit income. Fixed and variable living expenses reflect a person or household's lifestyle including consumption and saving. Loans can cause an artificially inflated lifestyle!

The Economic Dimension

Illustration I

Sheffer el al. determined that in human societies the elite has the lion's share of the wealth and in nature, a small fraction of species dominates the biomass. Based on data gathered in the Amazon rainforest, roughly 1% of the tree species account for 50% of the total stored carbon. As seen in the following graph, the similarity between human societies and nature is striking.

Figure 6.0 Comparison of Society with Nature*

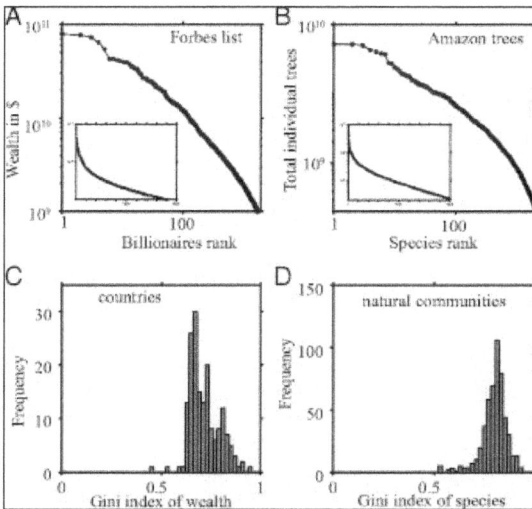

The left side shows inequality in society and the right side show inequality in nature. The upper panels illustrate the similarity between the wealth distribution of the world's 1,800 billionaires (A) and the abundance distribution among the most common trees in the Amazon forest (B). The lower panels illustrate inequality in nature and society more systematically, comparing the Gini index of wealth in countries (C) and the Gini index of abundance in a large set of natural communities (D).

The similarity of the pattern of inequality between the human species and nature is astonishing. It is generally accepted that 1% of the population owns 50% of the wealth. In Nature, 1% of the trees account for 50% of the total stored carbon. But there is a common belief that order and balance of the ecosystem are the hallmarks of Nature. In the words of Marcus Aurelius, the last of the five good emperors of Rome, "Nature insists upon whatever benefits the whole system". Implicit in this quote is a fair distribution of resources for the benefit of the whole community. Nature confirms that wealth inequality is inevitable.

The comparative analysis of the profile of nature and society eliminates many misconceptions and reinforces realities that may be difficult to admit. According to Sheffer et al, the drivers of inequality are the particular traits and the competitive powers among the actors. In nature, some species may have traits that make them prone to dominance. In society, stamina and business acumen make a difference among actors. In a nutshell, traits, power and chance are the drivers of wealth inequality in society. Wealth leads to power which facilitates access to the means to increase wealth. In nature, the population composition is not homogenous. The notion of abundance particularly in sub-species could be an unbalanced issue but this was dealt with naturally in the analyzed communities. Dominant species are more vulnerable to the vagaries of the environment e-g hurricane, earthquake.

Figure 6.1 Inequality Unifying Mechanisms and their Drivers

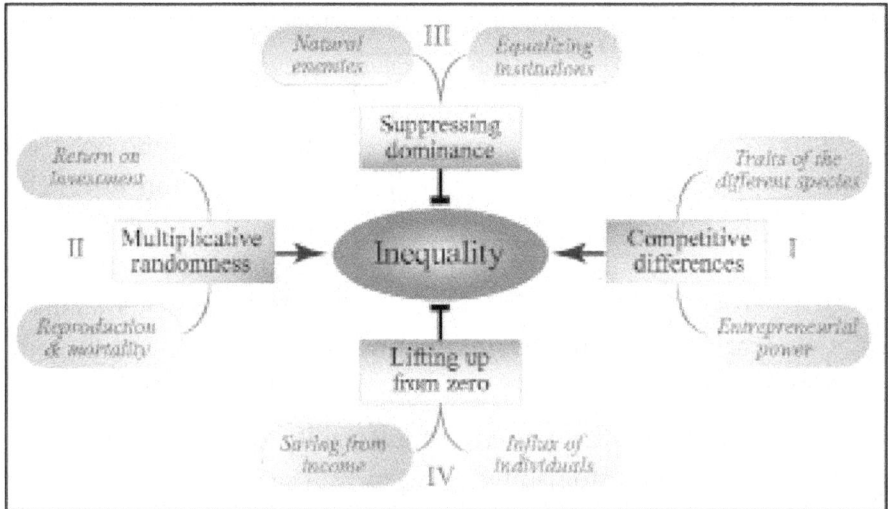

Chance is another driver of inequality. Business and financial transactions have gains and losses which have a multiplicative effect. Similarly, in nature, variations in weather and natural enemies such as diseases have a multiplicative effect on the population size of all species. Multiplicative gains and losses follow a Bell or Gaussian curve distribution. The extent of inequality depends on the size of the dispersion of the distribution of the gains and losses. Extreme inequality is the result of the expansion of multiplicative random processes.

As illustrated in Figure 6.1 suppressing dominance and lifting the majority affected by inequality from zero are Sheffer et al' two strategies to reduce inequality. In Nature, this can be achieved by increasing the population size. In society, more savings from middle-class people can reduce the previous upper-class dominance. Conceivably people do not save for the future because of high consumption or because they rely on social welfare for their future needs. It is an established fact that the wealthy save and invest not necessarily because they can but because it is in their culture. The propensity to spend is less in rich than in poor people. Permanent accumulation resulting from return on investment, which is negligible or absent in the lower class, keeps wealth concentration in the elite class.

Rolling the dice in a small sample of people that each of them was given a fixed amount of money at the start will result in only one of them winning all the money. Statistics application results could be very surprising!

Repression of dominance and leveling society is a mechanism to remedy inequality. In nature, this correction is made automatically. The most abundant species becomes victims of natural enemies and die thereby permitting other species to share the resources. It would be unrealistic and amoral to wish this to happen in human society. However, war and natural disasters have the same effect but only temporarily since inequality returns to its former level preceding these events.

In conclusion, Sheffer et al suggests implementing a global-wealth-equalizing institution to alleviate inequality through a taxation system of inheritance and property rights.

Illustration II

As an example of the ubiquity of inequality is it follows the Power Law. This latter means a relative change in one quantity which results in a proportional relative change in another. This can be seen in the number of copies sold of bestseller books and the 1% rule in the internet culture (only 1% of the users of a website actively create new content, while the 99% are only readers). Another area of application comes from the 80-20 rule. Known as the Pareto principle, it means that for many events roughly 80% of the effects come from 20% of the cause. Inequality is so common and complex I believe it is helpful to understand the underlying mechanism of its functioning and the required policy decision for those affected by it.

Illustration III

I will elaborate on the nature of inequality by another mathematical approach. A fractal is a pattern or system that repeats itself at a different scale. At first glance, the design may look complex but it is simply an effect of repetition of a simple process. The term fractal coined by the mathematician Benoit Mandelbrot derives from the Latin verb *frangere*, meaning to break into, to create irregular fragments like a broken stone. Mandelbrot defined fractal as a "shape made of parts similar to the whole in some way." An example would be the human brain which is comprised of approximately 100 billion neurons with about 100 trillion synapses connecting them to each other. Another example is the circulatory system with its arteries and veins etc. Fractals in nature figure in trees, clouds and mountains.

It may be helpful to describe the fractal development process to understand its correlation with inequality. For fractals constructed algorithmically way, also known as deterministic fractals, the functioning of the iterative system requires a generator as the main design element (B. B. Mandelbrot 1983: p.62). After the first repetition, this generator is replaced by multiple initiators having the same design characteristics as the generator. When the system repeats itself these initiators become generators on their own with the same design. Deterministic fractals look the same regardless of scale every time the system is reproduced. In other words, self-similarity is the basic concept in this repetition. As can be seen in the following image successive repetitions of the system can produce a very complex design that is simple for the experienced observer.

Figure 6.2 The Mandelbrot fractal set

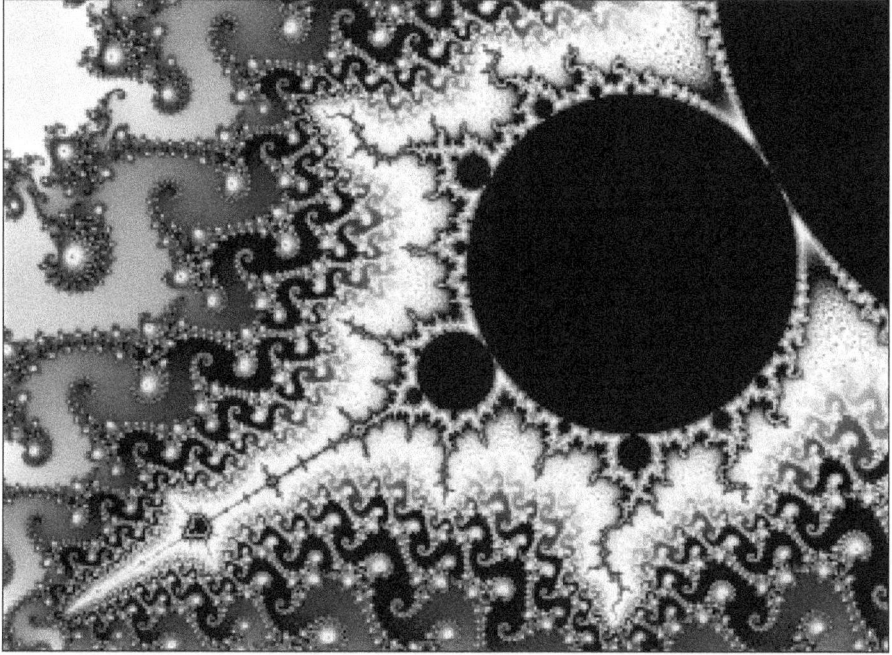

The similarity between fractal and income inequality within each decile is astonishing. Most social inequalities are derived from a differential treatment affecting a particular layer of a country's society. This is true regardless of whether a country's economy is developed, developing or less developed. This differential treatment replicates, like a virus, to all layers of this society. This is part and parcel of humanity's socioeconomic history which started as (mostly) egalitarian followed by ranked then stratified. Special treatment and benefits were attributed to members of the last two stages of this cultural evolution. With the passage of time, this tolerated attribution became the norm reversed by some revolutions but furtively re-emerged as time went by.

Today, income and wealth inequality resides not only in the elite, middle and lower classes but also within classes. There is a great discrepancy between the fortune of the top 1%, the .1% and the 0.01% of the upper class. The World Top Income Database indicates that the 2012 average household in the top 1% was $1,264,065 and $6,373,782 for the top 0.1%. The bottom 90% of household income figures at $30,438 which means that people in the 10% have a higher household income. The pattern is quite clear; It's a similar inter and intra economic class repetition that by definition is a fractal. This confirms that inequality has a fractal-like structure.

Illustration IV

The growth of wealth inequality in many countries has led to the development of a number of theoretical tools to describe wealth inequality. The conventional assumption has always been to control the distribution of income through taxation or other macroeconomic policy instruments to regulate wealth distribution. These are useful in identifying the driving forces of wealth inequality and the effectiveness of measures to calibrate wealth inequality to prevent long term economic and social structure instabilities. Scholars like T. Piketty have underscored the divergent trend of wealth inequality and personal savings. In most western countries where wealth inequality had dramatically increased during the last three decades, personal savings had substantially decreased. It appears that any policy invoked to increase saving from the second to the tenth decile should reduce wealth inequalities.

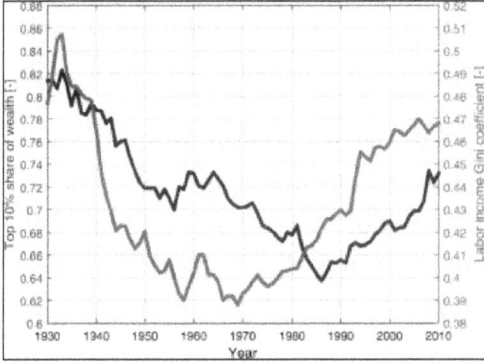

Berman et al took up this challenge by reviewing the income distribution and wealth in the United States from 1930 to 2010. They were able to describe the effects of personal savings and income distribution on wealth inequality.

The Wealth (black) and labor income (grey) inequality (pre-taxes) in the US for 1930–2010. The wealth inequality is quantified by the share of wealth owned by the richest 10% of the population. The income inequality is measured using the Gini Index. Data is taken from Piketty and Saez and Saez and Zucman. https://doi.org/10.1371/journal.pone.0154196.g001

In the above graph, wealth and income inequalities are closely related because labor is a major source of wealth at the beginning of the accumulation process. However, despite the relationship between them, they differ considerably. This differentiation is important since changes affecting one may not affect the other and vice versa. It is also evident that wealth inequality is always higher than labor inequality due to income generated from wealth or capital income such as rents, dividends or royalties and the increase in asset values. Despite the magnitude of labor income in the national account, only a small fraction of it contributed to accumulated personal wealth due to taxation and spending.

The calculation of the correlation between wealth and income inequalities in the US, led to a moderate level because of the differences between them. This imperfect correlation implies that the effect of controlling the income distribution on the wealth distribution is limited. It also suggests that the recent wealth inequality surge in the US is only partially related to the income inequality surge as shown in Figure 6.4. This means some factors may have played a major role while others played a secondary role in the structure of this inequality. This has led to the development of a mathematical model to provide a theoretical framework to quantify the contributions of the factors affecting wealth inequality and to offer a test-bed for predicting the effect of various policies on wealth inequality.

The Wealth (black) and disposable income (grey) distributions representing the distributions from which the initial individual wealth and income values are drawn in the model. The wealth and income were normalized for proper display. These distributions depict the realistic 1930 wealth and income distributions in the US.

Based on this model, it was found that the dependence of savings on income is due to the tendency of individuals with higher income to save a larger fraction of it. In the same way, the dependence of capital value change on wealth is mainly due to different asset classes owned by wealthier individuals compared to poorer individuals, in addition to better terms of investments and investment possibilities accessible to rich individuals but inaccessible to the poor.

Figure 6.4 The Initial Distributions of Wealth and Income

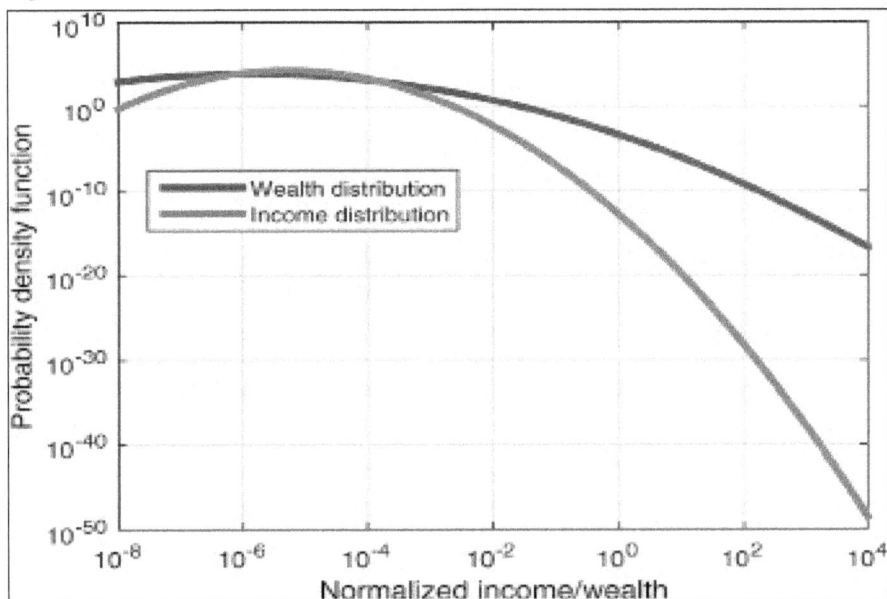

Increased savings lead to decreased wealth inequality. This confirms that the inception of the wealth inequality surge in the US can be primarily associated with the decrease in personal savings. The model is sufficiently robust to be used for predicting wealth and income inequality. This can be seen in the following graph showing the high correlation between the model results and the historical reconstructed Gini index (.94)

The dark and grey lines represent the historical wealth inequality behavior and the model behavior for the historical values of the parameters, respectively. The black line depicts the model results when the savings in the period 1980–2010 are taken as constant and equal to 10%, while the other model parameters are considered with their historical values. The dotted gray line separates the calculation using historical parameter values and with the altered parameters.

Figure 6.5 Effect of Personal Savings on Wealth Inequality

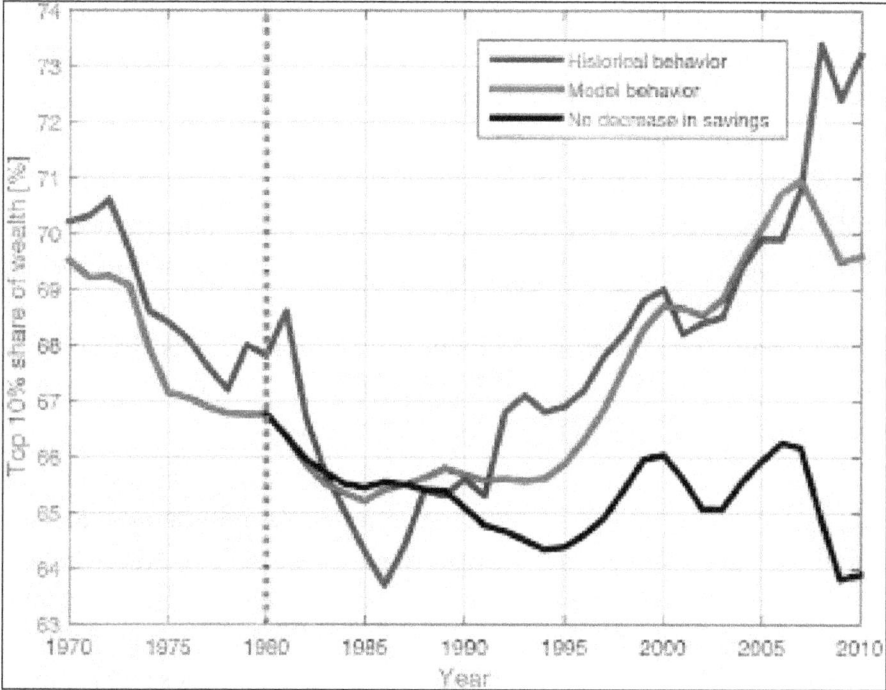

The observed effect may seem counterintuitive due to the effect of the non-uniform distribution of savings. It may seem that the rich use their money to earn larger returns and the poor have no savings with which they can produce returns or eliminate debt. However, the imperfect correlation between wealth and income allows for the possibility of savings to reduce the relative gap between deciles. These results do not imply that extremely poor individuals can become rich if they work and save a large portion of their income. It only accounts for the possibility of mainly middle and higher wealth deciles to narrow the relative gap between their wealth and the wealth of richer individuals. This is the effect observed in the above figures, driven by personal savings.

The substantial effect of personal saving on wealth inequality is well known. Let's now review the effect of income tax and income inequality on wealth inequality more specifically. The consensus is that increasing income tax progressively contributes to lowering wealth inequality. And, increasing the average tax rate reduces disposable income, effectively reducing savings. But, increasing progressive income tax rates does reduce income inequality. In short, taxation reduces savings but redistributes income more equally. The bottom line is that increasing progressive income tax creates a trade-off between the effect of the decreased savings and the decreased income inequality.

The distribution of income tax has a small effect on the dynamics of wealth inequality due to the imperfect correlation mentioned earlier. Similarly, changing the income distribution has only a small effect on wealth inequality. These implications are valid as long as the correlation between wealth and income remains low. As income inequality increases, this correlation is also likely to increase.

I must emphasize that this model and analysis were conducted for the United States only. Furthermore, inheritance, inheritance tax and population growth were not incorporated in the model. Nevertheless, the model does provide a realistic tool to estimate the effect of income tax and personal savings on wealth inequality. Wealth inequality in most developed countries has gradually increased since the 1980s and resulted in a decrease in personal savings particularly between the highest deciles and the middle class, which is expected to continue to grow in the US.

Another noteworthy fact is the limitation of progressive income tax to reduce wealth inequality. On the one hand, when income tax is increased, the top earners, who are not necessarily the wealthiest individuals in the population, have a greater difficulty accumulating wealth. On the other hand, it barely affects the wealthiest individuals. Therefore, an increase in income tax might widen deepen the wealth gap. When decreasing income tax, the opposite effect will therefore occur. In addition, progressive taxation, which might have a significant effect on the distribution of income, will also have a small effect on wealth inequality. Therefore, adjusting progressive income tax rates or changing the average income tax to reduce wealth inequality in developed countries are likely to be ineffective.

Are there any potential solutions to address this issue? Many attempts have been made by many governments around the world to alleviate this dangerous imbalance between the haves and the haves-not. The difficulty resides in finding a permanent solution to a moving target. No society can flourish and be happy if most of its members are poor and miserable. This was the sentiment of Adam Smith, the father of modern capitalism. A good starting point would be to eliminate the maleficent practices and tax havens. The funds recuperated therefrom could be used where needed to reduce economic inequality. In tandem with this initiative, an optimal rate of inequality can be used to monitor the expansion or contraction of the economy. More on this concept in the next few pages.

I have extensively described the origin and development of inequality and presented the analogy of the forest ecosystem. Inequality per se is not the challenge. The problem arises when the discrepancy between the different layers of society become out of proportion. Based on the 2019 Oxfam report, 26 of the richest people on Earth had almost the same net worth as the poorest half of the world's population. To be more precise $8.5 trillion own by the richest people on the planet slightly exceed half of the world's wealth estimated at $16.7 trillion.

The magnitude of this disproportion also creates political inequality. The political power of the elite is significant and can adversely affect the needs of the rest of society. Political inequality is another kind of inequality that needs to be controlled.

An egalitarian society should not be sought because it is a utopia. Recent research has revealed that a classless society is a negation of reality. Upper and lower classes will always exist. I believe the emotional and economic challenges of a classed society reside not in this classification but in the limitations that it creates because of the imbalance in resource distribution which in turn affects social standing.

Austrian historian Walter Scheidel calls lethal pandemics the fourth horsemen of leveling, the other three being mobilization warfare, trans-formative revolution and state collapse (W. Schneidel 2017 pp. 335). The Black Death pandemic of the middle age had a substantial leveling effect that did occur reverse itself until a century later. On the one hand, the upper-class members feel they deserve their spontaneous or gener-ational wealth because of their hard work and a sense of corporate and global responsibilities. Indeed, many billionaires have created or support philanthropic organization; ignore for the moment how it really costs their corporations. On the other hand, the lower class members feel powerless to improve their status and climb the social ladder because the rungs between the financial levels are too far apart. This situation threatens social peace. People feel that their governments have aban-doned them and became predisposed to change. This is a legitimate democratic option. There is a large body of literature about the ascen-dance of populism around the world. Dis-satisfaction is the source of it. Dissensions can become toxic particularly in a period of low economic performance.

Signatories of the United Nations' Declaration of Human Rights all have laws affirming the equality and freedom of their citizens and their right to pursue the full measure of happiness. However, while everyone is equal under the law, economic inequality remains an impediment to that goal. Surely, different people have different skills*, talents and capacities to work allowing them to make a different and unequal contribution to society and therefore are compensated accordingly. Inequality generated by productive activity is considered fair. Problems emerge from devia-tions to this principle such as arbitrary privilege in the form of access to information resulting in financial gains. An experiment reported in the Proceeding of the National Academy of Science of the United States of America has revealed a significant neuronal response to "deviations" from the distribution of income that was proportional to work effort (Alexander et al. PNAS 2014).

It is one thing to describe an existing problem and quite another to propose a practical solution. Humanity has been struggling with all forms of inequality for millennia. Most social scientists agree that re-making society egalitarian is at best a fantasy, a fairy tale not worth pursuing. So how much inequality is unfair? As a starting point let's look at the concept of fairness in the context of income-distribution. Money is a means to an end. The lack of income, not because of one's own doing, covers many grounds. Although the following analysis looks at both wealth and income, data limitations for the former makes it less thorough than the latter.

A couple of examples will facilitate the understanding of fairness used in this book.

In a 2014 study of 1600 people in 44 countries including the United States, respondents were asked how much they thought the pay ratio of CEOs to low-skill factory workers was and how much it should be. The actual ratio at the time of the study varied from a top 354 for the USA and a low 28 for Poland. However, the response from the interviewees to the first part of the question ranged between 4.3 for Norway to 40 for Australia. With respect to the second part of the question (What should the ratio be?), their answers varied between 2.2 for Sweden to 8.3 for Australia. Obviously, people substantially underestimate the actual pay inequality.

In another study, 5,500 people were randomly selected out of a population of 1 million Americans arranged to be gender-balanced. They were presented with three pie charts showing different percentages of wealth distribution of the five quintiles of different unidentified societies. One pie mimicked an egalitarian society with five equal slices of the pie representing the five quintiles. The second one representing the five quintiles portrays but with unequal slices representing the wealth distribution of a particular country around the globe. Similarly, the third pie represents the slightly unequal wealth distribution of another country. The people were asked to choose the society in which they would rather live, unaware of which slice would find themselves in that society. This, in essence, is an application of the Veil of Ignorance* of the late political philosopher John Rawls. The people overwhelmingly selected the slightly unequal society regardless of sex. This choice seems to suggest that Americans prefer some inequality to perfect equality.

Fairness has different meanings depending on the field of application. In our economic context, it rests on three principles: equality, proportionality and arbitrariness respectively, meaning equal pay for an equal amount of the same work. As a result, proportionality means you earn more for doing more. Arbitrariness, as one of the basic foundations of fairness, rejects the baseless choice of candidates or requires solid pieces of evidence in support of decision making or it would violate the first principle.

A broader view of fairness would proscribe advantages or privileges to any particular business. This is important because leveling the market this way through the pricing strategy would positively impact the consumer. Fairness is a good companion to capitalism.

As can be seen, inequality means many things depending on the context. The magnitude and characteristics of the inequality problem require a global approach. It is evident that developed and developing countries require a flexible framework fair to each economic stratum of their respective societies.

Maleficent business practices were identified as contributing to inequality. I have also pointed out the negative impact of globalization in both developed and developing countries. Technological development is another factor which has enormously affected the middle class. Repetitive work, formerly performed by less educated people has been replaced by automation. Finding an economic solution to these categories of challenges requires policy changes, retraining to alleviate the burden of inequality on the lower classes. A good starting point would be to reduce the political power of the elite by means of policy and regulatory changes. The voices of professional associations and trade unions should also be heard to provide another balancing weight to adjust the economic system. This would reduce the farming out or export of some of the middle-class jobs.

The goal is to reinforce the need for reducing the magnitude of the gap between the 1% and the lower layers of society. The urgency for initiating this change can be found in the statistics. In Canada, the average net worth of the 87 wealthiest families from 1999 to 2016 amounts to

$259 billion almost equivalent to what everyone in Newfoundland and Labrador, Prince Edward Island and New Brunswick collectively owns, that is $269 billion*. Between 2012 and 2016, the average net worth of these families rose by 37% while the net worth of the middle-class families increased by 16% over the same period. As a result, Canada's wealthiest 87 families hold 4,448 times more wealth than the average Canadian family. In the United States, the gap is even bigger. Of the richest people, 10% control almost 70% of the country's total wealth. In 2016 the top 1% of household net worth exceeded the average net worth by 15,045 times. This is the magnitude of economic inequality that needs to be adjusted.

Where do we go from here?

I have stated many times that eliminating economic inequality is a utopian dream. That said, many strategies can be implemented to economically elevate the middle class, the largest stratum of most societies. In PART V, I have provided the means for doing so through stricter monitoring of rent-seeking, globalization policies and enforcement of tax haven regulations.

The basis of this approach rests on Adam Smith's principles of taxation: fairness, certainty, convenience and efficiency. As the father of capitalism, he surely knew that no government could run a country without the equitable tax contribution of its citizens and commercial regulations.

But complementary to the above strategies, there is a need to institutionalize the monitoring of inequality like it is done for other ailments of the economy such as inflation and unemployment. The inverted U-shaped graph shows the variation of income at different stages of economic development. A low level of income inequality reflects an inefficient economy that is the workforce is not fully utilized and the Gini Coefficient is high. As the economy performs better, more people are employed and the income expands. However, there is a level of inequality, called the optimal rate of inequality (ORI), which maximizes both the economic growth and the workforce's income. The ideal then for any country is to strive to maintain its optimal rate of inequality.

Simon Kuznets, a Nobel Prize-winning economist developed this hypothesis in 1954. He raised the question "Does inequality in the distribution of income increase or decrease in the course of a country's economic growth?" This was echoed by the labor economist Richard Freeman who wrote in 2011:" Is there a level of inequality that optimizes economic growth, stability, and shared prosperity?   Yes. The relation between inequality and economic outcomes follows an inverted U-shaped graph so that increases in inequality improve economic performance up to the optimum and then reduce it."

Figure 6.6 Kuznets Inverted U-shaped graph.

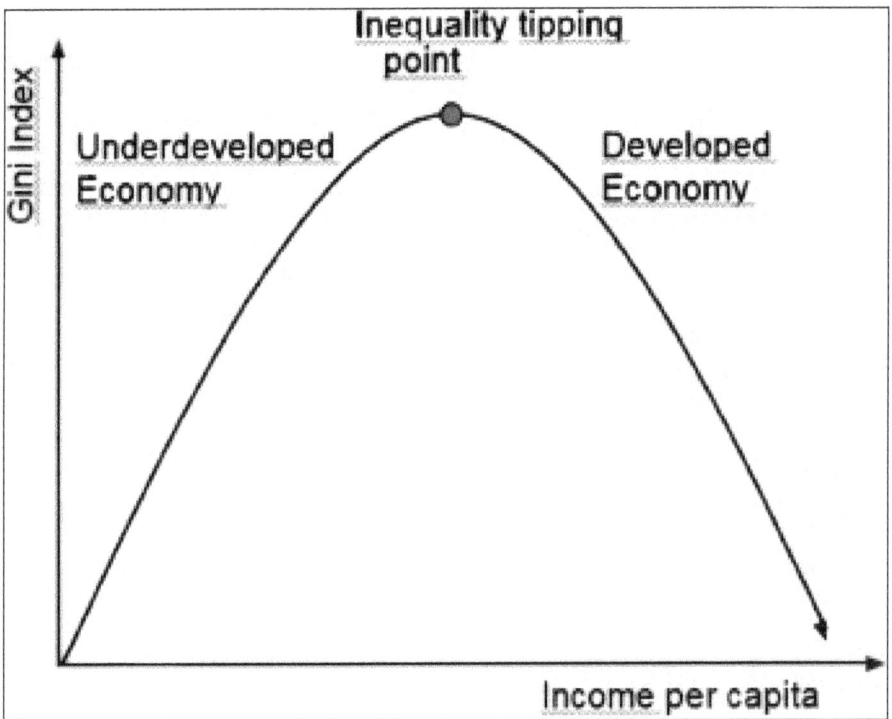

A proliferation of papers and books have surged in the current decade including "The Optimal Rate of Inequality: A framework for the relationship between income inequality and economic growth" Jorge A. Charles-Coll, 2010); Is there an Ideal Amount of Inequality by Venkat

Venkatsubramanian, 2017 followed by *How much Inequality is Fair?* *Mathematical Principles of a Moral, Optimal, and Stable Capitalist Society*; The Optimum level of Income inequality: Evidence from Panel Data, 2018 by Syed Yusul Saadat, 2018 and many others. These publications stress the need to address inequality on a scientific and robust basis.

Although each of these studies has its own merit, Saadat's study has caught my curiosity. Based on an econometric model, his study has revealed that the optimal level of income inequality occurs at the Gini value of .383691. The author posits that "lower levels of income inequality may lead to higher saving and greater capital accumulation which may result in higher growth". His statement is consistent with the dependence of savings on income as shown earlier in Illustration IV in Part VI.

Inequality is either tolerated or despised. The advocates of the former see in it a constructive way to enhance competition and motivate people to get to a better place in society. The advocates of the latter see the disastrous impact of inequality on the lower classes and the overall economy. At the risk of repeating myself, I have argued many times against the magnitude of inequality in our society. The Gini value of .383691 calculated by the author rests on a strong foundation and may set a benchmark but for a particular period of time and place due to the prevailing socio-economic and political circumstances. However, I see ORI as a moving target. As such, I suggest the establishment of a permanent and apolitical agency to institutionalize this task. That said, this new agency has a lot of work ahead to build the credibility of the Kuznets number by submitting realistic projections supported by sound economic policies.

The socioeconomic and technological environment of our current time is different than three of four decades ago taking into account automation, artificial intelligence, globalization and labor force skill diversity. However, while economic inequality between countries is on a downtrend, inequality within countries is still on the rise. Milanovic describes this event as a second Kuznets curve (B. 2016: pp. 50-57). According to various sources, the Gini Index for the United States in 2019 varies between .38 and .48. In Kuznets's inverted U-shaped concept, the former number would be similar to Saat's ORI study if his model was updated to include the data of the most recent years. However, if the latter number is considered, a decrease in inequality will occur when the economy grows. It is difficult to expect such a scenario on a short-term basis because of the wealth concentration in the elite and their power, the productivity and the political environment. Recall Scheidel's hypothesis for leveling inequality. Warfare and pandemic were two of the four horsemen of the apocalypse. There is no war on the horizon but the COVID-19 pandemic is affecting the demographic profile of many countries and their productivity. The many forms of financial relief programs provided by the government of some developed countries may reduce the economic class differentiation profile but on a short term basis. Different and robust macropolicies are required for the long term. Permanent financial incentives cannot be the solution.

The Political Dimension

"What is most important for democracy is not that great fortunes should not exist, but that great fortunes should not remain in the same hands, in that way there are rich men, but they do not form a class.

Alexis de Tocqueville*-
Democracy in America – Volume I

At the end of 2017, of 167 countries with a population greater than 500,000, 57% were democracies of some sort, 28% were anocracies, and 13% were autocracies. Democracy being defined as a political system with institutions that allow citizens to express their political preferences and includes some constraints on the power of the executive by the separation of power among the three branches of the government.

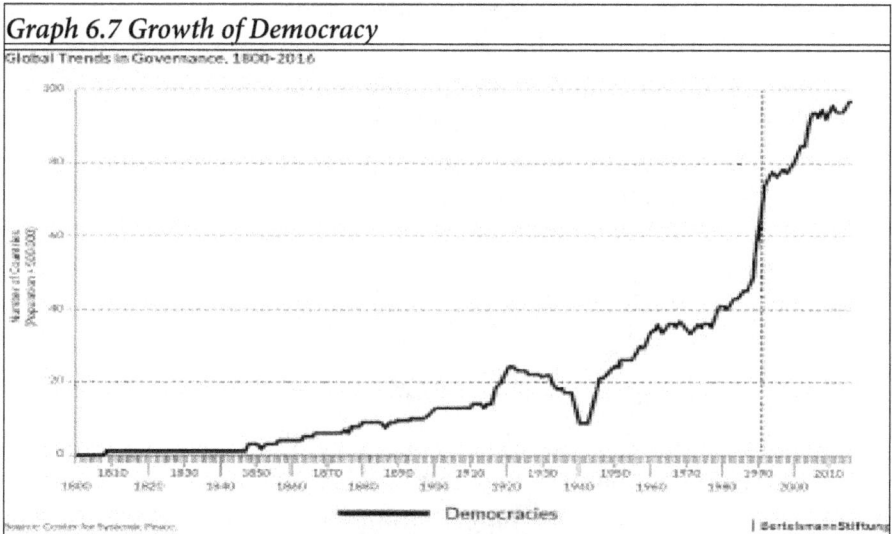

Source:Systemic Peace Polity IV dataset. Reproduced with permission

The surge of democracy shown in the above graph is very encouraging. It illustrates its recent growth since the First Industrial Revolution. From a modestly flat beginning, it grew in the first decade of the 20th century, declined on the eves of the First World War and the Great Depression, vigorously surged after World War II and the Cold War period. Democracy's exponential growth became particularly evident after the fall of the Berlin Wall.

In a democracy, people are the source of authority. Citizens directly and freely exercise their power and right to elect representatives who collectively create a government body for the nation. The government is thus ruled by the people and for the people. In a democracy, citizens have basic rights that are recognized and guaranteed. A representative democracy occurs when people freely choose to vote who will represent them in a parliament based on the political platform of the running candidate. Most representative democracies consider themselves to be liberal democracies because they tend to practice classical liberalism. This is grounded in the respect of the rule of law, freedom and tolerance and a free market economy. The legitimacy of an elected leader to govern is based on his/her adherence to the political platform presented to the electorate.

At the conclusion of the preceding part, I discussed what obviously needs to be done to address inequality and why it is so difficult to implement the required changes in a democratic environment. Democracy is greatly coveted around the world but it has also become the panacea to all political ills forgetting the cunningness of human beings and the mutability of the political environment.

Relationship between democracy and economic development.

Does democracy lead to economic development?
Some scholars, including the eminent sociologist S. M. Lipset, suggest a strong relationship between economic development and democracy. This echoes Max Weber who suggested that that modern democracy in its purest forms can only occur under the unique set of conditions of

capitalist industrialization. Perhaps a fuller explanation would be that "industrial capitalism creates conditions that facilitate the organization of the working class stratum, making it much more difficult for the elite to exclude this group politically" (Stephen J. D 1989: p. 1024). However, it has also been observed that many countries that are at their highest levels of economic development are also the ones that began to develop in the early historical periods (Bollen K. A. 1979: pp.573, 584). This begs the question as to whether it is the level of development that causes democracy or the timing. If it is the level of development, democracy would be largely dependent on economic changes. If it is the timing, that would be equivalent to a nation missing a "one-time" opportunity. The consensus is that the level of economic development better substantiates the path to democracy than the timing, with the caveat that specific cultural systems and economic dependence also have an effect.

Nonetheless, the road to democracy until the 1890s was bumpy. At the beginning of the 20th century, only a handful of countries besides the United States, Canada, UK, France, Germany and the Scandinavian countries were democratic even based on a loose definition of this system of governance. By the beginning of the 21st century, 57% of sovereign states were democratic. With the passage of time, it seemed that economic development led to modernization with the momentum to support democracy. In this context, modernization refers to the transitional process of moving from a traditional agrarian, rural society to an urban industrial society.

An analogy can be made with technology (including information technology). We become what we behold. We shape our tools and then our tools shape us. Empirical evidence suggests that modernization changes people's ways of living and affects their perception of the world around them and their culture in terms of self-expression, traditional values, civic responsibilities and attitude towards authority.

In the preceding paragraph, I conveyed the relationship between modernization and democracy. However, modernization does not automatically lead to democracy but rather facilitates it by bringing social and cultural changes that make it increasingly probable (R. Inglehart and C Welzel 2009: p. 38-44). Economic development brings financial freedom, self-confidence and social and cultural changes to the lower levels of the elite class making it difficult for the political system to ignore the requests of the majority.

It should be noted that wealth does not necessarily bring democracy. According to the 2019 Democracy Index Study, Israel, which is not a wealthy country, is the only flawed democracy in the Middle East. If wealth were a determining factor Saudi Arabia would be classified as a democratic country but it is not.

Relationship between Democracy and Economic Inequality

If modernization, resulting from economic development supports democracy there is an expectation that it would also reduce economic inequality. But, does democracy alleviate or exacerbate economic inequality?

Recent research does not support any systematic relationship between democracy and inequality. The World Income DataBase's statistics show a decline in inequality occurring before the countries were democratized (democratization J. F. Timmons 2006: p. 742). Acemoğlu et al (2015 Vol.2B) found that democracy had a limited effect on inequality perhaps due to the complexity of this relationship. In fact, democracy seems unable to counteract economic inequality.

The natural inclination would be to consider them as having an endo-symbiotic relationship. Low economic inequality should occur in periods of stable democracy inferring that a government has heard the voice of its people in terms of their pressing economic needs. However, the overall verdict varies from mutual exclusivity between economic inequality and democracy to a mild dependence.

It is getting increasingly common to view democracy as a self-contained mode of governance independent of inequality. Neither a correlation nor a (re)distributional effect could be established. At best, there is a strong positive relationship between growth and reduction of poverty, if the re-distribution of wealth reaches the right class of people.

The 1990s were a period of economic recovery and macroeconomic and political stability. During this period there was a surge of democracy in Argentina, Bolivia, Brazil, Chile, Nicaragua, Paraguay and Peru. However, a reduction in inequality preceded the surge of democracy such as happened in East Asian countries during 1970 to the 1990s. The conclusion is clear: "... nothing indicates a systematic relationship between democracy and lower economic inequality" (J. F. Timmons 2010: p. 742).

A survey of 17 Latin American countries for the period described above was conducted by the Inter-American Development Bank for this purpose. It showed a strong negative effect of inequality on poverty reduction. The report concluded that "a favorable macroeconomic context, such as that experienced by Latin America in the 1990s, does create favorable conditions for poverty reduction. But a significant proportion of the gains for the poor was swept away by an increase in inequality. This can be interpreted as the gains being taken by the upper class. In this case, democracy and economic inequality behave in opposite direction.

Contrary to expectation, democracy and inequality must be dealt with separately. Their emergence, developmental processes and implementation are very different. Inequality is amorphous and its pernicious effect can flourish in all political systems.

What then justifies democracy's attraction and reputation and makes it the most sought-after political system? A short answer is democracy sustains liberty, freedom (election, choice) and other attributes found in modern advanced societies. History has proven that all other systems, anocratic or autocratic have spectacularly failed over time. But in the context of inequality, democracy is not at stake. Political scientists recognize that the consequences of inequality are deeper. Christian Houle in his detailed paper "Why Inequality Harms Consolidation but Does Not Affect Democratization" substantiates my point. This robust study found no relationship between democracy and inequality. He contrasted the emergence and maintenance of democracy in Costa Rica, India and the swing between dictatorship in Nigeria, Peru, and Turkey. Houle stressed the difference between creating democracy and the ability to maintain it. The maintenance of democracy requires enough revenues to ensure that the state can fulfil its responsibility to provide public goods and services. In addition, the state must avoid excessive inequalities in its distribution of wealth and power. Inequality may cause backsliding from democracy to dictatorship. Recall my conclusion preceding modern Peru. Following World War II, two periods of military junta followed civilian governments trying to maintain order and democracy in Peru.

Inequality is independent of democracy. A responsive democratically elected government *may* accept the petition of his/her citizens regarding social benefits or abuse of power. But an elected leader may also disregard the people's demands and become authoritarian. In other words, democracy can produce a monster*. History reminds us of many democratically elected leaders transformed into dictators.

Today, in many countries people freely choose their government without the risk of violence. People in democratic systems also assume that their civil liberties are protected by the government. More countries are democratic now than at the beginning of the 20th century. But elected political leaders through a democratic process, do not necessarily guarantee the protection of citizens against abuses from the democratic majority leader (F. Zakaria 2003: p. 17). Freedom of speech and religion, absence of coercion regardless of source, protection of properties are the domain of civil liberties in a liberal constitution, but not part of those governing systems. They fit in the definition of illiberal democracy. The association of political rights guaranteed under liberal democracy with civil liberties covered by constitutional democracy can be found in the classical republic definition: "a mixed constitutional government" which embodies civic duty, virtue, social cohesion and where there is devotion, fidelity and regard for the rule of law. Since liberalism is an offshoot of classical republicanism, the term republic has been confused with the ideas of democracy and liberalism (W. Lindsay Wheeler 2016). According to a 2019 Freedom House report, more than half of the countries around the world are illiberal democracies.

But along with this trend, society is also witnessing the resurgence of another type of political concept: populism. It is difficult to define populism because, in contrast to a doctrine, populism is based on disparate facts appealing to a segment of a population yet not universally common around the globe. Some of its main characteristics are anti-elitist, anti-pluralist and nationalist. In the words of the German political philosopher Jan-Werner Müller, "populism is a particular moralistic imagination of politics, a way of perceiving the political world that sets a morally pure and fully unified - but ultimately fictional – people against the elite who are deemed corrupt or in some other way morally inferior". Müller suggests that criticizing the elite does not necessarily make someone a populist although it is a necessary but insufficient requirement to identify a populist. The repeated bashing of the elite as one of the hallmarks of this movement resonates well in those who feel left out by the mainstream political parties.

Political impact

It is important to reconsider the ascent of populism from a broader perspective. As indicated in the Greek root of the name democracy (the combination of demos (people) and kratos (rule)), is the political system of a government ruled by the people and for the people. If people feel left out, conceivably there is a contradiction in the representative democracy which political scientist Natalia Letki calls a democratic deficit. Although mostly used in the context of European Union institutions and policy-making, the democratic deficit may also describe the asymmetry between governmental decisions and the electorate's interest. Research undertaken by political scientist Armin Schäfer has shown that "political decisions are biased in favor of better-off citizens across rich democracies".

Why then do political leaders give preferential treatment to the wealthy? Generally, not all leaders were wealthy before becoming the head of a nation. Some have a modest economic background but still, they embrace the interests of the 1%. One reason that comes to mind is the enormous financial donations that they receive from this particular stratum of society. Support for political parties and individuals is a hallmark of the wealthy and this type of expenditure is legal*. This practice is not exclusive to developed countries but also to developing countries and less-developed countries where the donation rules imprecision leave room for misinterpretation therefore difficult to enforce.

But, more important are the ramifications of these donations*. On the one hand, political campaigns become more and more expensive influencing leadership races and the political platform of the candidates. On the other hand, the elected leader becomes indebted to his/her donors hence Shaffer's statement. The roots of some of the advantages given to a few at the expense of society come from this practice. A solution must be found to address this dependence. Perhaps the financing of political parties should come from the public fund with the appropriate criteria for eligibility.

Back to populism, populist leaders position themselves as the exclusive representative of the real people. The strongman governing style eliminates the need for dialogue with other parties on policy issues which is an impediment to democracy. And migration is seen as a threat to economic and cultural security. Modernization theorist, Seymour Lipset describes populism as a political expression of the anxieties and anger of those wishing to return to a simpler, pre-modern life. Since 1980, the economic situation of the middle class has worsened. They feel their government has abandoned them. The resentment of the have-nots has reached a paroxysm when they consider the economic distance between them and the upper haves. Nature abhors a vacuum and so do voters.

Populism emerged in the United States in the mid19th century and almost 30 years later in Canada (See populism in the note section of Appendix I). However, it is my assessment that the recent resurgence of populism is the lack of focus by political parties on their ideology. The report of the Tony Blair Institute for Global Change states that "populism's appeal is often based on real concerns about the failure of mainstream parties to address issues that citizens are worried about and the failure of institutions to deliver policy outcomes that matter to citizens". These flaws become part of the populist' political platform. It gives this movement the flexibility to adapt to every situation if they choose to.

Populism ideology has gained traction because of the deficit in the working of representative democracy.

Could the real issue be functioning of the two dominant modes of governance modes of modern civilization namely capitalism and democracy? What would happen if they worked in harmony? What is the impact of a complete disconnect between them?

Opinions widely vary on the complementarity or disjunction of capitalism and democracy since the last two centuries. From the analysis of the late political scientist Gabriel G. Almond that capitalism supports democracy and conversely capitalism subverts democracy with the same reversal role for democracy. The neutral and debatable conclusion was that democracy and capitalism are both positively and negatively related and they both support and subvert each other.

Time gives porosity to historical events making them more penetrable for analysis. Democracy inherited from the Greek civilization in the 6th century B.C. is still coveted by most societies but whether the power in place can accommodate its requirements is a different story. A 2018 Pew survey covering 27 countries has revealed 51% are dissatisfied with the functioning of democracy and an increasing disinterest of the millennials in capitalism. A similar result in the same year was found by the Freedom House organization. Capitalism challenges continued with the passage of time. According to an October 2019 Pew Research Center poll, one-third of Americans have a negative opinion about capitalism and this opinion is linked to inequality and corruption. Indeed capitalism in its essence supports inequality. Nevertheless, the two-thirds support for profit resulting from hard work and ingenuity is robust enough for maintaining capitalism in the foreseeable future.

Originated from Europe in the Late Middle Ages, capitalism has reached a dominant position for the last two hundred and twenty years. Instead of a graph that would show the hiccups in the ascending trend of capitalism, I thought it would be more relevant to briefly describe the major events of the past and current centuries of this system of governance. In Canada six recessions, one long depression occurred in the 19th century and the impact of those in the United States have affected this economic system. In the 20th century, three events namely the end of World War I and World War II and the fall of the Berlin Wall were more political than economic. In fact, due to the participation of the allied forces, following each of these events capitalism has grown stronger than before. The 1929, 1987, 2008 market crashes causes were caused by the flaming passion or in the words of the economist and former Chair of the USA Federal Reserve Bank, by the irrational exuberance of the investors. The capitalism* rebounding each time has proven that central planning is no match to the free market economy.

By the forces of four Industrial Revolutions and socioeconomic evolution, both democracy and capitalism transform each other to their current areas of responsibilities. However, since the last decade, both have been under assault. In the United States, as shown by many scholars and surveys, public policies tend to favor the affluent of this society. Finally, an article from Harvard Business Review in which five top political scientists give their opinion, the question raised was whether capitalism and democracy need each other. The result was inconclusive. Those who recognize a need for a bijective relationship also require more protection for democracy and capitalism because of the rise of populism and the unrealistic promises of the Democratic Party left wing. Those who deny that capitalism needs democracy or vice versa still want certain characteristics of either capitalism such as the competitive market or democracy such as the maintenance of civil liberties or equality of all citizens before the law.

In this discourse, the role of the state, the visible hand of human agents in the government, was not often mentioned. Capitalism is not only a system of economic relations that are coordinated through the invisible hand of the pricing mechanism in markets but also an indirect system of governance because the economic actors are governed by laws and rules that set conditions for acceptance behavior (B. R. Scott 2011 pp. 37, 39).

With respect to democracy, it is worth repeating Joseph Schumpeter's definition given in PART II as the democratic method is that institutional arrangement for arriving at (political) decisions in which individuals acquire the power to decide by means of a competitive struggle for the people's vote. Democracy can be seen as a three-level system of governance with its own markets regulated by the appropriate institution under the state authority. The late professor B. R. Scott clearly differentiates these markets: the electoral markets which provide a structure for competition among candidates for office and the legislative markets which dictate the distribution of power within various government branches.

So, do capitalism and democracy need each other? The orientation of these two systems of governance could potentially have a detrimental effect on society if they don't work in harmony in the absence of state authority. On the one hand, capitalism in its application can lead to inequality by its strict obligation to the shareholders for profit and exploitation of the working class. On the other hand, a failure of democracy to giving a voice to the people in the production process, better redistribution of resources and producing a government by the people and for the people could lead to anarchy. Over the last two centuries, they have transformed each other into the mixes as known today. It also means that the economic power of the elite may swing the political process in their favor.

Corruption of the opportunity to earn a living or to vote remains one of the biggest challenges to the legitimacy of capitalism and democracy creating thereby a cardinal inequality. The following graph shows an era of modest economic growth for both the 10% and 90% of the American society from 1947 to 1980. This was the beginning of rampant economic inequality in recent times. What did happen? The rise of neoliberalism.

Graph 6.10 Gain of the Top 1 Percent 1980-2015

Income Gains at the Top Dwarf Those of Low- and Middle-Income Households

Percent change in real after-tax income since 1979

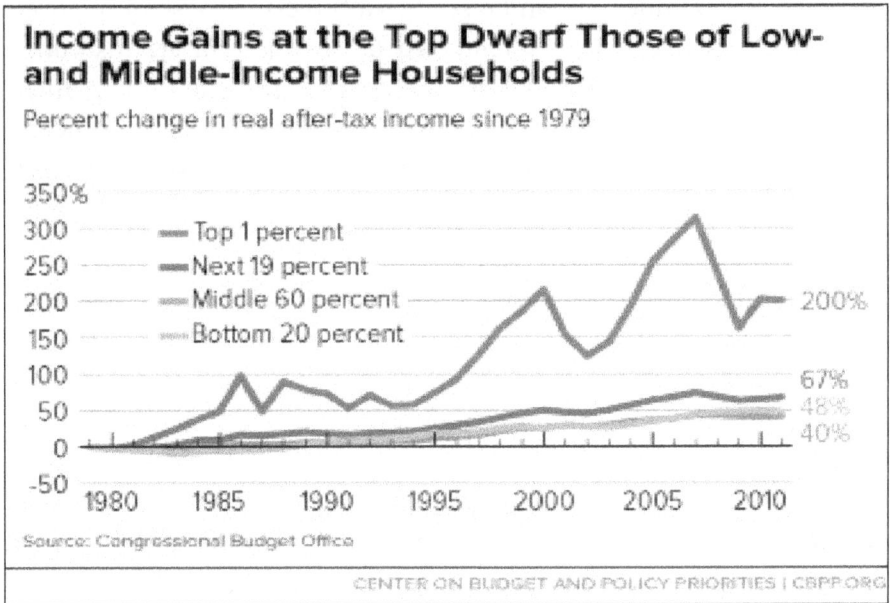

Source: Congressional Budget Office

CENTER ON BUDGET AND POLICY PRIORITIES | CBPP.ORG

The conflation of many factors in the United States and the rest of the world can explain this loss of shared prosperity. Among those factors, technological development, deregulation of financial markets, union's declining power, lack of protection from globalization are often mentioned. But this graph shows the magnitude of the gap between the top 1 percent and the rest of American society.

The two-digit increase of the lower classes from 1980 to 2015 is pale in comparison with the one of the one percent. It also means that the economic power of the elite has substantially increased to a point that it may swing some economic decisions in their favor.. More wealth in the top social stratum means more economic inequality. You will recall the A. Schäfer earlier quote that political decisions are biased in favor of better-off citizens across rich democracies. In other words, economic inequality creates political inequality.

The working group on political inequality led by Joshua K. J. Dubrow defines political inequality as the unequal influence over decisions made by political bodies and the unequal outcomes of those decisions. It is my assessment that more will be said on this issue in the near future.

Endnotes

6a. This comparison of nature and society focuses on wealth instead of income which adds to the originality of Sheffer et al study compared to many others on this subject. Inequality in wealth is greater than in income and this latter is poorly correlated with wealth inequalities across countries. At the turn of the new millennium, the Gini coefficient of wealth was almost twice the one on income in both advanced and developing countries. Developing countries include China. India, Pakistan, Thailand, Turkey Argentina, Mexico, Indonesia and Brazil.

6b. It is also important to emphasize that not all income differentials are necessarily bad for examples: higher pay for special trade works -. The status of a position can be justified by a combination of hard work and special skills.

6c. The veil of ignorance is a hypothetical social construct designed to overcome our tendency to self-projection and create a fair to all way of living. A rich person may naturally propose a society with all the amenities of luxurious living with some limited advantages to the poor. Conversely, a poor person may prevent any person from being very rich and a more balanced share of the available primary goods. Conceived by the late Harvard academic John Rawls in his book "A Theory of Justice", the designer does not have any information about himself or herself and the future position he/she will occupy in that society (rich or poor, educated or illiterate, physically impaired or athlete, man or woman, religious or not, etc). This theory rests on two principles of justice: liberty and utility. The former means freedom of belief, speech and political choice; the latter also called the difference principle recognizes that some inequalities can exist only if they maximize the benefits of everyone's position and the least advantaged provided that they are consistent with equal liberty and fair opportunity (Rawls 1999: p. 131). It is a safeguard that any reasonable person would propose in his/her original position.

6d. Source: Born to Win. Wealth Concentration in Canada since 1999. Canadian Centre for Policy Alternatives (CCPA

6e In my opinion, the above quote must be understood as a path to economic distribution efficiency, social justice and individual liberty. There is no evidence in de Tocqueville's abundant work that he was adverse to wealth accumulation but a balanced socioeconomic structure was ideal.

6f. Source: Ian Kershaw. "How democracy produced a monster." New York Times. February 3, 2008

6g. In the Citizen United v Federal Election Commission, the Supreme Court of United States has ruled on January 21/2010 that labor unions and corporations can spend money on electioneering communication and directly advocate for the election or defeat of candidates.

6h. For more information on the magnitude of these donations see Thomas B. Edsall's article: "Why Is It So Hard for Democracy to Deal with Inequality?" New York Times, February 15, 2019, based on data from Bonica et al.

6g. Indeed, capitalism does not appear to have a competitor. However, it is more accurate to use the position of Francis Fukuyama in *The End of History* that humanity has reached"the end-point of mankind's ideological evolution and the universalization of Western liberal democracy as the final form of human government.

The Corona Pandemic

A s I was completing this manuscript, rumors of the coronavirus (COVID-19) emerged. Shortly thereafter the World Health Organization declared a pandemic. Travel bans, library closures, delivery delays, availability of post-graduate researchers are a few of the impediments that authors have encountered. On the positive side, this hiatus in 'business as usual' delay brought the opportunity to reflect on the socio-economic impact of this pandemic.

COVID-19 is not the first pandemic that has stricken humanity. The 1918 influenza pandemic, affected 500 million people and killed 40 million worldwide (675,000 in the United States) over 12 months. It followed the end of World War I which took the lives of ~116,000 soldiers and wounded ~320,000. Ironically, more soldiers died of the disease than in combat. And, seven centuries earlier, the Black Death (1343 -1353) killed 50 million in Europe*. The mortality rate of this pandemic in human lives is still unknown.

A 2007 report of the Federal Reserve Bank of St Louis looked at the mortality rates, income, place of residence and economic impact of the 1918 influenza pandemic. This report posits that mortality rates are influenced by population density, place of residence, race and access to health care. But more specifically, racial differences in influenza mortality rates reflected some degree of differences in population, density and geography (T.A. Garett 2008: 84). This is an issue under close consideration in the COVID-19 pandemic. The demographic profile of the victims of the 1918 pandemic is bizarre given the average age profile of the population. The mortality rate was 49% for people between the age of 18 and 40 but only 18% for those under age 5 and 13% for those over age 50. The report states that "in general, death was not caused by the influenza virus itself, but by the body's immunological reaction to the virus. Individuals with the strongest immune systems were more likely to die than individuals with weaker immune systems. Understandably, the economic impact was substantial at family and business level" (T. A. Garett 2007: p.9).

The 1918 influenza pandemic was relatively short. It ended approximately 12 months after it began. The emotional impact was significant on those who survived and the economic impact was substantial. It may have cost the United States economy between $166 to 200 billion but this is difficult to confirm because of the lack of data. Some businesses such as drug stores thrived but many others lost money. Through the supply and demand mechanism, wages increased before plateauing for decades after. Recall, feudalism became no longer viable because of this wage increase. It sounds like a repeat of the impact of the Black Death

The Federal Reserve Bank of St Louis report also noted that cities and states with higher mortality rates experienced a greater increase in manufacturing wage growth over the period 1914 to 1919. Moreover, states that experienced larger numbers of influenza deaths per capita experienced higher rates of growth in per capita income after the pandemic.

The 2007 report sheds light on the potential state of affairs after COVID-19. Physical distancing, public health planning and education, inter-governmental planning are all happening on a broader scale. However, government readiness for a second wave of COVID-19 and future pandemics remains a work in process. Given the advances in medical technology and procedures and the government support for businesses and workers, the performance of the economy depends on the duration of the current pandemic. Nonetheless, there was a change following both the Black Death and the 1918 influenza that is related to the theme of this book: the reduction of economic inequality resulting from the gains of the labor force.

By the beginning of the 14th century, Europe's population had reached 100 million. This demographic explosion was due to the favorable climatic and political environment. The labor force consisting of peasants and farmers made up 85% of the population. The Black Death killed huge numbers of people, shrinking family size. It was not uncommon that a distant family member of a landowner changed social status by becoming property owner by inheritance in a relatively short period of time. But the greatest proportion of the people killed were farmers and peasants. A new situation emerged in which there was more work than workers. The supply and demand mechanism mentioned earlier pushed the wages three to four times what they were before the plague. In England, the Statutes of Labourers of 1351 prohibited requesting or offering wages higher than the pre-plague period. Needless to say that the law could not be enforced. Some landlords opted to pay their workers in product and money. As a result, a new class of wealthy people emerged, changing the resource distribution in European society.

Austrian historian Walter Scheidel examined the extent of post-Black Death leveling. As an example, he cites a 1336 decree of the English Parliament that only nobles and clerics whose incomes were greater than £1,000 per annum could wear furs. This law was replaced in 1363 with one allowing everyone, except the lowliest manual laborers, to wear furs. Ridiculously the furs of different animal species represented the social order. Mustelidae furs were at the top, rabbits and cat furs at the bottom (W. Schneidel 2017: p.305).

So far, it seems that the 1918 pandemic was more severe than the COVID-19 pandemic. At the time of the 1918 pandemic, despite the limited resources of the government due to WWI, the early intervention of civilians and public health-related organizations reduced the number of deaths which by extension mitigated the economic impact of the pandemic. It is premature to speculate on the potential socioeconomic leveling that COVID-19 may bring as the ramifications depend on the duration of this pandemic.

Epilogue

Humankind has come a long way since its first sociocultural and economic incarnation. But the fight for equality persists mostly because of humanity's perseverance and resilience comparable to a stubborn boxer whose efforts are redoubled by each knockdown. Inequality remains one of the socio-economic frontiers to cross on the road to human flourishing. Approximately one hundred and fifty years ago Abraham Lincoln expressed his insight about the enemies of the young nation in the quote that "America will never be destroyed from the outside. If we falter and lose our freedoms it will be because we destroy ourselves". I suggest that inequality is one of those enemies from within. Undoubtedly, this quote also applies to most nations depending on the magnitude of the economic inequality in their society. Wall Street Occupy protest (2011) and the Yellow Vest movement (2018) expressed the deep concern of the middle class with economic inequality. The rise of populism can also be explained by the failure of goverments to deliver on electoral promises, neglecting the working class. Populism put them in the forefront by calling them the real people, the pure people versus the corrupt elite.

While it is correct to say that there will always be lower classes. But the concept of social justice requires a substantial rebalancing of their burden by reducing the extravagant differences between the 1% and the 99%.

The notion of fair inequality may be a more acceptable way to describe the required adjustments. That said, the recurring question has always been by how much? The optimal rate of inequality along with the other suggested corrective measures. By these strategies, everyone wins from top to bottom. Enough funds will be available to facilitate accessibility to education, housing and healthcare of the lower classes based on certain criteria.

Some authors have a knack for leaving a permanent mark on our psyche. One such author is Nigel Warburton. His book, *A little History of Philosophy* provokes deep thinking about pressing and complex subjects such as the meaning of life or a need for a just society. Warburton brilliantly summarizes these philosophical concepts with Socrates in *The Man Who Asked Many Questions*, *with Hannah Arendt in The Man Who Didn't Ask Question* by Hannah Arendt and with John Rawls's *Theory of Justice*.

In 2,400 BC, Socrates was sentenced to death for asking too many questions. Socrates is credited for having the insight that people know more than they can tell. He believed that questioning someone's assumptions is the best approach to help him/her discovering the truth. Needless to say pointed and insistent questions at best make people uncomfortable and at worst, annoyed.

Fast forward to modern time, Adolf Eichmann, the lethal Nazi bureaucrat, failed to ask any questions and in December 1961 he was sentenced to death by the Jerusalem District Court of Israel for his participation in the murder of millions of Jews. Eichmann believed that the carrying out of an order which entailed the efficient and effective transportation of Jews to Poland's concentration camp was the end of his responsibility – without question. For the German Jewish philosopher Hannah Arendt reporting on Eichmann's trial for the New Yorker magazine, obedience to regulations required Eichmann to turn a blind eye to people on their way to death. Understandably, this mindset made it possible for him to look at himself shamelessly in the mirror daily. To paraphrase John Stuart Mill, a person may cause evil to others not only by his actions but by his inactions, and in either case, he is justly accountable to them for the injury that he caused.

This may be a cynical comparison but I could not avoid seeing a similarity between the attitudinal behavior of these two agents and the traditional approach to address economic inequality in our society.

This issue has been in the forefront at the World Economic Forum in 2013 and 2017 by Christine Lagarde, then Managing Director of the International Monetary Fund, currently President of The European Central Bank. Much rhetoric, no action. Economic inequality within countries continues to rise. This issue will not go away unless appropriate measures are implemented and consistently monitored. It is worth repeating this quote from Adam Smith "No society can surely be flourishing and happy, of which the far greater part of the members are poor and miserable".

Acknowledgments

If I have seen farther, it is by standing on the shoulders of giants

Isaac Newton

This book was written over the last two years and many people contributed to this undertaking. Listing all of them would be an abuse of your patience as a reader. Nevertheless, this does not diminish my obligation to acknowledge the contributions of the many scholars and institutions upon whose writings I have had the opportunity to reflect or adapt to the context of this book.

More specifically, I am indebted to Pascal Boyer PhD for using his conceptual approach to religion which facilitates the understanding of the religious imperatives and the leadership continuity in the pre-state polity period. I would like to thank Anna Belfer-Cohen PhD of the Hebrew University of Jerusalem for sharing her insights into the Natufian civilization. My conversations with the late Robert L. Carneiro PhD on the origin of the state polity were inspirational. Mapping the evolution of democracy would not be possible without the extensive data provided by Monty G. Marshall PhD of the Center for Systemic Peace. My appreciation goes to Gabriel Zucman PhD for shedding light on Tax Haven's opacity by his robust study on this subject. Finally, and not least, I thank my editor and book designer for their arduous work.

APPENDIX I
Glossary and Notes

Glossary

Aggressive Tax Planning

It refers to domestic and international strategies that "push the limits of acceptable tax planning." When a series of transactions are undertaken not for a genuine business purpose but to obtain a tax benefit, the CRA can invalidate the tax-free consequences of the transaction or series of transactions, and taxes may be owed. There is also the General Anti-Avoidance Rule (GAAR) in our tax law, which is available to the CRA to help deal with unanticipated circumstances. The GAAR provides the CRA with broad powers to challenge tax avoidance activities including those of financial advisors who set up schemes to hide their clients' or employers' money. Source: taxfairness.ca

Anocracy

Anocracy is a form of government loosely defined as part democracy and part dictatorship or as a "regime that mixes democratic with autocratic features". This type of government is characterized by institutions and political elites that are far less capable of performing fundamental tasks and ensuring their own continuity. Anocratic regimes very often reflect inherent qualities of instability or ineffectiveness and are especially vulnerable to the onset of new political instability events, such as outbreaks of armed conflict, unexpected changes in leadership, or adverse regime changes.

Autocracy

Institutionalized Autocracy ("Authoritarian regime" in Western political discourse) is a pejorative term for some very diverse kinds of political systems whose common properties are a lack of regularized political competition and concern for political freedoms. We use the more neutral term Autocracy and define it operationally in terms of the presence of a distinctive set of political characteristics. In mature form, autocracies sharply restrict or suppress competitive political participation. Their chief executives are chosen in a regularized process of selection within the political elite, and once in office, they exercise power with few institutional constraints. In a fully institutionalized autocracy, citizens' participation is sharply restricted or suppressed (Monty G Marshall – Polity IV).

Cosmic Egg

Current cosmological models maintain that 13.8 billion years ago, the entire mass of the universe was compressed into a gravitational singularity, the so-called *cosmic egg*, from which it expanded to its current state following the Big Bang. This latter is a theory describing the expansion of our Universe from a point of origin roughly 13.8 billion years ago.

Monsignor Georges Lemaître was a Belgian Roman Catholic priest, physicist and astronomer. He is usually credited with the first definitive formulation of the idea of an expanding universe and what was to become known as the Big Bang theory of the origin of the universe, which Lemaître himself called his hypothesis of the primeval atom or the "Cosmic Egg".

Cosmic Time Scale

The history of the beginning of our universe is one of convergence starting with the Big Bang, the most popular theory. Imagine this history being compressed into one year, with the Big Bang corresponding to the first second of New Year's Day, and the present time to the last second of December 31 (midnight). Using this scale of time, each month would equal a little over a billion years. The late astrophysicist Carl Sagan has compressed in one year the time from the creation of the universe to the preceding century. On the basis of that scale the first human appeared on December 31 at 10:30 pm. From this perspective, the appearance of Homo sapiens is relatively recent.

Cultural Fractals

Cultural fractals represent the traditions transmitted from one generation to another. They are built by simple lines which are repeated and manifest themselves in the specific way in which things are done within a social group. (*Sabrina Farías-Pelayo*. Characterization of Cultural Traits by Means of Fractal Analysis. DOI: 10.5772/67893)

Democracy

Democracy is conceived as three essential, interdependent elements. One is the presence of institutions and procedures through which citizens can express effective preferences about alternative policies and leaders. Second is the existence of institutionalized constraints on the exercise of power by the executive. Thirdly, is the guarantee of civil liberties to all citizens in their daily lives and in acts of political participation. Other aspects of plural democracy, such as the rule of law, systems of checks and balances, freedom of the press, and so on are means to, or specific manifestations of, these general principles.

(Representative) Democracy

Representative democracy, the majority of currently established democracies, takes place when people choose to vote for who will represent them in a Parliament. This is the most common form of democracy around the world. It takes advantage of the division of labor: a small group of representatives can use their expertise in policy-making, freeing everyone else to pursue other tasks. In addition, it emphasizes on protecting the rights of not only the majority of the people of the state but also the minorities. By electing a more qualified representative, a minority population would be able to vocalize its grievance in a more efficient manner.

(Direct) Democracy:

A form of democracy in which people decide on policy initiatives directly as in referenda. Direct democracy serves as remedies for the ills of representative democracy such as backtracking from the campaign commitments.

Demography

Demography is the scientific study of human populations primarily with respect to their size, their structure and their development; it takes into account the quantitative aspects of their general characteristics. (iussp.org)

Radiocarbon dating

Many methods are used for dating fossilized remains including Radiocarbon dating (~60,000years), Luminescence (~600,000 years), Uranium-series (500,000years), Electron spin resonance (~2 million years), Argon-argon (~6 million years). Each of them has its specific time range shown in brackets. Radiocarbon dating is used to know the age of a biological specimen. It works by comparing the three different isotopes of carbon. Isotopes of a particular element have the same number of protons in their nucleus, but a different number of neutrons. This means that although they are very similar chemically, they have different masses.

Depression

A depression is a sustained downturn in the economic activity of one or more economies, lasting two or more years.

FATCA - Foreign Account Tax Compliance Act

The Foreign Account Tax Compliance Act (FATCA) is a law that was passed in the United States. U.S. Persons are taxed on their worldwide income regardless of where they live. FATCA aims to combat U.S. tax evasion by U.S. Persons with financial assets outside the U.S. Therefore, FATCA is meant to encourage proper reporting of all investment income and all dispositions of securities by a U.S. person no matter where in the world the investment is held. Beginning July 1, 2014, non-U.S. financial institutions are required to identify, document and report on accounts held by U.S. Persons. To learn more about FATCA, visit the Canada Revenue Agency's website.

Along with many governments, the Canadian government has entered into an Intergovernmental Agreement (IGA) with the U.S. to establish a simplified reporting process. Information on accounts held by U.S. persons will be reported to the Canada Revenue Agency (CRA) and not directly to the Internal Revenue Service (IRS). The CRA will then exchange the information with the IRS through the existing provisions of the Canada-U.S. Tax Convention, which is consistent with Canada's privacy laws. (https://www.bmo.com/home/about/banking/foreign-account-tax-compliance)

Inequality: Social and Economic Inequality

While social inequality is different from economic inequality, the two are linked. Social inequality refers to disparities in the distribution of economic assets and income as well as between the overall quality and luxury of each person's existence within a society, while economic inequality is caused by the unequal accumulation of wealth; social inequality exists because the lack of wealth in certain areas prohibits these people from obtaining the same housing, health care, etc. as the wealthy, in societies where access to these social goods depends on wealth.(https://www.sciencedaily.com/terms/social_inequality.htm)

Phyletic Gradualism

In modern biology, phyletic gradualism refers primarily to a pattern of sustained, directional, and incremental evolutionary change over a long period during the history of a species.

Polity/Republic

From the Greek word "*politeia*" which means citizenship or government, *polity* refers to a political group of any size or shape — it can be a government, a state, a country, or even a social group.

Republic

In Latin res-publica embodies civic duty, virtue, social cohesion and a high devotion for the rule of law and distinction of rank

Punctuated Equilibrium

A theory of evolution that claims change happens suddenly over short periods of time followed by long periods of inactivity.

Recession

Recession can be defined as a significant decline in economic activity characterized by a decrease in the real Gross Domestic Product over two consecutive quarters lasting more than a few months or rarely years such as the recession of 1987.

Social Fractionalization:

The basic idea of how social fractionalization hinders economic growth is that when there is a higher number of groups with different racial, languages, values and beliefs, it is more difficult to coordinate and communicate, these costs could be a high transaction cost. This would also raise uncertainty and instability, thus lower investment. In the game theory, when the number of competitors rise, the harder for the society to achieve the cooperative Nash equilibrium. Therefore, social fractionalization causes political instability and is harmful to economic growth. The most important religious tensions in the world can be found in Lebanon and Israel, where there are conflicts among religious communities; in Malaysia with tension between Christians and Muslims; in India, between Hindus and Muslims.

Systemic Peace

The Polity data series is a widely used data series in political science research. The latest version, Polity IV, contains coded annual information on the level of democracy for most independent states with greater than 500,000 total population and covers the years 1800–2018. Source: Systemicpeace.org.

Tax Avoidance

The CRA defines "tax avoidance" as any taxpayer activity that minimizes tax payable by contravening the object and spirit – but not necessarily the letter – of the law. It occurs when the taxpayer does not provide false information to the CRA, but the provisions of the law are used in a manner that was not intended by Parliament. The taxpayer is deemed to be innocent if it is unclear whether abusive tax avoidance has occurred.

Tax Evasion

Outright "tax evasion" involves concealing income or assets, or by making false statements to deliberately avoid tax on them. Tax evasion violates the object, spirit and letter of the law. Both tax advisors and taxpayers can be prosecuted because the law specifies that every person who has "made, or participated in, assented to or acquiesced in the making of, false or deceptive statements in a return, certificate, statement or answer filed or made as required by or under this Act or a regulation, … is guilty of an offence." However, up to now, advisors have faced "administrative" penalties instead of the full brunt of the law.

Tax Haven

There is no legal or internationally agreed definition of a tax haven. Nevertheless, there is broad consensus that a tax haven has one or more of the following characteristics:

- No, or low taxes.
- Ring fenced tax systems.
- Lack of effective exchange of information with other governments.
- Lack of transparency on ownership, accounting and other essential business information to be registered in the host country. This country by legal or illegal methods reduces or eliminates the payment of taxes otherwise due on revenue and earn to the home country by the individual or corporation.

Notes

Egypt Chronology

Date	the cultural background	the kings	Duration
before 8000 BC	Palaeolithic		
8000-5200 BC	Epipalaeolithic (Tarifian; Qarunian - Fayum B - 6000-5000 BC)		3000 years
6000-5000 BC	Nabta Playa		1000 years
5200-4000 BC	Fayum Neolithic (Fayum A)		1200 years
4800-4200 BC	Merimde		600 years
4600-4400 BC	El Omari		200 years
4400-4000 BC	Badarian		400 years
4000-3300 BC	Maadi		700 years
4000-3500 BC		Naqada I	500 years
3500-3200 BC	Egypt in the Naqada Period	Naqada II	300 years
3200-3100 BC		Naqada III	100 years
3100-2686 BC	Egypt in the Early Dynastic	Early Dynastic	400 years
2686-2181 BC	Egypt in the Old Kingdom	Old Kingdom	500 years
2181-2025 BC	Egypt in the First Intermediate Period	First Intermediate Period	150 years
2025-1700 BC	Egypt in the Middle Kingdom	Middle Kingdom	325 years

1700-1550 BC	Egypt in the Second Intermediate Period	Second Intermediate Period	150 years
1550-1069 BC	Egypt in the New Kingdom	New Kingdom	500 years
1069-664 BC	Egypt in the Third Intermediate Period	Third Intermediate Period	400 years
664-525 BC	Egypt in the Late Period	Late Period	139 years
525-404 BC	Egypt in the first Persian Period	First Persian Period	121 years
404-343 BC	Late Dynastic Period in Egypt	Late Dynastic Period	61 years
343-332 BC	Egypt in the second Persian Period	Second Persian Period	11 years
332-305 BC		Macedonian Period	27 years
323-30 BC	Ptolemaic Period	Ptolemaic Period	293 years
30 BC - 640 AD	Egypt in the Roman Period	Roman/ Byzantine Period	670 years
640-1517		Islamic Period	877 years
1517-1805		Ottoman Period	288 years
1805-1919	Egypt in the Islamic Period	Khedival Period	114 years
1919-1953		Monarchy	34 years
1953-today		Republic	50+ years

Dates are only certain after 664 BC. The earliest dates are often very obscure.
Reproduced with Permission - Source: Digital Egypt, Petrie Museum, UCL

****

- Paleolithic (c. 700,000-7000 BP)
- Saharan Neolithic (c. 8800-4700 BC)
- Lower Egyptian Neolithic and Chalcolithic (c. 5300-3200 BC)
- Pre-dynastic (c. 6000-3000 BC):
- Naqada I (c. 3900-3650 BC) –Naqada II (c. 3650-3300 BC) –Naqada III (c. 3300-2950)

Mesoamerican Chronology

Based on archeological, ethnohistorical, and modern cultural anthropology research, Mesoamerican chronology divides the history of pre-Hispanic Mesoamerica into several periods:

- The Paleo-Indian Period - first human habitation (3500 BC); the Archaic Period (before 2600 BC)
- The Pre-classic or Formative Period (2000-AD 250); the Classic Period or late formative Period (250 – AD 900)
- The Post-Classic Period (900- AD 1521; the Colonial Period (1521-1821
- The Post-Colonial Period (1821- present).

Latin American Chronology

https://www.yachana.org/teaching/resources/chron.html

Ancient America

Also see comparative Ancient America Time Line

https://www.yachana.org/teaching/resources/timeline.html

Paleo-Indian

30,000 BCE (Before the Common Era): Highly mobile hunting and gathering groups crossed the Bering Strait land bridge in pursuit of large game and enter North America.

10,000 BCE: A second migration crosses the Bering Strait and joins the first one. Groups spread all the way down to Chile in southern South America.

Archaic or Preceramic

8000-2000 BCE: Disappearance of large game leads to switch to small game, gathering, fishing, and beginnings of agriculture and village life.

Formative or Pre-classic Period

2000-200 BCE

Classic Period

200 BCE-1000CE

Post-classic Period
AD 1000-1532

1345-1521 CE: The Mexicas (Aztecs) form a militaristic tribute empire in Mexico.

1325: Founding of Tenochtitlán

1440-1487: The Aztecs greatly expand their power and empire under Emperor Moctezuma I.

1487: Dedication of the Great Temple in Tenochtitlán.

1502: Montezuma II becomes emperor of Tenochtitlán.

1200-1532 CE: The Inka form the Tawantinsuyu empire in the Andes with sophisticated and very efficient organizational and administrative structures.

1200-1225: Manco Capac and Mama Ocllo found Cuzco and begin the Inka Empire.

1425-1438: Viracocha Inka establishes the cult of Viracocha & panaqa tradition.

1438-1471: Pachacuti Inka begins expansion begins out of Cuzco valley to the south.

1471-1493: Tupac Inka defeats Chimu (1476) and extends the empire south (Chile) and to the coast.

1493-1527: Huayna Capac expands north to Ecuador and Colombia; dies in a smallpox epidemic which launches a civil war between his two sons Huascar (Peru).

1532: Atahualpa wins the civil war and becomes the leader of Tawantinsuyu.

Conquest Period
1415-1534

1492: Christopher Columbus is lost at sea and is rescued by Arawak Indians in the Bahamas (October 12).

1493: Columbus' second voyage.

1498: Columbus sent back to Spain in chains after his third trip to the New World.

1502: Columbus is marooned for a year in Jamaica during his fourth trip, but is unable to fix his ships or feed the crew.

1519-22: Hernándo Cortés enters, lays siege to, and conquers Aztec capital Tenochtitlán.

1532: Francisco Pizarro captures Atahualpa, ending the Inca Empire.

Colonial Period
1524-1781

1571-72: Revolt of Tupac Amaru I in Peru.

1780-81: Indian revolt led by Tupac Amaru II in Upper Peru

Independence

1821: Agustín de Iturbide declares Mexico independent with his Plan of Iguala

1823: United States issues the Monroe Doctrine which warning Europe against the recolonization of the newly independent Spanish American republics.

1824: Peru declared independence from Spain

Brain Projects

Understanding the amazingly complex human cerebral cortex requires a map (or parcellation) of its major subdivisions known as cortical areas. Recently, 97 new areas in the cortical zone have been identified as part of the Human Connectome Project. *(Matthew F. Glasser et al. A multi-modal parcellation of the human cerebral cortex - Nature 536,171-178 Aug 11.2016)*

An ongoing international Brain Mapping Project to be completed in the next decade will also help neuroscientists understand the origins of cognition, perception, and other enigmatic brain activities.

Religion

A simplistic and common feature of all religions and related rituals, although not universal, seems to be the belief that human affairs are controlled by supernatural agent(s) namely gods, spirits, ancestors or other powerful invisible entities. In turn, they establish some norms, values, emotion and behavior transmitted over generations like a meme.

With regard to this modus vivendi, some comments are necessary. In the first place the reciprocal obligations between rulers and ruled have, of course, an asymmetrical character; put in a simple way, it is an exchange of goods for 'Good'. The existence of a common ideology does not necessarily mean that rulers and ruled have an identical ideology. The elite and commoners' views on Christianity differed greatly in medieval West Europe – and yet, they shared the same Christian doctrine (Duby 1985). As long as there exists a certain overlap between the views of both categories, small differences in ideology will not endanger the legitimacy – and thus the stability – of the (early) state. Secondly, a sound economy does contribute greatly to the acceptance of the rulers; as long as there is available sufficient food and goods for all, the legitimacy of the government will be easily accepted and maintained.

Human Sacrifice

A Few Examples of Human Sacrifice around the World

Stonehenge – England

Stonehenge was constructed between roughly 5,000 and 4,000 years ago and was part of a sacred landscape that included shrines, burials and additional circles made of stone or wood. Not all archaeologists are convinced that human sacrifice took place at Stonehenge, but future research into the nearby landscape and its burials may help resolve the debate.

The skeleton of a man found buried in a ditch at Stonehenge has been interpreted by Jacqueline McKinley, an osteo-archaeologist with Wessex Archaeology, as a sacrificial victim. The man, who McKinley said was 5 foot 10 inches and had a robust muscular build, was shot repeatedly with arrows. McKinley interprets the location of his burial and the nature of his execution as indicating that he was killed as part of a human sacrifice. Her research was featured in 2014 in a Smithsonian Channel documentary showing a re-creation of his sacrificial execution.

Mound 72 – North America

A 10-foot (3 meters) mound called Mound 72 by modern-day archaeologists holds the remains of 272 people, many of them sacrificed. It is located at Cahokia, a city located near modern-day St. Louis that flourished from A.D. 1050 to 1200.

The archaeology of the mound is complex, but it appears as if people were sacrificed gradually in a series of episodes. In one episode, 52 malnourished women ages 18 to 23, along with a woman in her 30s, were sacrificed at the same time. In another episode, it appears that 39 men and women were clubbed to death. The mound also holds the remains of two individuals who were buried with 20,000 shell beads. It's possible that some or all of the sacrifices were dedicated to the two individuals.

Hitobashira - Japan

Depending on how the term human sacrifice is defined, the kamikaze pilots who tried to crash their planes into Allied ships during World War II could be defined as human sacrifices. Their planes sometimes had images of cherry blossoms, which historically symbolized a samurai who gave his life for the emperor.

Other examples of human sacrifice can be found in the stories of Hitobashira — human sacrifices found within the walls or floors of important structures like castles. How often this practice occurred and which structures actually had human sacrifices built within them is a matter of debate. According to legend, Maruoka Castle (constructed in 1576) contains the sacrifice of a peasant woman named Oshizu, who agreed to be sacrificed so that her son could become a member of the samurai class.

Tanzania

The ritual sacrifice of people with albinism, a condition that leaves someone without pigment in their skin or hair, has been an ongoing problem in the East African nation of Tanzania.

Some individuals in the country believe that rituals that involve the sacrifice of albinos, or the use of their body parts, can bring good fortune. Then Guardia reported in 2015 that Tanzanian officials had arrested 32 "witch doctors" who were allegedly involved in the rituals or trade in body parts.

Source: https://www.livescience.com/59514-cultures-that-practiced-human-sacrifice.html

Homo ergaster

The species name originates from the Greek ergaster meaning "Workman". This name was chosen due to the discovery of various tools such as hand-axes and cleavers near the skeletal remains of H. ergaster. http://imagingmylife.blogspot.com/2012/12/hominini.html

Homo sapiens

The binomial name Homo sapiens was coined by Linnaeus, 1758 translated from Latin as wise man or modern man. The species was initially thought to have emerged from a predecessor within the genus Homo around 300,000 to 200,000 years ago.

Taxonomic Ranks

The basic ranks are species and genus. When an organism is given a species name it is assigned to a genus, and the genus name is part of the species name.

Main taxonomic ranks			
Latin		English	
regio		domain	
regnum		kingdom	
phylum	divisio	phylum (in zoology)	division (in botany)
classis		class	
ordo		order	
familia		family	
genus		genus	
species		species	

Warka Vase

In this artwork of 5000 BC, a glimpse of the social class can be seen. The sumptuous of the King's wedding. Then a group of nine identical men, each holding a vessel which appears to contain the products of the Mesopotamian agricultural system: fruits, grains, wine, and mead. The men are all naked and muscular and, like the sheep beneath them, are closely and evenly grouped, creating a sense of rhythmic activity. Nude figures in Ancient Near Eastern art are meant to be understood as humble and low status, so we can assume that these men are servants or slaves. (Warka Vase – Dr. Sentra German).

Narmer Palette
This image depicts the unification of upper and lower Egypt by King Narmer.

Sykes-Picot Agreement
The Sykes-Picot Agreement (officially the 1916 Asia Minor Agreement) was a secret agreement reached during World War I between the British and French governments pertaining to the partition of the Ottoman Empire among the Allied Powers. Russia was also privy to the discussions. The agreement became official in an exchange of notes among the three Allied Powers on April 26 and May 23, 1916.

Traded Goods between Europe and the OLD World
Silk, porcelain, precious stones, precious metals, woolen goods, spices, fruits, nuts, religion, philosophy, technology

The Balfour Declaration

Analysis of the embarrassment caused by this letter in one of the McMahon-Hussein Correspondence and the Question of Palestine.

Foreign Office,

November 2nd, 1917.

Dear Lord Rothschild,

I have much pleasure in conveying to you, on behalf of His Majesty's Government, the following declaration of sympathy with Jewish Zionist aspirations which has been submitted to, and approved by, the Cabinet

His Majesty's Government view with favour the establishment in Palestine of a national home for the Jewish people, and will use their best endeavours to facilitate the achievement of this object, it being clearly understood that nothing shall be done which may prejudice the civil and religious rights of existing non-Jewish communities in Palestine, or the rights and political status enjoyed by Jews in any other country"

I should be grateful if you would bring this declaration to the knowledge of the Zionist Federation.

McMahon letter

Sir,

Many references have been made in the Palestine Royal Commission Report and in the course of the recent debates in both Houses of Parliament to the 'McMahon Pledge', especially to that portion of the pledge which concerns Palestine and of which one interpretation has been claimed by the Jews and another by the Arabs.

It has been suggested to me that continued silence on the part of the giver of that pledge may itself be misunderstood.

I feel, therefore, called upon to make some statement on the subject, but I will confine myself in doing so to the point now at issue—i.e. whether that portion of Syria now known as Palestine was or was not intended to be included in the territories in which the independence of the Arabs was guaranteed in my pledge.

I feel it my duty to state, and I do so definitely and emphatically, that it was not intended by me in giving this pledge to King Hussein to include Palestine in the area in which Arab independence was promised.

I also had every reason to believe at the time that the fact that Palestine was not included in my pledge was well understood by King Hussein.

Yours faithfully,

5, Wilton Place, S.W.1.   A. Henry McMahon.
July 22.

Indus Valley

PART III - Differences between Caste and Class

SR. NO	Caste	Class
1	Membership of a cast is hereditary and no amount of struggle can change it.	A person is placed class by virtue of his acquisition of education, wealth or other achievements.
2	There is no social mobility.	Social mobility is possible, i.e. it is possible to improve social status
3	Members are normally not conscious of their social status.	Members are generally conscious of their social status.
4	The caste system expects members to follow certain customs, folkways, rituals, etc.	Social class has no prescribed customs rituals and folkways
5	Inter-caste marriage is not possible, because it will earn the wrath of society	Marriage between two individuals belonging to different classes is possible without earning the displeasure of society
6	The caste system is based on the inferiority or superiority of human beings. Therefore, does not promote democracy.	Social classes are based on the superiority or inferiority of the social status of an individual. Social classes help in the working of democracy.
7	In the caste system, the members must follow a particular religion.	Members of social classes may follow any religion
8	The caste system is a closed class system in which hereditary status is the lifetime status.	Social classes are an open class system in which movement from one class to another is completely unrestricted.
9	In the caste system, there is no occupational mobility, i.e. one has to follow the occupation of ancestors and it cannot be changed	As a member of the social class, one can adopt any occupation and change it at will.
10	The social gap between members of different castes is too wide.	The social gap is not so wide as in the caste system.
11	The caste system is supported on religious grounds as a manifestation of God's will.	Social classes have no such religious support.

The 42 Divine Principles of the Maat

In Chapter 125 of The Papyrus of Ani, we find the petitioner led by Anubis into duat and pronouncing his/her 42 affirmative declarations, listed below from Budge's public domain translation of the 42 Divine Principles of Maat:

I have not committed sin.

I have not committed robbery with violence.

I have not stolen.

I have not slain men or women.

I have not stolen food.

I have not swindled offerings.

I have not stolen from God/Goddess.

I have not told lies.

I have not carried away food.

I have not cursed.

I have not closed my ears to truth.

I have not committed adultery.

I have not made anyone cry.

I have not felt sorrow without reason.

I have not assaulted anyone.

I am not deceitful.

I have not stolen anyone's land.

I have not been an eavesdropper.

I have not falsely accused anyone.

I have not been angry without reason.

I have not seduced anyone's wife.

I have not polluted myself.

I have not terrorized anyone.

I have not disobeyed the Law.

I have not been exclusively angry.

I have not cursed God/Goddess.

I have not behaved with violence.

I have not caused a disruption of peace.

I have not acted hastily or without thought.

I have not overstepped my boundaries of concern.

I have not exaggerated my words when speaking.

I have not worked evil.

I have not used evil thoughts, words or deeds.

I have not polluted the water.

I have not spoken angrily or arrogantly.

I have not cursed anyone in thought, word or deeds.

I have not placed myself on a pedestal.

I have not stolen what belongs to God/Goddess.

I have not stolen from or disrespected the deceased.

I have not taken food from a child.

I have not acted with insolence.

I have not destroyed property belonging to God/Goddess.

After the petitioner's testimony containing the 42 affirmative declarations, the weighing of the ka for truth, and the reading of the scales, it is said that the doer of Maat is administered by Maat. If the petitioner is deemed by the Goddess Maat to be in substantial compliance with the 42 Laws of Maat the petitioner passes from duat to the Field of Reeds (Arus) where Osiris sits as the final gatekeeper.

If the King could not achieve balance and promote harmony, then it was a clear sign that it was not fit to rule. Maat and the vital concept she embodied was crucial to the King success

Buddhism

In the sixth century BCE, a prince of India named Siddhartha Gautama is said to have given up his throne, left behind his family and his palace, and set out into the forest to seek answers to the haunting questions of suffering, disease, old age, and death. Through this ardent search and his deep meditation, he gained great insight. He became known as the Buddha, an honorific title meaning the "Enlightened One" or the "Awakened One," and is considered by many to be one of the archetypal spiritual pathfinders of history.

Within his own lifetime, the Buddha attracted a considerable following in India with his understanding of the suffering of living beings and his teachings about overcoming suffering through moral living, meditation, and insight into reality.

Source: https://rlp.hds.harvard.edu/religions/buddhism

Populism

Populist around the World

Types of Populism

Populism varies according to the portrayal of which actors in society belong to the pure people and which to the outsiders. Populism manifests itself so differently across contexts that it is hard to think about its effects on political institutions without taking these variations into account. There are three broad ways of demarcating the people and the elite, frequently used by populist candidates and parties: cultural, socio-economic and anti-establishment. These types of populism are distinguished by how political elites use populist discourse to sow divisions (see table 1).

Table 1: Three Ways That Populists Frame 'Us vs. Them' Conflict

	Cultural Populism	Socio-Economic Populism	Anti-Establishment Populism
The people	'Native' members of the nation-state	Hard-working, honest members of the working class, which may transcend national boundaries	Hard-working, honest victims of a state-run by special interests
The others	Non-natives, criminals, ethnic and religious minorities, cosmopolitan elites	Big business, capital owners, foreign or 'imperial' forces that prop up an international capitalist system	Political elites who represent the prior regime
Key themes	Emphasis on religious traditionalism, law and order, national sovereignty, migrants as enemies	Anti-capitalism, working-class solidarity, foreign business interests as enemies, often joined with anti-Americanism	Purging the state from corruption, strong leadership to promote reforms#

Populism in Europe, Americas and Asia

Country	Leader or Party	Years in Office	Type of Populism
Argentina	Carlos Menem	1989–1999	Anti-establishment
Argentina	Néstor Kirchner	2003–2007	Socio-economic
Argentina	Cristina Fernández de Kirchner	2007–2015	Socio-economic
Belarus	Alexander Lukashenko	1994–	Anti-establishment
Bolivia	Evo Morales	2006–	Socio-economic
Brazil	Fernando Collor de Mello	1990–1992	Anti-establishment
Bulgaria	Boyko Borisov	2009–2013, 2014–2017, 2017–	Anti-establishment
Czech Republic	Miloš Zeman	1998–2002	Anti-establishment
Czech Republic	Andrej Babiš	2017–	Anti-establishment
Ecuador	Abdalá Bucaram	1996–1997	Socio-economic
Ecuador	Lucio Gutiérrez	2003–2005	Socio-economic
Ecuador	Rafael Correa	2007–2017	Socio-economic

Country	Leader or Party	Years in Office	Type of Populism
Georgia	Mikheil Saakashvili	2004–2007, 2008–2013	Anti-establishment
Greece	Syriza	2015–	Socio-economic
Hungary	Viktor Orbán	1998–2002, 2010–	Cultural
India	Narendra Modi	2014–	Cultural
Indonesia	Joko Widodo	2014–	Anti-establishment
Israel	Benjamin Netanyahu	1996–1999, 2009–	Cultural
Italy	Silvio Berlusconi	1994–1995, 2001–2006, 2008–2011, 2013	Anti-establishment
Italy	Five Star Movement/ League coalition	2018–	Anti-establishment
Japan	Junichiro Koizumi	2001–2006	Anti-establishment
Macedonia	Nikola Gruevski	2006–2016	Cultural
Nicaragua	Daniel Ortega	2007–	Socio-economic
Paraguay	Fernando Lugo	2008–2012	Socio-economic
Peru	Alberto Fujimori	1990–2000	Anti-establishment
Philippines	Joseph Estrada	1998–2001	Anti-establishment
Philippines	Rodrigo Duterte	2016–	Cultural
Poland	Lech Walesa	1990–1995	Anti-establishment
Poland	Law and Justice party	2005–2010, 2015–	Cultural
Romania	Traian Basescu	2004–2014	Anti-establishment
Russia	Vladimir Putin	2000–	Cultural
Serbia	Aleksandar Vucic	2014–2017, 2017–	Cultural
Slovakia	Vladimír Meciar	1990–1998	Cultural
Slovakia	Robert Fico	2006–2010, 2012–2018	Cultural
South Africa	Jacob Zuma	2009–2018	Socio-economic
Sri Lanka	Mahinda Rajapaksa	2005–2015, 2018–	Cultural
Taiwan	Chen Shui-bian	2000–2008	Anti-establishment
Thailand	Thaksin Shinawatra	2001–2006	Socio-economic
Thailand	Yingluck Shinawatra	2011–2014	Socio-economic

Country	Leader or Party	Years in Office	Type of Populism
Turkey	Recep Tayyip Erdogan	2003–	Cultural
United States	Donald Trump	2017–	Cultural
Venezuela	Rafael Caldera	1994–1999	Anti-establishment

Military expenditure by country as percentage of gross domestic product, 2008-2018 - SIPRI 2019

Middle East	2008	2009	2010	2011	2012	2013	2014	2015	2016	2017	2018
Bahrain	2.8%	3.6%	3.3%	3.6%	3.8%	4.1%	4.4%	4.6%	4.7%	4.4%	3.6%
Egypt	2.2%	2.0%	2.0%	1.8%	1.6%	1.6%	1.7%	1.7%	1.7%	1.4%	1.2%
Iran	2.8%	3.2%	2.9%	2.4%	2.8%	2.2%	2.3%	2.8%	3.0%	3.1%	2.7%
Iraq	2.4%	2.9%	2.7%	2.3%	1.9%	3.3%	3.0%	5.3%	3.5%	3.8%	2.7%
Israel	6.6%	6.8%	6.2%	6.2%	6.0%	5.9%	6.0%	5.6%	4.6%	4.4%	4.3%
Jordan	6.2%	6.6%	5.9%	5.5%	4.8%	4.3%	4.3%	4.3%	4.6%	4.8%	4.7%
Kuwait	3.0%	4.0%	3.8%	3.5%	3.4%	3.3%	3.6%	5.0%	5.8%	5.6%	5.1%
Lebanon	4.0%	4.0%	4.1%	4.1%	4.0%	4.2%	4.7%	4.5%	5.2%	4.6%	5.0%
Oman	5.7%	7.0%	6.3%	7.4%	12.1%	11.1%	10.1%	10.8%	12.0%	9.6%	8.2%
Qatar	2.0%	2.0%	1.5%	..	..	..	..	..	..	..	..
Saudi Arabia	7.4%	9.6%	8.6%	7.2%	7.7%	9.0%	10.7%	13.3%	9.9%	10.3%	8.8%
Syria	3.6%	4.0%	4.1%	..	..	..	..	..	..	..	..
Turkey	2.2%	2.5%	2.3%	2.1%	2.1%	2.0%	1.9%	1.8%	2.1%	2.1%	2.5%
UAE	3.7%	5.5%	6.0%	5.5%	5.1%	6.0%	5.6%	..	..	..	..
Yemen	4.4%	5.7%	4.7%	4.9%	4.6%	4.1%	4.0%	..	..	..	..

NOTES
1) Countries are grouped in region and sub-region.
2) Figures in Italic Blue are SIPRI estimates. Figures in gray indicate highly uncertain data
3) Dots (…) indicate "Data Not Available"
SIPRI (Stockholm International Peace Research Institute) Military Expenditure Database. https://www.sipri.org/databases/milex

Country	Leader or Party	Years in Office	Type of Populism
Venezuela	Hugo Chávez	1999–2013	Socio-economic
Venezuela	Nicolás Maduro	2013–	Socio-economic
Zambia	Michael Sata	2011–2014	Socio-economic

Table 2: Populists in Power, 1990–2018

Source: Tony Blair Institute for Global Challenges – Populism in Power around the World.

The Decimation of the Mexican Population

The 16th-century population collapse in Mexico, based on estimates of Cook and Simpson (1). The 1545 and 1576 Cocoliztli epidemics appear to have been hemorrhagic fevers caused by an indigenous viral agent and aggravated by unusual climatic conditions. In 1520 Smallpox killed ~8 million people; ~Cocoliztli ~12-15 million in1545 and ~ 2 million in 1576.

Venezuela

Johannes Alvarez James Fiorito. *Venezuelan Oil Unifying Latin-America.* Stanford University 2005

The inhabitants of Venezuela have a long relationship with oil even preceding the Age of Discovery. Christopher Columbus has found in his third voyage to America in 1498 that indigenous Venezuelan used hydrocarbon on the surface of their land for medicinal, and illumination purposes. They also used the asphalt they found for caulking their canoes. The medical application has caught the attention of Johanna, Queen of Spain for alleviating the gout of Emperor Charles V. Later in 1878 the first oil company was created in Venezuela, Compania Nacional Petrolia del Tachira" by Antonio Pulido using drilling imported from Pennsylvania.

At that time, Venezuela's oil production was still a small operation largely overridden by agricultural production. The economical production of petroleum products started with the Royal Dutch-Shell Company in the large oil reserve in Mene Grande near the Gulf of Lake Maracaibo. World War I and II made Venezuela an important oil supplier in the world. Oil export grew from 1.9% in 1920 to 91.2% in 1935. This endowment has influenced economic policies since early 1940. In fact, a decision was made at that time to importing rather than producing some goods locally.

Venezuela became the most secure oil supplier to the United States. Petroleos De Venezuela SA (PDVSA) – Oils of Venezuela created in 1976 for planning, coordinating and supervising the oil industry became one of the most important companies in the world through its acquisition of refineries and gas distribution in the United States, Europe and South America. In 1998 PDVSA has a production capacity of 4 million barrels per day (BPD); actually, its production exceeds 3 million BPD and 8.81 billion standard cubic feet/day of gas. Also, PDVSA is among the leading corporations in the refining business, with a petroleum processing capacity of 3,285,000 BPD (1,285,000 BPD in Venezuela and 2 million BPD outside the country) through 24 refineries: six complexes in Venezuela, one in the Caribbean, eight in the United States and nine in Europe. Moreover, PDVSA generally exports 93% of its total hydrocarbon production. Approximately 54 % of these hydrocarbon exports go to the U.S. and Canada. Just to the U.S. PDVSA exports 1.5 million BPD. It seems Chavez believed a leftist politically driven oil revolution of state-owned oil company coalitions offers a greater economic benefit in the future.

The fall and rise of oil prices in the 1970s and 1980s did not convince the policymakers that the country was infected with the Dutch diseases even if agriculture production was down by half and the industrial sector by one third.

I thought it useful to provide this background information which makes the Venezuela Dutch disease almost inconceivable. Fast forward to 1999, Hugo Chavez a career military became President of the Bolivarian Republic of Venezuela. Rising oil prices allowed him to implement his Bolivarian socialist program for low-income people. Indeed, has decreased. The Gini coefficient index moved from 49.5 in 1998 to 41 in 2009. Some improvement also occurred in the level of poverty; from 42% in poor household families in 1999 to 17% in 2007. In education, university enrollment rose 86% in 2006-2007 from the 1999-2000 level.

More boys and girls attended primary education and high school; free meals were served like in all modern societies. A combination of political strategies he also became an important political figure internationally through his agreement with OPEC and energy arrangements with South America and Caribbean head of states. In 2001 after signing a law on a tax increase to companies for exploitation in Venezuela, H. Chavez said: "This new law will permit using our oil and the refineries activities as an instrument of the national development and the diversification of the production of the country". I want to underline that this economic strategy was considered slow and arduous particularly in the context of an upward oil price trend. Hugo Chavez died on May 5/2013. He was succeeded by his vice president Nicolas Maduro.

Unfortunately, all these social improvements, economically speaking, were made in a fragile and risky environment. A fifty percent drop in oil price in 2014 caused Venezuela's export revenues to slide down from $74 Billion in 2014 to $37 Billion in 2015. The oil production went from 3.2 million barrels per day in 2001 to 2.6 million barrels per day in 2015.

Venezuela appears to be in a very tight budgetary constraint. According to Urdaneta-Zubalevich "Revenues from oil exports at current prices (about $50 per barrel of WTI) are about $3 billion. Net revenues, excluding costs, are lower, about $1.5 to $1.8 billion a month, while the average monthly expenditure for payment of debts is $0.75 billion". The PDVSA assets value may calm the creditors on a short term but the future of Venezuela on a long term is unclear unless an agreement can be reached with the International Monetary Fund.

Maritime Silk Road

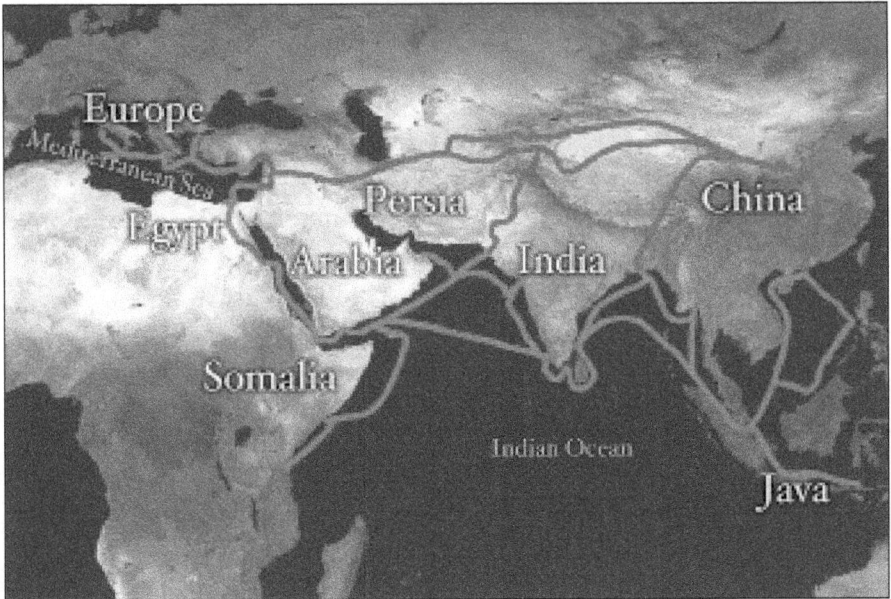

Silk Road and Spice trade, ancient trade routes that linked India with the Old World (Africa, Asia & Europe); carried goods and ideas between the ancient civilizations of the Old World and India. The land routes are red, and the water routes are blue

From 220 to 1453 BC, a variety of commodities were traded through the Silk Road (Land and Sea): Europe, among the most important products, imported silk, lacquerware, pearl and gems, tea, salt, sugar, spices, porcelain, carpets, other fabrics and gunpowder. China and other countries of the Far East imported cotton, ivory, wool, gold, silver, gems and glass.

From a cultural aspect, the Silk Road also contributed to the development of religion and technology. Buddhism entered China from India via the Silk Road, while Islam later made inroads into China through the trade routes across Central Asia. Zoroastrianism and Manicheism, mostly from Iran, and of the Christian Church of the East, based in

Syria, also moved along these Central Asian trade routes. Technological advances in the science of navigation, in astronomy, and also in the techniques of shipbuilding combined to make long-distance sea travel increasingly practical. Knowledge about science, arts and literature, as well as crafts and technologies was shared across the Silk Roads, and in this way, languages, religions and cultures developed and influenced each other. One of the most famous technical advances to have been propagated worldwide by the Silk Roads was the technique of making paper, as well as the development of printing press technology.

Comparison of Europe and China Feudalism

Under the Zhou feudal society, the relationship was based on kinship and the contractual nature was not precise whereas in the European model, the lord and vassal had specific mutual obligations and duties. Medieval European feudalism realized the classic case of the 'noble lord' while, in the middle and later phases of the Chinese Feudal society, the classic case of the landlord system was to be found. Chinese history from the Zhou the Qin dynasty has been termed a feudal period by many Chinese historians due to the custom of enfeoffment (deed by which a person was given land in exchange for a pledge of service) of land similar to that in Europe. Scholars have expressed some reservation about this attribution based on the following differences:

In Europe, the feudal lordships were hereditary and irrevocable and were passed on from generation to generation, whereas the Zhou lordships were not hereditary, required reappointment, and could be revoked.

The medieval serf was bound to the land and could not leave or dispose of it, whereas the Zhou peasant was free to leave or, if he had the means, to purchase the land in small parcels.

In Europe, feudalism was also considered to be a part of an economic system in which the lords who were at the top of the structure, followed by the vassals, and then the peasants who were tied to the land and were responsible for the production.

In addition, in Zhou's rule, the feudal system was not responsible for the economy. The European towns could grow outside of the feudal system instead of being integrated with them since the landed aristocrats were settled in the manors.

Thus, the towns were independent of the influence of the feudal lords and were solely under the authority of the Kings and the kingdoms. In China, these conditions were non-existent and the King and his officials depended greatly on the landed gentry. No political power was available to encourage the growth of the merchant class in an independent manner. Towns and villages were an integrated system and merchants remained under the control of the gentry class instead of setting up an independent trade and economy.

Regardless of the similarities of the agrarian society being dominated by the feudal lords in both societies, the application of the term 'feudal' to the Western Zhou society has been a subject of considerable debate due to the differences between the two systems. The Zhou feudal system was termed as being 'proto-bureaucratic' (The Prehistory and Early History of China – by J.A.G. Roberts) and bureaucracy existed alongside feudalism, while in Europe, bureaucracy emerged as a counter system to feudal order. Therefore, according to some historians the term feudalism, is not supposed to be an exact fit to the Western Zhou political structure but it can be considered a system analogous to the one that existed in medieval Europe

Mercantilism

Navigation Acts

The Navigation Acts, or more broadly The Acts of Trade and Navigation were a long series of English laws that developed, promoted, and regulated English ships, shipping, trade, and commerce between other countries and with its own colonies.

The Navigation Act of 1663

The money from the taxes went to England, not the colonies from where they originated. Other, **non**-specified goods, could go directly to foreign ports from English colonies in English ships. The Navigation Act of 1663 was also called the Act for the Encouragement of Trade or the Staple

The Navigation Acts of 1763

They had several regulations: Colonists had to sell certain products (sugar, tobacco, indigo) only to England or English colonies. The Act was also designed to help pay the war debt created by the French and Indian War, Parliament (British Government) decided to enforce the laws more so than it had in the past.

The Sugar Act

The American Revenue Act of 1764, the so-called Sugar Act, was a law that attempted to curb the smuggling of sugar and molasses in the colonies by reducing the previous tax rate and enforcing the collection of duties on molasses imported from non-British isles. This affected Boston and New England greatly because the colonists there used sugar and molasses to make rum. This law gave British sugar growers in the West Indies a monopoly on the colonial market. The new law added several products such as hides, skins and potash to the list of enumerated commodities that could be legally exported under the Navigation Acts.

Military Expenditures 2008-2018

Military expenditure in local currency at current prices is presented according to both the financial year of each country and according to the calendar year, calculated on the assumption that, where financial years do not correspond to calendar years, spending is distributed evenly through the year. Figures in constant (2017) and current US $, as a share of GDP and per capita are presented according to calendar year. Figures as a share of government expenditure are presented according to the financial year.

Democratic Waves

As written by the political scientist Samuel P Huntington in the respected Journal of Democracy and further detailed in his 1991 book, *The Third Wave: Democratization in the Late Twentieth Century,* a wave is a group of transitions from non-democratic to democratic regimes that occur within a specified period of time and that significantly outnumber transitions in the opposite directions during that period of time. He posited that the first wave extends from 1826 to 1926, the second from the end of World War II to the early 1960s and the third from 1974 to the 1990s. The number, definition, time period and the analytical substantiation of these waves of democracy have been the subject of long debates among scholars. For instance, Seva Gunitsky, a political scientist at the University of Toronto has identified 13 democratic waves between 1776 and 2012, the first from 1776 to 1798. Another divergence of opinion is the inconsistent application of Dahl's definition of democracy used by Huntington in the *Third Wave* as posited by Renske Doorenspleet in her reassessment of Dalh's three waves of democracy. Nonetheless, the attention raised by this book underlines its influence and Huntington's lasting contribution to political science.

The Thirteen Waves of Democracy of Seva Gunitsky

In a 2018 study, Seva Gunitsky of the University of Toronto identifies thirteen waves of democracy. By contrast, Huntington used the much narrower criteria of voting rights for the majority of men.

1. *The Atlantic Wave (1776-1798)*
2. The Latin American Wars of Independence (1809–1824)
3. The First Constitutional Wave (1820–1821)
4. The Romantic-Nationalist Wave (1830–1831)
5. The Spring of Nations (1848)
6. The Second Constitutional Wave (1905–1912)
7. The post-WWI Wave (1919–1922)
8. The post-WWII Wave (1945–1950)

9. The African Decolonization Wave (1956–1968)

10. The Modernization Wave, also known as the "Third" Wave (1974–1988)

11. The Post-Soviet Wave (1989–1994)

12. The Color Revolutions (2000–2007)

13. The Arab Spring (2011–2012)

Perspectives on Politics (Page 38). Volume 16, Issue 3, DOI: 10.1017/S1537592718001044

APPENDIX II
Bibliography and Online Resources

Abdul & Abdul Azim Islahi. Thirty Years of Research in the History of Islamic Economic Thought: Assessment and Future Directions. Academia. edu/30693363/

Acemoglu Daron and James Robinson. The Economic Impact of Colonialism. Volume I. A Global View p. 81. A VoxEU.org Book. CEPR Press. London, UK 2017.

Acemoglu D, S Johnson and J. A. Robinson (2001). The Colonial Origins of Comparative Development: An Empirical Investigation. American Economic Review, 91, 1369-1401.

Acemoglu D, S Johnson and J. A. Robinson. Reversal of Fortune: Geography and Institutions in the Making of the Modern World Income Distribution. Quarterly Journal of Economics, 118, 1231-1294. 2002

Acemoglu Daron and Robinson A. James. Why Nations Fail. The origins of Power, Prosperity, and Poverty. Crown Business New York. 2012

Acemoglu Daron, James A. Robinson. The Narrow Corridor – States, Societies, and the Fate of Liberty. Penguin Press. New York 2019

Acemoglu D, S Johnson and J. A. Robinson (2002). Reversal of Fortune: Geography and Institutions in the Making of the Modern World Income Distribution. Quarterly Journal of Economics, 118, 1231-1294.

Acemoglu Daron, Suresh Naidu, Pascual Restrepo, James Robinson. Feb 07/2014. Can democracy help with inequality? VOX, CEPR Policy portal

Africa's Legacy in Mexico – A Legacy of Slavery http://www.smithsonianeducation.org/migrations/legacy/almleg.html

Alesina Alberto and George-Marios Angeletos. Corruption, Inequality and Fairness. Massachusetts Institute of Technology. Department of Economics Working Paper Series Paper No. 05-16 and Hier Harvard Institute of Economic Research. Discussion Paper No. 2070, 2005

Allen O. Ralph et al. Impact of the Environment on Egyptian Civilization before the Pharaohs – Analytical Chemistry Vol. 65, No 1, American Chemical Society. January 1, 1993

Almazán A. Marco. The Aztecs State-Society: Root of Civil Society and Social Capital. Volume: 565 issue: 1, pp. 162-175. Sage Journals. September 1, 1999

Almond Gabriel A. *Capitalism and democracy. Political Science and Politics.* Vol 24, No 3 pp.467-474. American Political Association. Cambridge University Press. September 1991

Altman Ida et al. *The Ancient History of Greater Mexico-The Conquest of New Spain* [abridged edition of The True History of the Conquest of Mexico], trans. J. M. Cohen (London, 1963), pp 232-5.

Altman Ida. *The Hispanic Historical Review*, Vol. 71, No. 3, pp. 413-445. Duke University Press, August 1991.

Altman Ida, Sarah Cline, Juan Javier Pescador. *The Early History of Greater Mexico.* Pearson Publishing 2003.

Anglim Simon. et al. *Fighting techniques of the ancient world 3000 BCE-500CE.* Amber Books, 2009

Angus Maddison. The world Economy: Historical Statistics, Organization for Economic Cooperation and Development, Paris 2003.

Anna Belfer-Cohen. The Natufian in the Levant. Annual Review of Anthropology. Vol. 20:167-186. October 1991

*Apostolou Mileanos. Sexual selection under parental choice: the role of parents in the evolution of human mating. Evolution and Human Behavior. 2007; 28:403–409

Aran Mary. Latin Americans Are Souring on Democracy https://time.com/5662653/democracy-history-latin-america/

Arnold J. E. The Archeology of Complex Hunter-Gatherers". Journal of Archeological Method and Theory. Vol. 3. No 2. 1996

Asimov Isaac. *Chronology of Science and Discovery*. Harper and Row Publishers, New York 1920.

Axelrod Alan. *The Middle East Conflict*. Alpha 2014

Axtell, James. "The Columbian Mosaic in Colonial America". Humanities Volume 12 No. 5, pp. 12–18. September-October 1991

Barker Ernest. Political Naturalism. Stanford Encyclopedia of Philosophy

Barett Justin L. *Why Would Anyone Believe in God?* Publisher Altamira Press. April 21 2004.

Barett Justin L. *Cognitive Science, Religion, and Theology: From Human Minds to Divine Minds*. Templeton Press; First edition Nov. 1, 2011

Baron Beth. *The Women's Awakening in Egypt: Culture, Society and the Press*. Yale University Press; Revised ed. edition (Aug. 25 1997)

Bartels L. M. Political Inequality in affluent society. Social Science Research Council. July 11, 2017.

Bartolomé de las Casas. *Indian Freedom: The Cause of Bartolomé de Las Casas, 1484-1566*: A Reader. Translation & Notes by Francis Patrick Sullivan S. J. Publisher Sheed & Ward Kansas City 1995.

Bartolomé de las Casas. *Brevísima relación de la Destrucción de las Indias. FV Éditions*. Published on May 11, 2018

Bell Catherine. *Ritual Theory, Ritual Practice*. New York, Oxford University Press 1992

Bell Duran C. Modes of Exchange: Gift and Commodity. University of California, Irvine. The Journal of Socio-Economics, Volume 20, Number 2, pp. 155-157. Jay Press Inc. 1991.

Benedictow Ole J. The Black Death: The Greatest Catastrophe Ever. History Today Volume 55 Issue 3 March 2005 https://www.historytoday.com/archive/black-death-greatest-catastrophe-ever

Bergreen Laurence. *Columbus: The Four Voyages, 1492-1504*. Penguin Books 2011.

Bill James A. Class Analysis and the Dialectics of Modernization in the Middle East. International Journal of Middle East Studies, Vol. 3, No. 4, pp. 417-434. Cambridge University Press. October 1972

Biraben Jean-Noel. The Rising Number of Humankind – Population & Society. No 394, October 2003

Blair Tony. Institute for Global Change. Populist in Power Around the World. November 7/2018 https://institute.global/insight/renewing-center/populist-power-around-world

Bloom Allan. The Republic of Plato. *Basic Books.* New York 1968

Bollen Kenneth A. Political Democracy and the Timing of Development. American Sociological Review 44 (4): pp. 572-88. 1979

Borah Woodrow Wilson. *Early Colonial Trade and Navigation between Mexico and Peru.* Cambridge University Press 1954. London England.

Bourguignon François. The Effect of Economic Structures on Social Growth in Handbook of Economic growth 2005. Science Direct –Elsevier. Chapter 3.

Boyer Pascal. *Religion Explained. The Evolutionary Origins of Religious Thought.* Basic Books 2001.

Brown Judith Margaret. *Modern India: The Origin of an Asian Democracy.* Oxford University Press 2004.

Brumfield Elizabeth M. Huitzilopochtli Conquest: Aztec Ideology in the Archeological Record. Cambridge Archeological Journal 8: pp. 3-14. 1998

Cantillon Richard. An Essay on Economic Theory. CreateSpace Independent Publishing Platform; Large type / Large print edition (Jan. 1 2010)

Cappelen Alexander W, Tom Eichele, Kenneth Hugdahl, Karsten Specht, Erik Ø. Sørensen, and Bertil Tungodden. Equity Theory and Fair Inequality: A Neuroeconomic Study. PNAS October 28, 2014.orkorkork First Published October 13, 2014 – https://doi.org/101073/pnas.1414602111

Carneiro Robert. *The Circumscription Theory: A Clarification, Amplification and Reformulation. Social Evolution & History,* Vol. 11 No 2, pp. 5-30 - Uchitel Publishing House. September 2012

Carneiro Robert A theory of the Origin of the State. Science, Vol. 169: pp. 733-736. 1970

Caroll Peter N. and Noble David W. *The Free and the Unfree: A Progressive History of the United States*, pp. 35-37 3rd edition. Penguin, New York. August 2001.

Castillos J. J. Upper and Lower Egypt in the Predynastic, Journal of the Society for the Study of Egyptian Antiquities 37, 2010.

Chard Chester S. Pre-Colombian Trade between North and South America. Kroeber Anthropological Society, Paper No 1, pp.1-27. Berkeley, 1950

Charles-Coll, Jorges A. The optimal rate of inequality: A framework for the relationship between income inequality and economic growth. University Autonoma de Tamaulipas. August27/2010.

Chide V Gordon. The Urban Revolution. Liverpool University Press April 1950

Claessen, H. J. M., and Skalník, P. *The Early State: A Structural Approach*. pp. 533–596. The Hague: Mouton. 1978

Clarke Steve et al. *Religion, Intolerance, and Conflict: A Scientific and Conceptual Investigation. Edited by Steve Clarke, Russell Powell, Julian Savulescu.* Oxford University Press June 30/2013

Classen Henry J, Renée Hajesteijn. *On State Formation and Territorial Expansion – Dialogue. Social Evolution and History* Vol. 11, 3-19. Uchitel Publishing House. March 2012

Classen Henri J. M. & Shalnik Peter. *The Early State. Theories and Hypotheses.* Mouton Publishers 1978

Cohen Yehudi A. *Man in Adaptation: The Cultural Present. Second edition.*

Aldine De Gruyter\New York. December 31, 1974

Coleman D.C. Proto-Industrialization: A concept Too Many. The Economic History Review. New Series, Vol. 36, No. 3, pp. 435-448. Aug., 1983

Coleman D. C. *Myth, History and the Industrial Revolution*. The Hambledon Press. London 1992. Rio Grande, Ohio USA.

Collier Paul and Hoefflery Anke. Greed and Grievance in Civil War. doi:10.1093/oep/gpf064. Oxford University Press 2004

Conrad Geoffrey W. Cultural Materialism, Split Inheritance and the Expansion of Ancient Peru Empire 1981

Correia Sergio, Stephan Luck, Emil Verner. Pandemic Depress the Economy, Public Health Intervention Do Not: Evidence from the 1918 flu. SSRN. March 26/2020

Croft William. Explaining Language Change: An Evolutionary Approach. Pearson Education ESL; 1 edition (January 5, 2001)

D'Acosta Krystal. Who are the Indigenous People That Columbus Met? Scientific American, October 12/2018.

De Tocqueville Alexis. Democracy in America. Volume I and II Combined. Translated by Henry Reeve. Solis Press, England 2013

Dahl R. A. Polyarchy. New Haven CT. Yale University Press 1971

Darwin Charles. *On the Origin of Species.* Oxford University Press 1859

Dascal Marcelo. Colonizing and Decolonizing Minds. Tel Aviv University.

De Chardin Pierre Teilhard. *The phenomenon of Man.* Harper Perennial Classic. New York. 2008

Deaton Angust. Rent seeking. Washington Center for Equitable Growth. March 7/2017.

Deininger, Klaus and Lyn Squire, "A New Data Set Measuring Income Inequality", The World Bank Economic Review, 10(3): pp. 565-91, 1996.

Delage Christophe. Some Thoughts Regarding the Research on the Natufian. Annual Meeting of the Society for American Archaeology 9/2001.

Dell Melissa. The Persistent Effects of Peru's Mining "MITA". Econometrica. Vol. 78, No. 6, pp. 1863-1903. Nov/2010

Deutsch Karl W. Mobilization and Political Development. The American Political Science Review, Vol. 55, No. 3, pp. 493-514. American Political Science Association Sept. 1961

Diamond Jared. *Guns, Germs and Steel –A Short History of Everybody for the 13,000 Years.* Vintage 1998.

Diamond Jared. *The Third Chimpanzee – The Evolution and Future of the Human Animal.* First Harper Perennial Edition 1993.

Diamond Larry. *The Spirit of Democracy – The Struggle to Build Free Societies throughout the World.* Holt Paperbacks and Company 2008.

Dunbar Robin. *Grooming, Gossip, and the Evolution of Language.* Harvard University Press. Cambridge Massachusetts 1996.

Durán Berios, Kevin. The Tainos: Mythology and Religious Beliefs https://encyclopediapr.org/en/encyclopedia/ the-tainos-mythology-and-religious-beliefs/

Douglas Theron Price, Feinman Gary M. Editors. *Fundamental Issues in Archeology. Pathways to Power New Perspectives on the Emergence of Social Inequality.* Springer 2010.

Durán Diego. *The History of the Indies of New Spain.* University of Oklahoma Press (Jan. 22 2010)

Earle Timothy K. Chiefdoms in Archaeological and Ethnohistorical Perspective: Annual Review of Anthropology, Vol. 16, pp. 279-308. 1987

Earle, Timothy K. *Chiefdoms: power, economy and ideology.* Cambridge and New York: Cambridge University Press 1991

Earle, Timothy. A reappraisal of Redistribution: complex Hawaiian chiefdoms. In. *T. Earle & J. Ericson (Eds). Exchange Systems in Prehistory.* New York: Academic Press 1977.

Earle Timothy. Wealth Finance in the Inka Empire: Evidence from the Calchaqui Valley, Argentina. American Antiquity, Vol. 59, No. 3. Cambridge University Press July, 1994

Earle Timothy K. Terrence N. D'Altroy. The Political Economy of the Inca Empire. The Archeology of Power and Finance 1989.

Elliott E. John, Joseph A. Schumpeter and the Theory of Democracy. Review of Social Economy. Vol. 52, No. 4. The Social Economics of Joseph A. Schumpeter (WINTER 1994). Taylor and Francis Ltd. https://www. jstor.org/stable/29769747

Ebenezer Sunder Raj. The Origins of the Caste System. Transformation, Vol. 2, No. 2, pp. 10-14. Sage Publications Ltd 1985.

Edelman M. Gerald and Tononi Giulio. *A Universe of Consciousness. How Matter Becomes Imagination.* Basic Books 2000

Eller Jack David. *Introducing Anthropology of Religion: Culture of the Ultimate.* Rootledge Publishing. New York 2007

Ekelund Robert B. Jr and Robert D. Tollison. *Mercantilism as a Rent Seeking Society.* Texas University Press 1981

Engerman Stanley L. and Sokoloff Kenneth L. Colonialism, Inequality and Long-Run Paths of Development. National Bureau of Economic Research. Cambridge Massachusetts, January 2005.

Fukuyama Francis. The end of History and the Last Man (in italic). Free Press; Re-issued edition (march 1, 2006)

Dubrow Joshua K. J. What is Political Inequality and How Unequal Are We? Working Group on Political Inequality. https://Joshuakjerulfdubrow.com/

Dubrow Joshua K. J. How Political Voice Fares in an Age of Rising Inequality: Frederick Solt's Research on Economic Inequality and Democracy. https://politicalinequality.org/2019/07/05/how-polit-ical-voice-fares-in-an-age-of-rising-inequality-frederick-solts-re-search-on-economic-inequality-and-democracy/

Engerman Stanley L, Kenneth L. Sokoloff. Colonialism, Inequality and Long Run Path of Development. National Bureau of Economic Research. Cambridge January 2005

Esposito John L. Women in *the Islamic World: Past and Present.* Esposito. *Oxford Islamic Studies Online,* http://www.oxfordislamicstudies.com/article/opr/t243/e370.

Ewell Frank W. 2013 "Robert Carneiro on the Rise of the State". http://www.faculty.rsu.edu/~felwell/Theorists/Essays/Carneiro1.htm

Facundo Alvaredo, Lydia Assouad, Thomas Piketty. Measuring Inequality in the Middle East – The World Most Unequal Region?

Fagan, F Brian. *The Long Summer: How Climate Changed Civilization.*

New York: Basic Books 2004

Ferraro Gary and Susan Andreatta Susan. *Cultural Anthropology: An Applied* Perspective. Wadsworth Cengage Learning 2012

Fish Steven. Islam and Authoritarianism. World Politics 55, pp. 4-37. October 2002

Flannery Kent V. The Cultural Evolution of Civilizations – Annual Review of Ecology and Systematics. Vol. 3, 1972.

Flannery Kent, Marcus Joyce. *The Creation of Inequality – How Our Prehistoric Ancestors set the Stage for Monarchy, Slavery, and Empire*. Harvard University Press. Cambridge, Massachusetts 2014

Freund Sigmund. *Civilization and its Discontents*. Martin Publishing 2010.

Fried Morton Herbert. *The Evolution of Political Society*. Random House. New York 1967.

Fukuyama Francis. The Origins of Political Order – From Pre-human Times to the French Revolution. Farrar, Straus and Giroux 2011.

Garrett Thomas A. Economic effects of the 1918 Influenza Pandemic. Implications for a Modern-day Pandemic. Federal Reserve Bank of St Louis. November 2007.

Garrett Thomas A. Pandemic Economics: The 1918 Influenza and Its Modern-Day Implications. Federal Reserve Bank of St Louis, March-April 2008

Ghanem Hafez. Improving Regional and Rural Development for Inclusive Growth in Egypt, Global Economy and Development. Global Economy and Development at BROOKINGS. Working Paper January 2014

Gibson Charles. The Aztecs under Spanish Rule: A History of the Indians of the Valley of Mexico, 1519–1810, Stanford: Stanford University Press 1964.

Goldman Irving. *The Cubeo Indian of the Northwest Amazon.* University of Illinois Press; 2nd ed. edition Nov. 1/ 1979.

Gould J. Stephen, Eldredge Niles. Punctuated Equilibria: An Alternative to Phyletic Gradualism, pp 82-115 in Models in Paleo-biology, edited by T. J. M. Schopf. San Francisco: Freeman Cooper. 1972

Gunder Frank Andre. *World Accumulation, 1492-1789* – Algora Publishing, New York. Feb. 13, 2008.

Gunitsky Seva . Perspectives on Politics. Volume 16, Issue 3, pp. 634–651. doi: 10.1017/S1537592718001044

Hamnett Brian. *A Concise History of Mexico. Second Edition.* Cambridge University Press May 4, 2006.

Harari Noah Yuval. *Sapiens. A Brief History of Humankind.* Penguin Random House 2011

Hatcher John. England in the Aftermath of the Black Death. Oxford University Press on behalf of The Past and Present Society, No 144 (August 1994).

Haywood John. *Chronicles of the Ancient World. Quercus.* November 1/2012.

Henry S. James. The Price of Offshore Revisited.: New Estimates for 'Missing' Global Private Wealth, Income. Inequality, and lostTaxes. Tax Jusstice Network, July 2012, http://www.taxjustice.net/cms/up-load/pdf/Price_of_Osfhore_Revisited_120722.pdf

Hershatter Gail. State of the Field in China's Long Twentieth Century. Published online by Cambridge University Press: 02 March 2007

Hickel Jason. *The Divide: Global Inequality from Conquest to Free Markets.* W. W. Norton, New York 2018

Himmerich Robert y Valencia. *The Encomenderos of New Spain, 1521-1555.* Foreword by Joseph P. Sánchez. University of Texas Press – Reprint 1996.

Hitler Adolf. *Mein Kampf* - Volume One, Chapter 11 – Nation and Race. https://www.csustan.edu/history/mein-kampf

Horvath Ronald J. A Definition of Colonialism: Current Anthropology, Vol. 13, No. 1, pp. 45-57. The University of Chicago Press on behalf of Wenner-Gren Foundation for Anthropological Research. Feb. 1972

Hunt Margaret & Philip J Stern. The English East India Company at the Height of Mughal Expansion. Bedford/St Martins Dec 28 2015.

Huntington Samuel P. *The Third Wave: Democratization in the Late Twentieth Century*

Huntington, S. P. (1996). *The clash of civilizations and the remaking of the modern world.* New York, NY: Simon & Schuster

Hur Johnson. History of the Stock Market. bebusiness ,com

Inglehart Ronald and Christian Welzel. How Development Leads to Democracy: What we know about Modernization. Foreign Affairs, Vol. 88 No 2, pp. 33-48. Council of Foreign Relations. March/April 2009

Jones G. D. and Kautz. *The Chiefdom Precursor of the State. The Transition to Statehood in the New World.* Cambridge University Press 1981

June Nash. The Aztecs and the Ideology of Male Dominance. Vol. 4, No. 2 (Winter, 1978), pp. 349-362. University of Chicago Press.

Karl, Terry Lynn. Economic inequality and Democratic Intavility. Journal of Democracy 11(1): pp.149-156. 2000

Kriedte, Peter, Hans Medick, and Jurgen Schlumbohm (KMS). *Industrialization before Industrialization.* Cambridge: Cambridge University Press and Paris: Editions de la Maison des Sciences de l'Homme. 1981

Kehoe Alice Beck. Humans - *An Introduction to Four-Field Anthropology.* Rootledge 1998

Kershaw Ian. "How democracy produced a monster." New York Times. February 3, 2008.

Kharas H. and Hamel Kristopher. A Global Tipping Point: Half the World is Now Middle Class or Wealthier. Brookings.edu Sept 27/2018

Khun Randall. On The Role of Human Development in the Arab Spring. https://www.jstor.org/stable/41811933?seq=1#page_scan_tab_contents. Volume 38 No 4, December 2012

Kidner Frank, Maria Bucur, Ralph Mathisen. Making Europe – *The story of the West-Volume 1, Second Edition.* Cengage Publishing 2013.

Kosambi D. D. *The Culture and Civilization of Ancient India in Historical Outline.* Routledge and Kegan Paul London 1965.

Kristal d'Acosta. Who are the Indigenous People that That Columbus Met? Scientific American., October 12/2018

Krueger A. O. The Political Economy of a Rent Seeking Society. American Economic Review, Vol 64 No 3. June 1974.

Kleiner M. Morris, Kruger B. Alan, and Mas Alexandre, "A Proposal to Encourage States to Rationalize Occupational Licensing Practices," in A Proposal to the Brookings Institution Hamilton Project, April 1, 2011.

Kulke Hermann and Rothermund Dietmar. *History of India. Fourth Edition.* Rootledge 2004. New York.

Kurzman Charles. Wave of Democratization. Studies in Comparative Analysis 33 (1): 44-64, 1998

Kuznets Simon and his Curve. Adam Smith Institute April 30/ 2019.

Lange Matthew, James Mahoney, and Matthias Hau. "Colonialism and Development: A Comparative Analysis of Spanish and British Colonies," American Journal of Sociology 111, no. 5, pp.: 1412-1462. March 2006

Lanning Edward P. *Peru before the Incas.* Prentice-Hall, Englewood Cliffs, N.J., 1967.

Mangan, Jane E. *Trading Roles: Gender, Ethnicity, and the Urban Economy in Colonial Potosí.* Duke University Press and Durham, London 2005

Lavinia Cazacu Andreea (Neamtu). The Role of Transfer Pricing in Economic Globalization International Journal of Business and Social Science Vol. 8, No. 3; March 2017.

Le Guin K. Ursula. *The Wave in the Mind. Talks and Essays on the Writer, the Reader, and the Imagination.* Shambala Publication Inc 2004.

Lenski Gerhard E. *Power and Privilege: A theory of Social Stratification.* Mc Graw-Hill. New York 1966.

Letki Natalia. *Encyclopedia of Governance.* Edited by Mark Bevir. Sage Publication 2017

Lindert Peter H. and Jeffrey G. Williamson. *American Growth and Inequality since 1700. Unequal Gains.* Princeton University Press – Princeton and Oxford 2016.

Linhares, Jane, "Egyptian Pieces of the Empire's Puzzle: Peasants, Women, and Students in British Official Documents Issued after the 1919 Revolution in Egypt". Trinity College, Hartford, CT 2018.

Lipset Seymour Martin. Some Social Requisites of Democracy: Economic Development and Political Legitimacy. The American Political Science Review, Vol. 53, No. 1. American Political Science Association. March 1959

Lipset Seymour Martin. *Political Man: The Social Bases of Politics.* New York: Doubleday, 1963.

Livi-Bacci Massimo. *A Concise History of World Population.* Wiley Blackwell 2012

Lockhart James. *The Nahuas After Conquest- A social and Cultural History of the Indians of Central Mexico Sixteenth Through Eighteenth Centuries.* California, Stanford University Press 2005.

Lussagnet Suzanne. Civilisations précolombiennes et métaux précieux. In: Annales. Economies, sociétés, civilisations. 3ᵉannée, N. 4, 1948. pp. 501-503; https://doi.org/10.3406/ahess.1948.2367

MacFarlane Alan. *The Riddle of the Modern World: Of Liberty, Wealth and Equality.* St Martin Press, New York 2000.

Mandelbrot B. Benoit B. *Fractal Geometry of Nature.* W. H. Freeman and Company. New York 1983

Mangan, Jane E. *Trading Roles: Gender, Ethnicity, and the Urban Economy in Colonial Potosí.* Duke University Press and Durham, London 2005

Manikumar k. A. Impact of British Colonialism on Different Social classes in the 19th Century Madras Presidency. Social Scientist Vol. 42, No 5/6. May–June 2014

Mark, Joshua J. War in Ancient Time. Ancient History Encyclopedia, 02 Sep 2009.

Matute Helena et al. Illusions of Causality: How they bias our everyday thinking and how they could be reduced. Frontier in Psychology. Doi: 10.3389/fpsyg.2015.0088

McCauley N. Robert. Why Religion is Natural, Science is Not. Oxford University Press October 2013

Means Philip Ainsworth. *Fall of the Inca Empire and the Spanish rule in Peru: 1530-1780.* Charles Scribner's Sons. New York 1932.

McEwan Gordon F. *The Incas – New Perspectives.* Publisher W. W. Norton New York 2008

McIntosh Jane. *The Ancient Indus Valley New Perspectives.* ABC-CLIO 1 Edition Nov 12/2007.

Meltzer, Edmund S. Horus. In D. B. Redford (Ed.): *The ancient gods speak: A guide to Egyptian Religion* (pp. 164). New York: Oxford University Press, USA. 2002

Mendels Franklin F. Proto-Industrialization: The First Phase of the Industrialization Process. The Journal of Economic History. Vol. 32, pp.241-261, No. 1. The Tasks of Economic History. 1972.

Mendonsa L. Eugene. *Greed Unbound. Official Misdeeds in Political Economies of Kin Groups and Chiefdoms.* Volume I. Lulu Publishing 2016.

Michalopoulos Stelios & Papaioannou Elias. The long economic and political shadow of history -Volume I: A Global View. A VoxEU.org

Milanovic Branco. *Capitalism Alone. The Future of the System that Rules the World.* The Belknap Press of Harvard University. Cambridge, Massachusetts 2019.

Milanovic Branco. *Global Inequality: A new Approach to the Age of Globalization.* Belknap Press: An Imprint of Harvard University Press April 9, 2018.

Milanovic Branco. Introducing Kuznets Waves: How income inequality waxes and wanes over the very long run, February/2016. VOX, CEPR Policy Postal.

Mitchell William P. The Hydraulic Hypothesis: A Reappraisal. Current Anthropology 14, no. 5: 532-534. https://doi.org/10.1086/201379. December 1973

Mortimer Wheeler. Civilization of the Ancient Valley and Beyond. Mc Graw Hill Book Company 1966

Mosely Michael E. *The Incas and their Ancestors- the Archeology of Peru (2001 Revised Edition).* Thames and Hudson, New York.

Müller Jan-Werner. *What is Populism?* University of Pennsylvania Press. Philadelphia 2016.

Mussa Michael. World Economic Outlook: Globalization: Opportunities and Challenges - Chapter III: Meeting the Challenges of Globalization in the Advanced Economies. IMF eLibrary. May 1997

Nash June. The Aztecs and the Ideology of Male Dominance. Vol. 4, No. 2, pp. 349-362. University of Chicago Press. Winter 1978

Niehans Jürg. *A History of Economic Theory: Classic Contributions, 1720–1980*, Baltimore, MD: Johns Hopkins University Press 1990.

Nunn Nathan. The Long-Term Effect of Africa's Slave Trades. NBER Working Paper No. 13367

Ogilvy Sheilagh, Durlauf N Steven, Blume E. Lawrence. *Proto-industrialization. From the New Palgrave Dictionary of Economics*, Second Edition, 2008

Ong Walter. Orality and Literacy. Rootledge Edition July 19/2002

Osterhammel Jürgen. *Colonialism: A Theoretical Overview*. Princeton, N.J.: Markus Wiener Publishers, 1997.

Piketty Thomas. *Capital in the Twenty-First Century*. The Belknap Press of Harvard University. Cambridge, Massachusetts 2014.

Pierson Paul. *Politics in time. History, Institutions, and Social Analysis.* Princeton University Press, 2004

Polanyi Karl. *The Great Transformation: The Political and Economic Origins of Our Time.* Beacon Press; 2nd Edition (March 28 2001).

Pringle Heather. The Ancient roots of the 1% - *AAAS* May 13/2014. Vol. 344, Issue 6186 DOI: 10.1126/science.344.6186.822

Ralph O. Allen O. Ralph, Hamroush Hany, Stanley J. Daniel. Impact of the environment on Egyptian civilization before the pharaoh. https://doi.org/10.1021/ac00049a002. January 1/1993

Rawls John. *A Theory of Justice*. Revised Edition. Belknap Press of Harvard University Press Cambridge, Massachusetts 1999eBook. CEPR Press. London UK. January 2017

Renske Doorenspleet. Reassessing the Three Waves of Democratization. World Politics. Vol. 52, No. 3. Cambridge University Press. April 2000

Reich Robert. *Saving Capitalism for the Many, Not the Few.* Vintage Books – New York 2016.

Reinhard Bendix. Inequality and Social Structure: A Comparison of Marx and Weber. American Sociological Review. Vol. 39, No. 2, pp. 149-161. April 1974

Revenka Ana & Dooley Meagan. Inequality beyond neoliberalism: Policies for more inclusive growth. Brookings May/2019

Revenka Ana and Meagan Dooley. Brookings. Is Equality Really on the Rise? https://www.brookings.edu/blog/future-development/2019/05/28/is-inequality-really-on-the-rise/

Rice Rob et al. Fighting Techniques of the Ancient World (3000 B.C. to 500 A.D.): Equipment, Combat Skills, and Tactics. Amber Books Ltd 2002.

Richards J. F. The Decline of the Tainos, 1492-1542. Cambridge Perseus Publishing 2003

Riello Giorgio. The Ecology of Cotton in the 18th Century: Possibilities & Potentials. GEHN, London School of Economics

Rivet Paul et H. Archambault. La métallurgie dans l'Amérique Précolombienne, Travaux et Mémoire de l'Institut d'Ethnologie de Paris

Roberts John A. G - *A Concise History of China.* Harvard University Press. Cambridge, Massachusetts 1999.

Robertson John. Iraq A History. One World Publication. London England 2015

Rodrigues Hillary P. *Introducing Hinduism.* Routledge 2006.

Rodrigues Vanessa et al. Homo sapiens, Homo neanderthalensis and the Denisovan specimen: New insights on their evolutionary histories using whole-genome comparisons. Genetic Molecular Biology; 35(4 Suppl): 904–911. Published online Dec 18/2012. PMCID: PMC3571422

Ross L. Michael. Does Oil Hinder Democracy? World Politics, Vol. 53, No. 3, pp. 325-361. Cambridge University Press. April 2001

Rousseau and Locke on Property and the State. https://blogs.harvard.edu/mattschrage/2018/04/26/rousseau-and-locke-on-property-and-the-state/

Rousseau Jean-Jacques. The Social Contract and The First and Second Discourses. Yale University Press. 1st edition. Feb 8/2002

Sahagún, Fray Bernardino de (1950-82) Florentine Codex, General History of the Things of New Spain. 12 books, Translated and edited by A. J.O. Anderson & C.E. Dibble. School of American Research & the University of Utah Press, Santa Fe & Salt Lake City.

Sangeetha Rao. R. Caste System in India: Myth and Reality. New Delhi India Publishers and Distributors 1989.

Scarborough Vernon L. & John E. Clark, editors. Political Economy of Ancient Mesoamerica: Transformation during the Formative and Classic Period. University of New Mexico Press 2007

Scott R. Bruce. Capitalism - Its Origins and Evolution as a System of Governance. Springer New York - Dordrecht Heidelberg London 2011.

Scott R. Bruce. Capitalism: The Indirect Economic Governance of a Visible Hand. Challenge. Vol 55, No 4 (July- August), pp.5-23. Taylor & Francis, Ltd 2012

Scheidel Walter. The Great Leveler – Violence and the History of Inequality From The Stone Age To the Twenty-First Century. Princeton University Press. Princeton and Oxford 2017

Schumpeter Joseph A. Capitalism, Socialism & Democracy. Harper, New York 1950.

Sen Amartya. The Idea of Justice. Belknap Press 2011. Harvard University

Service Elman R. Origin of the State and Civilization – The Process of Cultural Evolution. W. W. Norton & Company 1975

Seth Abrutyn and Kirk Lawrence. From Chiefdom to State: Toward an Integrative Theory of the Evolution of Polity. Sociological Perspectives, Vol. 53 No. 3. Fall 2010. Sage Publications Inc.

Shang Yang. The Book of the Lord Shang. Apologetic State Power in Early China. Columbia University Press. March 7, 2017

Schäfer Armin. Consequences of social inequality for democracy in Western Europe. *Z Vgl Polit Wiss* 6, 23–45 (2012). https://doi.org/10.1007/s12286-010-0086-6

Sheffer Marten, Bas van Bavel, Ingrid A. van de Leemput and Egbert H. van Nes. Inequality in Nature and Society. PNAS 2017 – www.pnas.org/cgi/doi/10.1073/pnas.17066412114. Proceedings of the Academy of Sciences. Supporting Information: www.pnas.org/lookup/suppl/doi:10.1073/pnas.1706412114/-/DCSupplemental

Sika, N. and Khodary, Y. One Step Forward, Two Steps Back? Egyptian Women within the Confines of Authoritarianism. *Journal of International Women's Studies.* 2012

Slavery. https://www.digitalhistory.uh.edu/disp_textbook.cfm?smtID=2&psid=3569

Smith Adam. *Wealth of Nations.* Oxford University Press. 1993

Smith Michael E. *At Home with the Aztecs.* Rootledge 2016. New York.

Smith Michael E. *The Aztecs. Third Edition.* Wiley Blackwell 2012. Ma -USA

Smith Michael E. The Aztecs Paid Taxes, not Tribute- Publisher: Mexicon, Vol. 36 No. 1, pp.19-22. Feb. 2014.

Smith Michael. The Aztecs -Third Edition. Wiley Blackwell Ma USA 2012

Smith Michael E. Rethinking the Aztecs Economy edited by Deborah L. Nichols, Frances F. Berden, M. E. Smith. American Studies in Anthropology. University of Arizona Press Tuckson 2017

Smith, Michael E. The Role of Social Stratification in the Aztec Empire: A View from the Provinces. *American Anthropologist, 88*(1), new series, 70-91. From http://www.jstor.org/stable/679280. March 1986

Sombart Werner. Modern Capitalism. Publisher K A Nitz. November 29/2019

Spencer, Charles S.; Redmond, Elsa M. Primary State Formation in Mesoamerica. Annual Review of Anthropology. 33: pp. 173–199. doi:10.1146/annurev.anthro.33.070203.143823. 2004

Spencer Charles. Territorial Expansion and Primary State Formation PNAS 2010.

Stanford Encyclopedia of Philosophy. Political Naturalism https://plato.stanford.edu/entries/aristotle-politics/supplement3.html

Stein Gil. Before the Pyramids – The origins of Egyptian Civilization. Oriental Institute Museum Publication 33. Oriental Institute of the University of Chicago 2011.

Steinmetz George. Empires and Colonialism. Oxford Bibliography- DOI: 10.1093/obo/9780199756384-0090. January 13, 2014

Stephen John D. Democratic Transition and Breakdown of Western Europe, 1870-1939: A Test of the Moore Thesis. American Journal of Sociology, Vol. 94. No 5, pp.1019-1077. University of Chicago Press. March 1989

Stiglitz Joseph E. *The Great Divide – Unequal Societies and What We Can Do About Them.* W. W. Norton & Company Ltd. New York, London 2015.

Stol Marten. Women in Mesopotamia. Journal of the Economic and Social History of the Orient. Journal of the economic and social history of the Orient. Vol. 38, No 2, women's history, pp. 123-124. E. J. Brill: Leiden 1995

Strausz-Hupe R. & H. W. Hazard. Editors. The Idea of Colonialism. New York: Praeger. 1958

Stringer Christ. *The Origin of Our Species.* Publisher Allan Lane 2011.

Stringer Christ. *Lone survivors. How We Came To Be The Only Humans On Earth.* St Martin's Press New York 2012

Suarez Steve. *Transfer Pricing in Canada.* Reprinted from *Tax Notes International,* p. 781. December 2, 2019

Sued Badillo J. General History of Autochthonous Societies. Paris and Oxford: UNESCO; Macmillan Caribbean, 2003

Székely, Miguel. The 1990s in Latin America: Another Decade of Persistent Inequality, but with Somewhat Lower Poverty. IADB Working Paper No 454. Washington D.C.: Inter-American Development Bank 2001.

Sørli et al. Why is there So Much Conflict in the Middle East? Mirjam E. Sørli, Nils Peter Gleditsch, Håvard Strand. Journal of Conflict Resolution, Vol 49 No 1, pp. 141-165. DOI: 10.1177/0022002704270824. February 2005

Swatos William H. JR. Encyclopedia of Religion and Society. Altamira Press 1998

Syed Yusuf Saadat. The Optimum Level of Income Inequality: Evidence from Panel Data - DOI: 10.21102/jbpr.2018.07.131.06.

Tallerman Maggie. *Language Origins – Perspectives on Evolution*. Oxford University Press. Aug. 11/2005

Taylor E. B. Primitive Culture: Research into the Development of Mythology, Philosophy, Religion, Art and Custom. Vol 1 London - John Murray, 1920.

Teeter Emily. Before the Pyramids – The origins of Egyptian Civilization. Oriental Institute Museum Publication 33 & The Oriental Institute of the University of Chicago 2011.

Tellier Luc-Norman. Urban World History: *An Economic and Geographical Perspective*. Press de l' Université du Quebec, Canada 2009

Thaddeus Metz. *Meaning in Life*. Oxford University Press. Oct. 8/ 2013

Timmons Jeffrey F. Does Democracy Reduce Inequality? British Journal of Political Science, Vol 40, No 4. Cambridge University Press. October 2010.

Tony Blair Institute for Global Change. Populist in Power Around the World. November 7/2018 https://institute.global/insight/renewing-center/populist-power-around-world

The Republic of Plato. Basic Books; 3rd edition, Nov. 22 2016.

Toussaint Carmel M. *Technology and Society – Rewards and Challenges*. Phronetech Writing, Toronto, Canada 2017

Trade-Related Illicit Financial Flows in 135 Developing Countries: 2008-2017. https://gfintegrity.org/report/trade-related-illicit-finan-cial-flows-in-135-developing-countries-2008-2017/

Tucker Judith. Decline of the Family Economy in Mid-Nineteenth-Century Egypt. Arab Studies Quarterly, Vol. 1, No. 3 pp. 245-271. Pluto Journals. https://www.jstor.org/stable/41857510. Summer 1979

Tullock, Gordon. *Rent Seeking*. Brookfield, Vt.: Edward Elgar, 1993.

Tylor Edward Burnett. *Primitive Culture, Researches Into the Development of Mythology, Philosophy, Religion, Language, Art, and Custom*, Volume 1. The University of Michigan. October 7/2008

Turner Victor. *The Forest of Symbols. Aspects of Ndembu Ritual.* Cornell University Press,1ˢᵗ Edition Feb 28/1970

Urbinati Nadia. Me the People: *How Populism Transforms Democracy.* Harvard University Press 2019. Cambridge Massachusetts

Verme Paolo et al. A World Bank Study: Inside Inequality in the Arab Republic of Egypt. Facts and Perceptions across People, Time and Space. 2014.

Vernon L. Scarborough and John E. Clark, editors. Political Economy of Ancient Mesoamerica: Transformation during the Formative and Classic Period. University of New Mexico Press 2007

Vincas P. Steponaitis Vincas P. Location Theory and Complex Chiefdoms: A Mississippian Example 1978 (corrected) ria.unc.edu

Wade Nicholas. The Faith Instinct- *How Religion Evolved and Why it Endures.* Publisher: Penguin Books; Reprint edition Sept. 28 2010

What evidence is there of human sacrifice? https://www.mexicolore.co.uk/aztecs/ask-us/what-evidence-is-there-of-aztec-human-sacrifice

Wallace A.F.C. Religion: *An Anthropological View. New York. Random House.* January 1, 1966.

Warburg R. Gabriel and G. G. Gilbar. Asian and African Studies. Journal of Israel Oriental Society. Institute of Middle Easter Study. Vol. 17 Nos 1-3. November 1883.

Warburton Nigel. *A little history of Philosophy.* Yale Universal Publications 2011

Watson James L. *Class and Social Stratification in Post-Revolution China. Cambridge University Press.* June 2010

Weber Max. *Politics as a Vocation - Macat Library*; 1 edition (August 8, 2017)

Webster David. Warfare and the Evolution the State. American Antiquity, Vol 40. No. 4. Cambridge University Pres1984.

Wheeler W. Lindsay. The classical definition of a republic. Academia.edu. 5ᵗʰ Revision. Feb 19/ 2016

Weidong Sun. Origin of Chinese Civilization. InsideHook.com

Whipps Heather. How the Hyoid Bone Changed History. Livescience.com. Feb 04/2008.

Williamson Jeffrey G. Latin America Inequality: Colonial Origins, Commodity Booms, or a missed 20th Century. National Bureau of Economic Research. January 2015.

Williamson Jeffrey A. Working Paper 20915 Latin American Inequality: Colonial Origins, Commodity Booms or a Missed 20th Century Levelling.

Wittfogel Karl August. Oriental Despotism – *A Comparative Study of Total Power.* New Haven, Conn.: Yale University Press. 1957

Venkatasubramanian Venkat. *How much Inequality is Fair? Mathematical Principles of a Moral, Optimal, and Stable Capitalist Society.* Columbia University Press 2019.

Wright Donald A. *The World and a Very Small Place in Africa: A History of Globalization in Niumi, the Gambia.* Third Edition. M E. Sharp inc. Armonk, New York 2010.

Yonathan Berman, Eshel Ben-Jacob, Yoash Shapira. The Dynamics of Wealth Inequality and the Effect of Income Distribution. PLOS. DOI 10.1371/journal.pone.0154196 April 22/2016

Zakaria Fareed. *The Future of Freedom – Illiberal Democracy at Home and Abroad.* W. W. Norton, New York. Revised edition Oct. 9/2007.

Zeder A. Melinda. The Domestication of Animals. Journal of Anthropological Research. Vol. 68, No. 2, pp. 161-190. University of Chicago Press. Summer 2012

Appendix III
Index

new, 46
Ottoman forces, 113
Ottoman's implication, 113
overseas possessions, 215
ownership, 32, 61, 186, 297
  claimed, 188
  corporate, 230
Oxfam report, 261

Paleolithic ice age, 13
Paleolithic period, 27, 48
Palestinians, 150–51
Pareto principle, 254
participation, female labor, 149
Partido Revolucionario Institucional, 203
parties, 21, 46, 49, 68, 121, 184, 196–97, 225,
  234, 276
Pascal Boyer PhD, 289
path, 82, 198, 271, 281
  migratory, 14
peace, 142, 197, 228, 247
period
  colonial, 51, 183, 204
  colonization, 159
  enlightenment, 221
  formative, 188
  medieval, 217, 224
  modern, 208
  post-conquest, 191
  pre-modern, 207
  recent, 52
Permanent accumulation, 253
Permanent financial incentives, 268
permanent settlement, 152, 161
  first, 190
perspective, 16, 20, 28, 30, 33, 52, 182, 184,
  218, 220, 225
  chronological, 210
  ethical, 86
  gender parity, 149, 166
  metaphysical, 15
  social, 115
  social class, 176
  sociopolitical, 27
pharaoh, last strong, 111
Pharoah Cleopatra, 107

Pharoah Hatshepsut, 107
philosophy, 139, 143, 204, 212
  ethical, 142
  utilitarian, 143
pictographic script, 176, 211
Piketty, Thomas, 240
Pizarro, Francisco, 188, 190, 193, 200
plague, 49, 104, 285
plants
  edible, 18
  tobacco, 160
plants cultivation, 33
plunder, 194, 247
pogroms, 159, 210
Poland's concentration camp, 287
Polanyi, Karl, 218
politeia, 295
political authority, 232, 234, 296
political campaigns, 276
political complexity, 60
political consolidation process, 168
Political Dimension, 5, 247, 269
Political Governance, 213
political ideologies, main, 5
political integration, 58, 61, 63
political organization, 28, 47, 60–61, 68, 75,
  150, 166, 179, 194
political process, 60, 279
political regime, 40, 90, 92, 98
political rights, 87, 209, 274
political structure, 27, 62, 72, 89, 105, 111,
  126, 197, 249
political power 58, 82, 115, 166, 261, 264
Polity 10, 22, 37, 42, 46, 58
populism ideology, 277
populism's appeal, 276
Portuguese trading posts, 218
post-classic period, 174
post conquest periods, 182
Potosi, 204, 212
Potosi silver, 204, 209
pottery, 49, 124, 127
poverty, eradicating, 148
Power (economic) 2, 141, 235, 279, 280
practices
  financial, 234